STUDY GUIDE

Pamela C. Regan
California State University, Los Angeles

W9-CVO-802

PSYCHOLOGY

Third Edition

Saul Kassin
Williams College

Prentice Hall, Upper Saddle River, New Jersey 07458

©2001 by PRENTICE-HALL, INC.
Pearson Education
Upper Saddle River, New Jersey 07458

ISBN 0-13-026946-8

Printed in the United States of America

Table of Contents

To the Student

Hi and welcome to psychology! This study guide was written to enhance your mastery of the material presented in the third edition of *Psychology*, written by Dr. Saul Kassin. It will help you to identify important information, terms, and concepts; evaluate and test your own knowledge of the chapter material; and stimulate your thinking about various psychological phenomena. Please keep in mind that the study guide is not intended to serve as a substitute for the textbook! Rather, use the study guide to supplement and to measure what you've learned from the textbook and your lecture notes. Each study guide chapter corresponds to a chapter in your textbook and is divided into several different sections. Specifically:

Chapter Overview

This section briefly summarizes the material covered in the chapter and serves as a general introduction to the theory and research topics discussed by the author.

Chapter Outline

Human behavior and the human mind are remarkably diverse and complex. As a result, psychology—the discipline that seeks to understand human behavior and the human mind—is a big field with a constantly changing base of theoretical and empirical (research) knowledge. As you read through each chapter, you may find yourself thinking that it contains a lot of information; so much so that it's hard to grasp the major points or "big picture" without getting confused by all the details. The chapter outline consists of the major section headings and subheadings from the textbook and is designed to serve as an organizational plan that presents the larger structure of each chapter. You probably will find it useful to supplement this general outline with more detailed notes of your own, both from the textbook and from lecture.

Learning Objectives

Unlike the chapter outline, the learning objectives provide a *detailed* list of the concepts, ideas, and points that you can expect to learn from the textbook. To assist you in mastering the material, page references are placed beside each objective. Take the time to go over the objectives carefully before you read the chapter; this will prepare you for what to expect and also will serve to guide your note taking and reading. Then, make sure to return to the learning objectives after you have read the chapter; this will allow you to determine whether you indeed have mastered the essential concepts of the chapter. If there is an objective that still seems unclear, reread that particular section of text and/or ask your instructor.

Key Terms

This section lists and provides page references for all the key terms and concepts from each chapter. Unlike a traditional glossary, the key terms are presented in order of appearance in the chapter rather than alphabetically so that you can work your way through the text chapter from beginning to end instead of jumping from section to section and topic to topic. After reviewing, you should be able to define these terms in a few sentences (and provide examples, if appropriate).

Practice Multiple-Choice, True-False, and Key Concepts Matching Exercises

In addition to outlining the chapter and reviewing basic concepts, this study guide allows you to test your knowledge of each chapter in two different formats. The first consists of practice multiple-choice questions, true-false questions, and key concepts matching exercises drawn from the material presented in the text. These questions are designed to test your mastery of factual information, your conceptual understanding of particular ideas or theories, and your ability to apply what you have learned to novel situations not explicitly discussed in the textbook. The answers (along with page references) to the practice questions are provided at the end of the study guide chapter.

Practice Essay Questions

Answering multiple-choice and true-false questions and matching up key terms with their definitions and/or key psychologists with their discoveries are important means by which you can test your knowledge of psychology. Writing about the concepts you have learned is another. This section consists of practice essay questions that allow you to test your ability to describe, explain, and illustrate the ideas and points of each textbook chapter. Some basic guidelines that might be helpful to you are: (1) State your answers in a clear and concise manner; (2) avoid the use of sexist or otherwise inappropriate language (for example, use the term "humankind" or "people" rather than "mankind;" refer to Chapter 7 for additional information on how to avoid sexist language); (3) use examples when relevant; and (4) make an outline before you begin writing so that you know exactly what points you wish to make to your audience. A sample answer with page references has been provided for each practice essay question and placed at the end of the study guide chapter. Of course, because some of the questions ask you to supplement your definitions or descriptions of a particular concept or idea with examples drawn from personal experience, several different answers may be appropriate for any one question.

Multimedia Study Resources

There are also two additional resources that may assist you in your study of psychology. The Psychology Place™ is a website that contains learning activities that explore key concepts, research, and current topics related to the material presented in the textbook. In addition, The Psychology Place™ also provides access to relevant news articles involving psychological issues, as well as opinion essays written by guest contributors and a collection of articles from *Scientific American* magazine. Mind Matters™ is a CD-ROM resource that contains modules devoted to several of the topics covered in your textbook. Each module combines text, graphics, and activities to allow you to more fully explore the science of psychology.

In order to allow you to efficiently utilize these resources, the Multimedia Study Resources section of your study guide will direct you to several activities in The Psychology Place™ that are related to the content of each textbook chapter. This section also will indicate which parts of the Mind Matters™ CD-ROM correspond to the chapters in your textbook. (Keep in mind that not all instructors will have chosen to utilize the Mind Matters™ resource, and the information contained in the CD-ROM corresponds to only a few of the textbook chapters. However, you all have access to The Psychology Place™ website, and this resource is relevant to each textbook chapter).

This study guide is intended to help you develop a knowledge base about psychology. If used in conjunction with a careful review of both the textbook and course lectures, it may enable you to increase your understanding of the material that Dr. Kassin presents in each chapter. I hope that your text, course, and this study guide introduce you to the breadth and depth of the exciting, rapidly growing field of psychology, and I wish you much success with your studies.

1 Introducing Psychology and Its Methods

Chapter Overview

The first part of this chapter introduces the field of psychology—its subject matter, its historical roots, and the individuals who established it as a legitimate arena of scientific inquiry. The major controversies that marked the beginnings of modern experimental psychology also are discussed, including the fundamental disagreement over what the "appropriate" goals, questions, and methods should be for this new science (e.g., subjective mental processes versus overt, observable behaviors). The text then explores some of the dramatic changes that have markedly altered the landscape of modern psychology, including the "cognitive revolution," the expansion of both basic and applied research areas, and increased diversity of members within the field. The second part of this chapter reviews the scientific methods used by psychologists in their quest to understand human behavior. Specifically, you will learn the difference between types of research settings (laboratory versus field), psychological measurements (self-reports, behavioral observations, and archival records), and research designs (descriptive, correlational, and experiment). The chapter concludes with a consideration of the ethical issues involved in using both humans and animals in psychological research.

Chapter Outline

I. *What's Your Prediction?* Thinking Like a Psychologist

II. What Is Psychology?

    A. Historical Roots
        1. Pioneers in the study of the mind
        2. The behaviorist alternative
        3. The "cognitive revolution"

    B. Psychology's Horizons Expand
        1. Basic areas of specialization

C. Practical Applications
   1. Values, ethics, and social responsibility

D. Diversity and Psychology

III. Scientific Methods

  A. Research Settings

  B. Psychological Measurements
    1. Self-reports
    2. Behavioral observations
    3. Archival records

  C. Research Designs
    1. Descriptive research
      a. Case studies
      b. Surveys
      c. Naturalistic observations
    2. Correlational studies
      a. Correlation and causation
    3. Experiments
      a. Control and comparison
      b. Random assignment
    4. Literature reviews

  D. Ethical Dilemmas
    1. Ethics considerations in human research
    2. Ethics considerations in animal research

IV. Psychology Today

  A. Biological Perspectives

  B. Sociocultural Perspectives

V. Thinking Like a Psychologist

Learning Objectives

By the time you have read and reviewed this chapter, you should be able to:

1. Define psychology and describe the three key elements in its definition (p. 4).

2. Discuss the historical roots (in philosophy, physiology, and medicine) of modern-day psychology (pp. 4-6).

3. Describe the contributions of Wundt and his students (Hall, Cattell, and Munsterberg) to the field of psychology (pp. 6-7). Compare the methods used by Wundt, James, and Freud to spark interest in psychology (pp. 6-7).

4. Describe the "behaviorist alternative" to the early focus on introspection and subjective experience (pp. 8-9). Define behaviorism and compare this approach to the introspective approach favored by early psychologists (e.g., Wundt) (p. 9).

5. Define cognition (p. 9) and compare the behaviorist and cognitive approaches to understanding human behavior (pp. 9-10). Describe three events or phenomena that incited the "cognitive revolution" (p. 9-10).

6. Explain the difference between basic and applied research (p. 10-11). Consider three ways in which psychology has developed since its original incarnation or conceptualization (p. 10-11).

7. Describe the five basic areas of specialization in psychology (i.e., biology, cognition/affect, human development, social psychology, and personality/clinical psychology) (p. 11-12).

8. Consider how psychological theory and research can be used in the domains of health, education, business, law, and the environment (p. 12-13).

9. Discuss the ways in which the field of psychology has benefited from the growing diversity of its members (pp. 14-15).

10. Discuss the difference between a theory and a hypothesis (p. 16).

11. Distinguish between laboratory and field research settings (pp. 16-17).

12. Define and consider the advantages and disadvantages of each of the three types of psychological measurement (p. 17). Consider the difference between self-reports, behavioral observations, and archival records (pp. 17-19).

13. Describe the three types of research design: Descriptive studies, correlational studies, and experiments (pp. 19-25).

14. Explain the difference between case studies, surveys, and naturalistic observations (pp. 19-21).

15. Define the concept of correlation (p. 22). Discuss the function of correlational studies and the types of conclusions that can be drawn from correlational evidence (pp. 23-24).

16. Define the essential aspects of an experiment (pp. 23-25). Consider the types of conclusions that can be drawn from experimental evidence (p. 24).

17. Describe a literature review (p. 25). Consider the importance of replication and generalizability for any research finding (p. 25).

18. Explain the three ethical concerns any researcher must address when conducting a study with human participants (p. 27). Consider the relation between deception, informed consent, and debriefing (p. 27).

19. Consider the three reasons why psychologists must sometimes make use of animals in research (p. 28). Discuss the ethical obligation that any researcher has when conducting a study on animals (p. 29).

20. Describe the influence of the biological and the sociocultural perspectives on modern psychology (pp. 30-32).

Key Terms

The following key terms and concepts are featured in this chapter and are important for you to know. Write out definitions of each term and check your answers with the definitions in the text on the pages listed.

Psychology (p. 4)
Dualism (p. 5)
Introspection (p. 6)
Psychoanalysis (p. 7)
Behaviorism (p. 9)
Cognition (p. 9)
Basic research (p. 10)
Applied research (p. 11)
Theory (p. 16)
Hypotheses (p. 16)
Laboratory research (p. 16)
Field research (p. 17)
Self-report (p. 17)
Behavioral observation (p. 18)
Archival research (p. 19)
Statistics (p. 19)
Case studies (p. 20)
Surveys (p. 20)
Epidemiology (p. 20)
Random sample (p. 20)

Naturalistic observations (p. 21)
Correlation (p. 22)
Scatterplot (p. 22)
Experiment (p. 23)
Independent variable (p. 23)
Dependent variable (p. 23)
Experimental group (p. 24)
Control group (p. 24)
Random assignment (p. 25)
Replication (p. 25)
Generalizability (p. 25)
Meta-analysis (p. 26)
Deception (p. 27)
Informed consent (p. 27)
Evolutionary psychology (p. 31)
Behavioral genetics (p. 31)
Behavioral neuroscience (p. 31)
Cross-cultural research (p. 31)
Multicultural research (p. 32)

Test Questions

Multiple-Choice Questions

Circle the correct choice for each question and compare your answers with those at the end of the Study Guide chapter.

1. According to your textbook, modern psychology is best understood as the scientific study of
   A. human behavior and the mind.
   B. biological and sociocultural influences.
   C. conscious and unconscious mental states.
   D. mental disorders and psychoanalysis.

2. Which of the following examples are behaviors that psychologists might study?
   A. an eye blink
   B. smiling
   C. the decision to attend college
   D. all of the above

3. Which of the following disciplines influenced the development of modern psychology?
   A. philosophy
   B. physiology
   C. anthropology
   D. A and B

4. Wilhelm Wundt (1832-1920) used the method of _____ to study the human mind.
   A. hypnosis
   B. introspection
   C. psychoanalysis
   D. systems classification

5. Which of the following early pioneers defined psychology as the study of conscious experience?
   A. James
   B. Freud
   C. Descartes
   D. All of the above

6. If the human mind is like an iceberg, then the very tip is the _____ part, and the huge area submerged under the water is the _____ part.
   A. penguin; whale
   B. unconscious; conscious
   C. conscious; unconscious
   D. surface; bottom

7. Dr. MustSee conducts his experiments by varying a stimulus in the environment and then observing a person's reaction. He thinks that motivations and feelings are interesting to talk about, but that such things cannot be studied scientifically and thus have no business in psychology. Dr. MustSee probably is best described as
   A. a behaviorist.
   B. a philosopher.
   C. a cognitive psychologist.
   D. a psychoanalyst.

8. Which of the following developments contributed to the "cognitive revolution"?
   A. the invention of the computer
   B. Piaget's studies on the development of thinking in children
   C. developments in the study of language
   D. all of the above

9. The goal of basic research is to
   A. discover general principles of human behavior.
   B. solve practical problems.
   C. examine human behavior in real-world settings.
   D. all of the above

10. Which of the following topics would be of interest to a biological psychologist?
    A. the situations that influence the expression of aggression
    B. the evolutionary origins of aggression
    C. the cross-cultural experience and expression of anger
    D. treatment programs for violent offenders

11. Psychologists develop theories from which of the following sources?
    A. research findings
    B. personal experience or observation
    C. other theories
    D. all of the above

12. If you were interested in studying the development of dominance hierarchies in wolf packs, the best type of measurement to use would be
   A. behavioral observation.
   B. self-reports.
   C. archival records.
   D. meta-analysis.

13. A psychologist is interested in studying beliefs about the elderly. To examine trends in stereotypes of the aged, she collects and examines portraits and drawings of elderly men and women engaged in a variety of activities across several historical eras. This psychologist is relying upon _____ for her study.
   A. self-report
   B. historical trend analysis
   C. archival records
   D. behavioral observation

14. In seeking to understand the factors that contribute to divorce, a researcher interviews a divorced couple at great length. Each member of the couple is asked to provide a detailed description of the reasons the marriage failed. This example describes a(n)
   A. meta-analysis.
   B. correlational study.
   C. experiment.
   D. case study.

15. Which of the following are examples of descriptive research designs?
   A. case study
   B. naturalistic observation
   C. survey
   D. all of the above

16. Brittney notices that the more time she spends reviewing her psychology text and lecture notes, the higher her quiz scores tend to be. Her review time and her quiz scores are
   A. randomly related.
   B. positively correlated.
   C. negatively correlated.
   D. causally connected.

17. The most significant disadvantage of a correlational study is that it
   A. is unable to examine the relationship between behaviors.
   B. has limited generalizability.
   C. cannot be used to explain the causes of behaviors.
   D. cannot be used to predict behavior.

18. Mark is interested in examining the relation between shyness and dating experience. He believes that shy people will have less dating experience than nonshy people. To test his hypothesis, Mark administers the "Bellvue Shyness Scale" to a sample of college students, and then asks them to report on the number of first dates they have had in the last year. He finds a negative relationship between shyness level and number of first dates. What can Mark conclude?
   A. Shyness causes dating anxiety.
   B. Dating experience is a function of shyness.
   C. People who date a lot become less shy.
   D. None of the above.

Questions 19-21 refer to the following scenario. Read it carefully!

Emma is working on her senior thesis. She believes that couples experience less physiological arousal when they are having a "positive" discussion than when they are having a "negative" discussion (in other words, type of discussion affects physiological arousal). To test this hypothesis, she asks 20 married couples to come into the laboratory. Upon arrival at the laboratory, the couples complete a "relationship satisfaction survey." Then, the couples are hooked up to machines that record their physiological arousal. At this point, Emma randomly assigns 10 of the couples to discuss an area of conflict in their relationships while the machines measure their heart rate and blood pressure. The other 10 couples are randomly assigned to discuss an area of pleasure in their relationship and their heart rate and blood pressure are assessed. Emma finds that the first group (conflict discussion) becomes more physiologically aroused during their discussions than the second group (pleasure discussion).

19. Describe Emma's study. What kind of research design, psychological measurement, and research setting has she used?
    A. descriptive; self-report; field
    B. experimental; self-report; field
    C. correlational; behavioral observation; laboratory
    D. experimental; behavioral observation; laboratory

20. What is the independent variable in this study?
    A. the type of relationship the couples have
    B. the couple's satisfaction
    C. the physiological arousal experienced by the couples
    D. the type of discussion in which the couples engage

21. What is the dependent variable in this study?
    A. the type of relationship the couples have
    B. the couple's satisfaction
    C. the physiological arousal experienced by the couples
    D. the type of discussion in which the couples engage

22. When all the participants have an equal probability of being placed in the experimental or control group, the procedure is called
    A. random sampling.
    B. random assignment.
    C. representative sampling.
    D. manipulation.

23. Matt has read Emma's published study. For his thesis, he decides to conduct a nearly identical study to see if the initial findings can be repeated. Matt is testing the _____ of Emma's study.
    A. replicability
    B. manipulability
    C. generalizability
    D. proof

24. Matt then decides to conduct the same study again, but this time using much older couples and a different measure of arousal. Matt is now testing the _____ of Emma's study.
    A. replicability
    B. manipulability
    C. generalizability
    D. proof

25. The set of procedures used to examine a research question by combining the results from multiple studies is called
    A. statistics.
    B. meta-analysis.
    C. literature review.
    D. correlation.

26. Ethical concerns raised by research involving the use of human participants include
    A. the participant's right to privacy.
    B. possible harm caused by experimental procedures.
    C. the use of deception.
    D. all of the above.

27. Informed consent refers to
    A. revealing in advance that an experiment will involve deception.
    B. informing participants that they are obligated to complete the experiment once it begins.
    C. fully explaining the experimental manipulation prior to participation.
    D. none of the above.

28. Your textbook author describes an example from his own experience as a research participant in which he agreed to be in an IQ study. He took a test and was told that his score was quite low, in the 25th percentile. On his way out, feeling bad about his poor performance, he was approached by a student who asked him to help out by completing a survey (your author refused). The experimenter then reappeared and revealed that there was no survey and the IQ feedback had been false. The study actually was designed to examine whether positive or negative experiences could influence helping behavior. This example demonstrates
    A. random assignment and debriefing.
    B. informed consent and the right to privacy.
    C. deception and debriefing.
    D. deception and the right to withdraw.

29. Animal researchers have a moral obligation to do which of the following?
    A. minimize pain and suffering
    B. ensure that animals receive adequate food and water
    C. ensure that animals receive adequate shelter and medical treatment
    D. all of the above

30. Psychologists who evaluate the generality of theories of human behavior by comparing people from different world regions are conducting _____ research.
    A. evolutionary   C. multicultural
    B. cross-cultural   D. behavioral neuroscience

True-False Questions

Indicate which of the following statements are true or false, and compare your answers with those at the end of the chapter.

T   F   1. The term "mind" in modern-day psychology refers only to conscious mental states.

T   F   2. Behaviorism is concerned with mental processes that connect a stimulus with a response.

T   F   3. Basic research is used to test theories and discover general laws of human behavior.

T   F   4. Some psychologists develop their theories of human behavior by examining existing theories and research.

T   F   5. A major disadvantage of self-report measurements is that people may distort their responses.

T   F   6. Behavioral observation can never be used to study subjective experiences like curiosity.

T   F   7. Case studies have played an influential role in the history of psychology.

T   F   8. Correlational studies provide an effective means of examining the causal relationship between two variables.

T F 9. It is possible to manipulate more than one independent variable in an experiment.

T F 10. One well-designed study can prove a hypothesis.

Key Concepts Matching Exercises

Exercise #1: Historical Foundations

Match the key people on the left with their contributions to psychology.

_____ 1. Descartes　　　　A. Founder of modern medicine

_____ 2. James　　　　　 B. Founded the APA

_____ 3. Freud　　　　　 C. Followed the philosophical position known as dualism

_____ 4. Calkins　　　　 D. Wrote the two-volume *Principles of Psychology*

_____ 5. Hippocrates　　 E. Established the field of psychoanalysis

_____ 6. Hall　　　　　　F. Viewed psychology as the study of observable behavior

_____ 7. Watson　　　　 G. Created the first psychology laboratory

_____ 8. Wundt　　　　　H. First woman president of the APA

Exercise #2: Scientific Methods

Match the key concepts on the left with the definitions on the right.

_____ 1. Archival measures　　A. Statistical measure of the relation between two variables

_____ 2. Case study　　　　　B. Used to describe the behavior of populations

_____ 3. Correlation　　　　　C. Examines cause-and-effect relations

_____ 4. Dependent variable　 D. Process of repeating a study

_____ 5. Replication　　　　　E. Testable prediction about the relationship between two or more variables

_____ 6. Experiment　　　　　F. What is manipulated by the researcher

_____ 7. Hypothesis　　　　　G. In-depth examination of one individual

_____ 8. Field research　　　 H. What is measured by the researcher

_____ 9. Survey　　　　　　　I. Research conducted in "real-world" settings

_____10. Independent variable　J. Set of principles that describes, explains, and predicts a phenomenon

_____11. Theory　　　　　　 K. Process of arbitrarily putting participants into the experimental or control groups

_____12. Random assignment　 L. Used to examine historical trends in human behavior

_____ 1. This graph illustrates a negative correlation.

_____ 2. This graph illustrates a zero correlation.

_____ 3. This graph illustrates a positive correlation.

Essay Questions

Write out answers to the following brief essay questions. Compare your responses with the sample answers at the end of the Study Guide chapter.

1. Your textbook author argues that psychology has "a long past but a short history." Explain what this statement means, using your knowledge of the historical foundations of modern psychology.

2. One of the most important events that shaped (and still is shaping) the face of modern psychology is the "cognitive revolution." What is cognition, and what is meant by the term "cognitive revolution"? What three events contributed to the cognitive revolution?

3. Upon receiving your Ph.D. in Psychology, you are hired by the owners of a large retail toy company to assist in the development of a new set of playground equipment that will be used in parks throughout the area. As a first step, you decide to explore the kinds of activities children actually engage in while playing with each other in park-like settings. Explain the difference between laboratory research and field research and provide an example of how you would use each setting to examine your research question. What are the advantages and disadvantages of each research setting? Is one research setting "better" than the other?

4. Many psychologists collect behavioral data from the participants in their studies. What is "behavioral observation"? What are some advantages and disadvantages of using this type of measurement?

5. What is a survey? Define this concept and give an example of a survey study or question that might be answered by a survey. What two factors are particularly important for psychologists who use surveys to consider? Use relevant examples when necessary.

Multiple-Choice Solutions

1. A (p. 4)	11. D (p. 16)	21. C (p. 23)
2. D (p. 4)	12. A (p. 18)	22. B (p. 25)
3. D (pp. 4-6)	13. C (p. 19)	23. A (p. 25)
4. B (p. 6)	14. D (p. 19)	24. C (p. 25)
5. A (p. 7)	15. D (p. 19)	25. B (p. 26)
6. C (p. 7)	16. B (p. 22)	26. D (p. 27)
7. A (p. 9)	17. C (p. 23)	27. D (p. 27)
8. D (p. 9-10)	18. D (p. 23)	28. C (p. 27)
9. A (p. 10)	19. D (pp. 16, 18, 24)	29. D (p. 29)
10. B (p. 11)	20. D (p. 23)	30. B (p. 31)

True-False Solutions

1. F (p. 4)	6. F (p. 18)
2. F (p. 9)	7. T (p. 19)
3. T (p. 10)	8. F (p. 23)
4. T (p. 16)	9. T (p. 24)
5. T (p. 17)	10. F (p. 25)

Key Concepts Matching Solutions

Exercise #1	*Exercise #2*	*Exercise #3*
1. C	1. L	1. B
2. D	2. G	2. C
3. E	3. A	3. A
4. H	4. H	
5. A	5. D	
6. B	6. C	
7. F	7. E	
8. G	8. I	
	9. B	
	10. F	
	11. J	
	12. K	

Essay Solutions

1. As a discipline, psychology has its roots in much older disciplines (in other words, psychology has a long past). For example, the ancient Greek philosophers Socrates, Plato, and Aristotle wrote a number of treatises about aspects of human behavior and the mind, including pleasure and pain, the five sensory systems, imagination, and the motivational state of desire. Similarly, Hippocrates and Galen (early physicians) formed theories about human behavior and consciousness. More recently (but still prior to psychology's actual "founding"), physiologists like Helmholtz and Fechner began to study the brain and the processes of sensation and perception. However, it was only in the late 1800s that modern experimental psychology was born when Wilhelm Wundt established the first laboratory specifically dedicated to the study of the human mind. Thus, psychology has a long past but a short history (only a little over a hundred years) (pp. 4-7)

2. Cognition refers to the mental processes that occur or intervene between a stimulus and a response (in other words, subjective phenomena like expectations, feelings, and images that lie between an environmental stimulus and our response to that stimulus). The term "cognitive revolution" refers to the reemergence of subjective, nonobservable phenomena (like expectations and affect) as suitable topics for scientific inquiry (remember that behaviorism and its emphasis on observable, overt behavior and stimulus-response patterns was the dominant perspective at the time; the cognitive revolution reinstated the primacy of the organism and the mind that lie between the stimulus and the response) (p. 9).

   Three events contributed to the cognitive revolution. The first was the invention of the computer; computers provided a new model for the human mind (an information-processing model). A second factor that contributed to the cognitive revolution was the cognitive theory of Piaget, who studied the development of thinking and reasoning in children. Piaget's writings were translated into English in the 1950s and 1960s, and they provided another source of inspiration for researchers interested in cognition. Finally, new research on language development demonstrated that language acquisition is not controlled by laws of learning (the behaviorist perspective) but rather is a function of specialized cognitive structures that are "hard-wired" into the human brain (p. 9-10).

3. Laboratory research involves collecting data from participants in a controlled environment in which the participant can be carefully observed. In this situation, you might recreate a park-like setting in the lab, bring children into this setting, videotape their interactions with each other, and then analyze their behavior (count, for example, the number of times children enter into a single as opposed to a group activity). The primary advantage of this type of research is that it offers a lot of environmental control (you can monitor all aspects of the children's behavior). The disadvantage is that a constructed laboratory setting is artificial and may actually cause participants to engage in unusual behavior: If the room in which children are playing is not at all like an actual playground, how do we know if we are really measuring "playground behavior?" (p. 16)

   The alternative to laboratory research is field research—this is research conducted in actual, real-world locations. In this situation, you could go to a playground that contains a mix of toys and children, observe several of these children over a specified period of time, and record various activities in which they engage. The advantage is that you would gain insight into what actually occurs in a park-like setting; the disadvantage is that you lose control over the situation and cannot precisely analyze every single aspect of the children's behavior (p. 17)

One setting is not necessarily better than the other. Both have advantages and disadvantages. Consequently, the best approach for answering any research question is to use both laboratory and field settings (p. 17).

4. Behavioral observations involve observing a participant's behavior firsthand, either openly or covertly. This type of measurement is the major alternative to self-report. An advantage of behavioral observation is that it allows psychologists to measure behavior objectively without relying on self-report data that may be distorted or inaccurate. For example, people may be unwilling to provide a truthful description of their drinking behavior; thus, a researcher who observes people in a bar may obtain a much more accurate assessment of drinking behavior than one who relies upon people's self-reports. The problem with using behavioral observation is that inner states (like feelings of anger or love) cannot be directly observed from behavior. Also, people may behave differently if they realize that they are being measured (for example, bar patrons might alter their drinking behavior if they become aware that a researcher is observing them) (pp. 17, 18).

5. Surveys are considered one type of descriptive research design. Their purpose is to describe an entire population by looking at many cases (p. 20). For example, a psychologist might investigate the percentage of husbands and wives who have an affair by calling 10,000 individuals and asking those who are married to provide an answer to this question.

There are two main factors that should be of concern to psychologists who use this research design. The first involves sampling issues (i.e., who the respondents are). To describe any group (like the population of married people), the researcher selects a subset of that group (the sample, 10,000 married people). For a survey to be accurate, the sample has to be as similar to or representative of the larger population as possible. In this case, it is important that the 10,000 married people surveyed by the researcher be randomly selected from the larger population so that they resemble that population in terms of age, race/ethnicity, region, income, and so on. If the researcher has only surveyed upper-income, middle-aged individuals, the results may not tell us much about the faithfulness of married people in general (pp. 20-21). Second, the researcher must consider how he or she words or frames the research questions. For example, respondents might provide quite different answers to the question, "Have you ever had an extramarital relationship?," than they would to the question, "Have you ever deliberately violated your sacred marriage vows by cheating on your beloved spouse?" (p. 22).

Multimedia Study Resources

The Mind Matters™ unit called "History and Methods" contains brief summaries of three key topics covered in your textbook: (1) Psychology's roots, (2) recent trends in psychology, and (3) the science of psychology. There is a brief quiz at the end of the unit.

Chapter 1 (Psychology, Research, and You) of The Psychology Place™ contains a variety of relevant activities and information. For example, the Research News section contains articles that discuss the use of animals in research ("Animal Rights Activists: Changing Views on Animal Research") and the controversy that often erupts when scientists draw research conclusions that go against public opinion ("Drawing Conclusions: The Child Sexual Abuse Controversy"). The Op Ed Forum includes personal biographies and interviews with some of today's leading psychologists ("How Did Leading Psychologists Find Psychology?"), and the Best of the Web section contains direct links to the American Psychological Association (www.apa.org) and the American Psychological Society (www.psychologicalscience.org).

Behavioral Neuroscience

This chapter focuses upon behavioral neuroscience, an area of psychology concerned with exploring the biological roots of human experience. Specifically, your text begins with an overview of the body's communication systems—the nervous system and the endocrine system—and the behaviors affected by different parts of those interconnected systems. The chapter then examines the structure and function of neurons (basic building blocks of the nervous system) and how neural communication influences our behavior through the release of neurotransmitters. The brain is the next topic of discussion. Your textbook author presents research methods available for studying brain activity and function (i.e., case study, experimental interventions, electrical recordings, imaging), discusses the various regions of the brain and the behaviors and events that each regulates, and explores the "split-brain" phenomenon and the notion of cerebral lateralization (brain function asymmetry). The chapter ends with an exploration of several topics that lie in the intersection between basic behavioral neuroscience and applied areas of psychology—handedness (i.e., being a "leftie" or a "rightie"), right-brain education, head injury in contact sports, and neurogenesis in adults.

Chapter Outline

I. *What's Your Prediction?* One Brain or Two?

II. The Body's Communication Networks

    A. The Nervous System

    B. The Endocrine System

III. The Neuron

    A. Structure of the Neuron

By the time you have read and reviewed this chapter, you should be able to:

1. Discuss the story of Phineas Gage and what his case revealed about the human brain and nervous system (pp. 40-41).

2. Distinguish between the various parts of the nervous system (pp. 41-42). Define the functions controlled by the central and peripheral nervous systems and list the different parts of these systems (pp. 41-42).

3. Define the elements and functions of the endocrine system (p. 42). Discuss how the nervous and endocrine systems communicate (p. 43).

4. Explain what a neuron is and list and define the different types of neurons (p. 43). List and explain the function of the structures of a neuron (pp. 45).

5. Explain how neurons communicate (pp. 45-47). Discuss the relationship between neurotransmitters and behavior (pp. 47-49).

6. Consider the various "tools" that psychologists have at their disposal for studying brain activity and function (pp. 49-53).

7. Explain the difference between case studies, experimental interventions, electrical recordings, and brain-imaging techniques (pp. 49-53). State the advantages and disadvantages of each method and what each reveals about the human brain.

8. Describe the regions of the human brain (pp. 53-60).

9. List the structures that comprise the brainstem and the function of each one (pp. 54).

10. List the structures of the limbic system and the function of each one (pp. 54-57).

11. Explain the differences in the cerebral cortex found in more complex as compared to less complex species (p. 57). List and describe the functional regions of the cortex (pp. 58-60).

12. Distinguish between the somatosensory and the motor cortex, and explain the functions controlled by each (pp. 58-59).

13. Describe the association cortex (p. 59).

14. Explain the difference between the two language areas of the cortex (Broca's area and Wernicke's area) (p. 60).

15. Discuss whether the functions of the human brain are localized or whether the brain operates as an integrated system (pp. 60).

16. Discuss the relation between handedness and health. Compare and contrast the longevity hypothesis and the modification hypothesis (pp. 61-62).

17. Describe the phenomenon of split-brain syndrome (p. 63). Discuss the "division of labor" in the brain (p. 63) and how this affects split-brain patients (pp. 63-64). Explain how subcortical structures may provide a means of hemispheric communication in split-brain patients (p. 65-66).

18. Consider the case for cerebral lateralization (pp. 66-67, 69).

19. Consider the topic of "right-brain education" and how this relates to cerebral lateralization (p. 68).

20. Define the concept of plasticity (p. 70) and discuss whether the adult human brain can be changed through enrichment experiences (pp. 70-72).

21. Discuss the signs of a concussion and the ways in which head trauma to athletes can be minimized (p. 73).

22. Consider developments in our ability to repair brain damage (e.g., neural grafts) (pp. 72-74). Discuss the ethical dilemmas raised by those developments (pp. 74-75).

23. Define the concept of neurogenesis and discuss whether this process occurs in the brains of adult humans (p. 75).

Key Terms

The following key terms and concepts are featured in this chapter and are important for you to know. Write out definitions of each term and check your answers with the definitions in the text on the pages listed.

Central nervous system (CNS) (p. 41)
Peripheral nervous system (PNS) (p. 41)
Somatic nervous system (p. 41)
Autonomic nervous system (p. 41)
Sympathetic division (p. 41)
Parasympathetic division (p. 42)
Endocrine system (p. 42)
Hormones (p. 42)
Pituitary gland (p. 42)
Neurons (p. 43)
Sensory neurons (p. 43)
Motor neurons (p. 43)
Interneurons (p. 43)
Glial cells (p. 44)
Reflex (p. 44)
Soma (p. 45)
Dendrites (p. 45)
Axon (p. 45)
Myelin sheath (p. 45)
Action potential (p. 46)
Threshold (p. 46)
Synapse (p. 47)
Neurotransmitters (p. 47)
Receptors (p. 47)
Acetylcholine (ACh) (p. 47)
Dopamine (p. 48)
Endorphin (p. 49)
Phrenology (p. 49)

Electroencephalograph (EEG) (p. 51)
Computerized tomography (CT) scan (p. 51)
Positron emission tomograph (PET) scan (p. 52)
Magnetic resonance imaging (MRI) (p. 53)
Brainstem (p. 54)
Medulla (p. 54)
Pons (p. 54)
Reticular formation (p. 54)
Cerebellum (pp. 54)
Basal ganglia (p. 54)
Limbic system (p. 54)
Thalamus (p. 55)
Amygdala (p. 56)
Hippocampus (p. 56)
Hypothalamus (p. 56)
Cerebral cortex (p. 57)
Somatosensory cortex (p. 58)
Motor cortex (p. 59)
Association cortex (p. 59)
Broca's area (p. 60)
Wernicke's area (p. 60)
Corpus callosum (p. 63)
Split brain (p. 63)
Cerebral lateralization (p. 66)
Plasticity (p. 70)
Neural graft (p. 72)
Concussion (p. 73)
Neurogenesis (p. 75)

Multiple-Choice Questions

Circle the correct choice for each question and compare your answers with those at the end of the Study Guide chapter.

1. Which of the following items does not belong with the rest?
   A. central nervous system
   B. peripheral nervous system
   C. somatic nervous system
   D. autonomic nervous system

2. Which of the following items is out of place?
   A. parasympathetic system
   B. autonomic nervous system
   C. somatic nervous system
   D. sympathetic system

3. Which one of the following experiences is regulated or controlled by the autonomic nervous system?
   A. the taste of a lemon
   B. the sound of a bird singing
   C. the beating of a heart
   D. the movement of a runner's legs

4. The endocrine system is involved in the regulation of human
   A. growth.
   B. sexual development.
   C. metabolism.
   D. all of the above.

5. Joanne is getting ready for her morning run. While she is sitting on her porch tying her shoes, her neighbor calls out a greeting. Joanne raises her head and replies, "Good morning!" The type of neuron that enables Joanne to tie her shoes is _____; the type of neuron that enables her to hear her neighbor's greeting is _____.
   A. sensory; motor
   B. motor; sensory
   C. sensory; interneuron
   D. motor; motor

6. The part of a neuron that receives impulses from organs or other neurons is called
   A. the dendrite.
   B. the axon.
   C. the soma.
   D. the nucleus.

7. The purpose of the myelin sheath surrounding a neuron's axon is
   A. to insulate the axon.
   B. to speed up the movement of electrical impulses.
   C. to prevent leakage of electrical impulses.
   D. all of the above.

8. Action potentials have which of the following characteristics?
   A. they are triggered any time a neuron is stimulated
   B. they are an all-or-none response
   C. they are reversible
   D. all of the above

9. Neurotransmitters have been implicated in a number of human behaviors and experiences, including
   A. depression.
   B. intelligence.
   C. growth.
   D. socioeconomic status.

10. Suppose that you are a researcher at a toxicology lab. One day, you accidentally inject yourself with curare, a poison that blocks the release of acetylcholine in the nervous system. What will you experience?
   A. violent muscle contractions
   B. hand tremors
   C. paralysis
   D. sleeplessness

11. Suppose that you receive immediate treatment for your curare poisoning, only to accidentally inject yourself with a solution that causes the release of serotonin. What will you feel now?
   A. depressed
   B. sleepy
   C. schizophrenic
   D. anxious

12. A teacher takes his class on a field trip to see the famous "Dr. Fantastik." For a small fee, Dr. Fantastik carefully examines the skull of each child and then makes a pronouncement about the characteristics that child possesses. The notion that physical features of the skull correspond to psychological characteristics is known as
   A. pseudoscience.
   B. phrenology.
   C. phenomenology.
   D. scientology.

13. Behavioral neuroscientists utilize a variety of research methods in their attempts to understand the human brain. Examples of experimental interventions include
   A. the creation of brain lesions.
   B. the administration of drugs.
   C. electrical brain stimulation.
   D. all of the above.

14. Some brain-imaging techniques can be used to map brain activity as it actually occurs over time. These techniques include
   A. CT scan.
   B. PET scan.
   C. functional MRI.
   D. B and C.

15. The _____ helps regulate "primitive" life-support functions like breathing, whereas the _____ controls "higher" mental processes like complex learning.
   A. brainstem; cortex
   B. limbic system; cortex
   C. brainstem; limbic system
   D. cortex; limbic system

16. A person who has difficulty focusing his or her attention and who is experiencing sleep disruptions may have sustained damage to the _____.
   A. medulla
   B. reticular formation
   C. cerebellum
   D. pons

17. Bart was in an accident that caused him to sustain some minor damage to his limbic system. The accident seems to have affected his ability to form new memories. What part of the limbic system is likely to have been involved?
    A. the amygdala
    B. the hypothalamus
    C. the hippocampus
    D. the thalamus

18. The limbic system plays an important role in regulating
    A. motivation.
    B. memory.
    C. emotion.
    D. all of the above.

19. Your textbook author believes that "if you had to sacrifice an ounce of brain tissue, you wouldn't want to take it from the hypothalamus." Why does he make this statement?
    A. The hypothalamus regulates higher thought processes.
    B. Stimulation of the hypothalamus causes pleasure.
    C. The hypothalamus helps us to retrieve important personal memories.
    D. Stimulation of the hypothalamus releases acetylcholine.

20. Which of the following statements about the cerebral cortex is accurate?
    A. The cerebral cortex is the innermost covering of the brain.
    B. The cerebral cortex is present in all mammals except dolphins and whales.
    C. The cerebral cortex constitutes about 10 percent of the human brain.
    D. None of the above.

21. The _____ lobe in the back of the brain is the primary visual cortex.
    A. temporal
    B. occipital
    C. frontal
    D. parietal

22. The _____ cortex communicates with the sensory cortex and the motor cortex and houses the brain's higher mental processes.
    A. somatosensory
    B. association
    C. broca
    D. Penfield

23. The _____ the need for precise control over a body part, the _____ is its area in the motor cortex.
    A. greater; smaller
    B. smaller; larger
    C. greater; larger
    D. There is no relation between need for control over a body part and size of motor cortex area.

24. Both Khaveri and Anupama have experienced brain damage. Khaveri does not understand what people are saying to her, but she speaks in complete sentences and produces fluent, grammatical speech. Anupama, on the other hand, understands what other people are saying to her, but she is unable to produce complete, grammatical sentences. Khaveri most likely has sustained damage to _____; Anupama most likely has sustained damage to _____.
    A. Broca's area; Wernicke's area
    B. Wernicke's area; Broca's area
    C. the left hemisphere; the right hemisphere
    D. the temporal lobe; the frontal lobe

25. The key language centers in the brain are located in the _____.
    A. corpus callosum
    B. occipital lobe
    C. right hemisphere
    D. left hemisphere

26. Jorge has severe epilepsy. One possible way of reducing the severity of his seizures is to sever the _____.
    A. limbic system
    B. frontal lobe
    C. corpus callosum
    D. Wernicke area

27. The primary function of the corpus callosum is to
    A. allow the two cerebral hemispheres to communicate.
    B. control the comprehension and production of language.
    C. produce emotional responses.
    D. regulate the body's hormone levels.

28. A split-brain patient is shown a slide of the words *puppy dog* in such a way that her right visual field (the left hemisphere of the brain) sees only the word *dog* and her left visual field (the right hemisphere of the brain) sees only the word *puppy*. When asked to tell what she sees, what will she say?
    A. puppy
    B. dog
    C. puppy dog
    D. dog puppy

29. Research on cerebral lateralization suggests that the right hemisphere plays a vital role in
    A. visual-spatial tasks.
    B. music.
    C. face recognition.
    D. all of the above.

30. Living in an "enriched" environment may produce
    A. dendritic growth.
    B. hemispheric specialization.
    C. neural grafts.
    D. split-brain syndrome.

True-False Questions

Indicate which of the following statements are true or false, and compare your answers with those at the end of the chapter.

T   F   1. Neural impulses are generally more rapid than hormonal messages.

T   F   2. The nervous system and endocrine system are in constant communication.

T   F   3. Each neuron is linked with no more than five other neurons.

T   F   4. Neural communication involves both chemical and electrical processes.

T   F   5. Each neurotransmitter is capable of binding only to certain receptors.

T   F   6. Phrenology is one of the primary methods utilized by modern neuroscientists.

T   F   7. In general, the more complex the species, the more convoluted the cortex.

T   F   8. Most psychologists prefer to divide the areas of the brain according to function rather than to actual physical region.

T F 9. Research on language disorders suggests that there is only one distinct cortical center for language.

T F 10. Current evidence on cerebral lateralization indicates that the left and right hemispheres of the brain are specialized to process different information.

Key Concepts Matching Exercises

Exercise #1: Pin the Name on the Skull

This is _____'s skull

A. Saul Kassin
B. Sigmund Freud
C. Phineas Gage
D. Mary Whiton Calkins
E. Wilhelm Wundt

Exercise #2: The Nervous System

Match the key concepts on the left with the definitions on the right.

_____ 1. Central nervous system

_____ 2. Somatic nervous system

_____ 3. Endocrine system

_____ 4. Parasympathetic division

_____ 5. Autonomic nervous system

_____ 6. Sympathetic division

A. Connects sensory organs and skin to the CNS

B. Connects the CNS to involuntary muscles and organs

C. The body's "department of peace"

D. Consists of the brain and spinal cord

E. Collection of ductless glands that secrete hormones

F. The body's "war department"

Exercise #3: The Neuron

Match the key concepts on the left with the definitions on the right.

_____ 1. Soma

_____ 2. Axon

_____ 3. Glial cell

_____ 4. Synapse

_____ 5. Interneuron

_____ 6. Dendrite

_____ 7. Axon terminal

_____ 8. Myelin sheath

_____ 9. Neurotransmitter

_____10. Action potential

A. The "glue" that provides neurons with structural support, nutrients, and insulation

B. Functions as the neuron's "antennae"

C. Fatty substance that insulates the axon and speeds neural communication

D. All-or-nothing burst of information that travels in the form of electrical energy

E. Knoblike "tips" that contain neurotransmitters

F. Fiber that sends information through one neuron to another

G. The cell body of a neuron

H. Narrow gap between neighboring neurons

I. Links sensory and motor neurons

J. Chemical substance that transmits information from one neuron to another

Exercise #4: The Brain

Match the key concepts on the left with the definitions on the right.

_____ 1. Brainstem

_____ 2. Reticular formation

_____ 3. Cerebellum

_____ 4. Limbic system

_____ 5. Hippocampus

_____ 6. Cerebral cortex

_____ 7. Motor cortex

_____ 8. Broca's area

_____ 9. Wernicke's area

_____10. Corpus callosum

A. Plays a key role in speech production

B. Damage to this structure impairs coordination and balance

C. Is involved in the formation of new memories

D. Portion of the brain that represents all 600 muscles in the human body

E. Plays a key role in speech comprehension

F. Netlike group of neurons that control sleep, arousal, and attention

G. "Bridge" that connects the two hemispheres

H. Regulates emotion, motivation, and memory

I. Outermost covering of the brain

J. Regulates primitive behaviors like breathing

Essay Questions

Write out answers to the following brief essay questions. Compare your responses with the sample answers at the end of the Study Guide chapter.

1. The pituitary gland has been called the "master gland" of the endocrine system. Why?

2. Discuss three types of experimental intervention that are commonly used by behavioral neuroscientists to explore the functions of the brain.

3. Is there a link between the amygdala and aggression? Explain why this part of the limbic system has been called an "aggression center."

4. "Each side of the brain is its own mind." Agree or disagree with this statement, using research on the split-brain phenomenon and cerebral lateralization.

5. What is plasticity? Define this concept and discuss whether the adult brain can be altered by environmental stimulation.

Test Solutions

Multiple-Choice Solutions

1. A (p. 41)	11. B (p. 48)	21. B (p. 58)
2. C (p. 41)	12. B (p. 49)	22. B (p. 59)
3. C (p. 41)	13. D (p. 50-51)	23. C (p. 59)
4. D (p. 42)	14. D (pp. 52-53)	24. B (p. 60)
5. B (p. 43)	15. A (p. 54)	25. D (p. 61)
6. A (p. 45)	16. B (p. 54)	26. C (p. 63)
7. D (p. 45)	17. C (p. 56)	27. A (p. 63)
8. B (p. 46)	18. D (p. 55)	28. B (p. 64)
9. A (p. 48)	19. B (p. 57)	29. D (p. 67)
10. C (p. 48)	20. D (p. 57)	30. A (pp. 70)

True-False Solutions

1. T (p. 42)	6. F (p. 49)
2. T (p. 43)	7. T (p. 57)
3. F (p. 46)	8. T (p. 58)
4. T (p. 47)	9. F (p. 60)
5. T (p. 47)	10. T (p. 66)

Key Concepts Matching Solutions

Exercise #1

1. C

Exercise #2	*Exercise #3*	*Exercise #4*
1. D	1. G	1. J
2. A	2. F	2. F
3. E	3. A	3. B
4. C	4. H	4. H
5. B	5. I	5. C
6. F	6. B	6. I
	7. E	7. D
	8. C	8. A
	9. J	9. E
	10. D	10. G

Essay Solutions

1. The pituitary gland is a small but powerful structure that sits at the base of the brain. When it receives the "go ahead," this gland releases a hormone that in turn stimulates the production and release of hormones in other endocrine glands. These hormones flow back to the brain, which then informs the hypothalamus to ask the pituitary for more or less hormone production. Thus, the pituitary gland is the master gland! (p. 42-43)

2. One experimental intervention involves purposefully disabling part of the brain by surgically destroying it (usually by means of a high-voltage electrical current). A second method is to administer drugs that are suspected of having effects on certain neurotransmitters; upon drug administration, behavior can be observed. A third method is to electrically stimulate the brain; specifically, a microelectrode is inserted into the brain and a mild electrical current is used to activate the neurons in a particular site (p. 50-51)

3. There does appear to be a link between the amygdala and aggression, although other structures and processes are involved in this human behavior (and the amygdala has other functions). In particular, stimulation of the amygdala can result in feelings of anger, fear, and anxiety, and in violent actions. For example, your text discusses research by Kluver and Bucy (1937), two scientists who found that lesions in the amygdala reduced aggression in rhesus monkeys. Similarly, Mark and his colleague (1970) demonstrated that electrical stimulation of the amygdala of a woman with epilepsy (Julia) caused violent episodes, whereas the destruction of part of the amygdala decreased her fits of rage. In sum, the amygdala does appear to be intricately associated with aggressive responses (pp. 56).

4. Well, you can agree or disagree with this statement—it's up to you! But to support your answer, you should note that there is a division of labor within the brain. For example, the left hemisphere receives information from the right side of the body, whereas the right hemisphere communicates with the left side of the body (p. 63). In addition, research on cerebral lateralization suggests that there are hemispheric differences in the connected brain; the left hemisphere controls verbal activities, whereas the right hemisphere plays a vital role in nonverbal activities (pp. 66-69). These two lines of evidence indicate that each side of the brain might be its own mind. Split-brain research, however, muddies the waters a bit. For instance, when the two hemispheres are separated by severing the corpus callosum, they are no longer able to work as a team by sharing information gathered from each side of the body (information sent to the right hemisphere may not cross over to the left hemisphere, and vice versa). In such cases, it is possible to create a situation in which the two halves function in complete ignorance of each other—each with its own mind (pp. 63-65). However, there is also evidence that some input from the environment may reach both

hemispheres through subcortical structures that remain connected when the corpus callosum is cut (p. 65-66). In sum, the halves of the brain are designed to receive information from different sources and to control different functions, but the fact that they are specialized does not necessarily mean that they are independent. In addition, even though split-brain individuals seem to have two independent streams of consciousness (and your text presents research on this point), their behavior is well-integrated and relatively seamless (you wouldn't know these people had a split brain in everyday situations). So, one mind or two, you decide!

5. Plasticity refers to the capacity of the brain to change as a result of practice, use, and/or experience (p. 70). Although psychologists used to believe that the adult brain was fully developed and incapable of change, research now suggests that it is much more plastic or flexible than had been originally thought. For example, research on rats indicates that exposure to an "enriched" environment (with ladders, toys, and other stimuli that promote curiosity and stimulate physical and mental exploration) causes the development of thicker, heavier brain tissue with more dendrites and synapses. In fact, the type of stimulation may cause specific brain transformations; for example, rats who receive a lot of visual stimulation experience more visual cortex growth, whereas rats placed in an environment that requires balance and coordination form a more well-developed cerebellum. In addition, some research on humans now suggests that repeated stimulation of a particular body part (like the tapping of fingers) causes enhanced brain activity and dendritic growth (p. 70). Thus, it appears that the adult brain can be altered by environmental input.

Multimedia Study Resources

The Mind Matters™ unit called "Biopsychology" presents a review of evolution and behavior, neurons and the endocrine system, and the brain. There is a brief quiz on these topics at the end of the unit.

Several activities and articles in Chapter 2 (Biological Foundations of Psychology) of The Psychology Place™ supplement the material covered in your textbook. "Action at the Synapse" is an animated learning activity that explores synaptic communication, neurotransmitter effects, and drug effects. Articles from *Scientific American* magazine discuss the cognitive changes associated with aging ("Aging Brain, Aging Mind") and cognitive variations between the sexes ("Sex Differences in the Brain"). And finally, there are informative research articles on neurogenesis ("Adult Brains Can Generate New Neurons") and the way in which learning a second language influences the physical development of the brain ("Second Languages and the Brain: New Organization for Later Learners").

3

Sensation and Perception

Chapter Overview

Building upon the information presented in Chapter 2, this chapter examines the psychology of sensation and perception, two interrelated processes that enable us to acquire information about the world. First, the chapter focuses on sensation, the process whereby receptor cells in our sensory systems (e.g., ears) gather information from the environment (e.g., vibrating air molecules) and send that information to the brain for further processing. Specifically, the text examines measurement issues including absolute thresholds and difference thresholds, as well as signal-detection theory. Then, each sensory modality is discussed in turn (i.e., vision, hearing, smell, taste, touch, temperature, pain, coordination). The second part of the chapter explores perception, the process in which sensory information is selected, organized, and interpreted (e.g., we "hear" a sound and recognize it as part of a song we've heard before). In turn, the chapter examines the process of perceptual organization, the phenomenon of perceptual constancy, and the factors involved in depth perception. The ways in which perception can be influenced by prior experience (called perceptual set) also are discussed, as are perceptual illusions. The chapter ends with a discussion of extrasensory perception, or perception in the absence of sensation.

Chapter Outline

I. *What's Your Prediction?* Does Culture Influence Depth Perception?

II. Measuring the Sensory Experience

    A. Absolute Thresholds

    B. Signal-Detection Theory

    C. Difference Thresholds

III. Sensation

    A. Vision
        1. Light
        2. The visual system
            a. The eye
            b. Visual pathways
            c. The visual cortex
        3. Color vision

    B. Hearing
        1. Sound waves
        2. The auditory system
        3. Hearing abilities
        4. Hearing disabilities

    C. *Psychology and ... Health* When is Noise Too Loud?

    D. Other Senses
        1. Smell
        2. Taste
        3. Touch
        4. Temperature
        5. Pain
            a. Gate-control theory
            b. Psychological control
        6. Coordination

    E. *Through the Global Window ...* Cultural Differences in Smell

    F. Sensation: Keeping the Signals Straight

IV. Perception

    A. Perceptual Organization
        1. Figure and ground
        2. Gestalt laws of grouping

    B. Perceptual Constancies
        1. Size constancy
        2. Shape constancy

    C. Depth and Dimension
        1. Binocular depth cues
        2. Monocular depth cues
        3. Origins of depth perception
            a. Perceptual experience
            b. Depth perception as inborn

Learning Objectives

By the time you have read and reviewed this chapter, you should be able to:

1. Distinguish between the processes of sensation and perception and consider whether these processes are separate or linked (pp. 82-83).

2. Explain the concept of absolute thresholds and how these are derived (p. 84). Consider the relation between absolute thresholds and signal-detection theory (pp. 84-85). Explain how difference thresholds are used to measure sensory capacities (pp. 85-86).

3. Discuss the visual sensory modality (pp. 86-95). Consider the properties of light waves (p. 87) and distinguish between the major structures of the human eye (pp. 88-89). Explain the processes of dark and light adaptation (p. 90).

4. Discuss how the eye, visual pathways, and the visual cortex are involved in visual sensation (pp. 87-89, 91-92). Compare the trichromatic and opponent-process theories of color vision (pp. 93-94).

5. Discuss the auditory sensory modality (pp. 95-100). Consider the properties of sound waves (pp. 95-96). Examine the auditory system, including the structures of the ear and the auditory cortex (pp. 96-97).

6. Discuss the adaptive aspects of normal hearing, including auditory localization (p. 97). Consider types of hearing impairment (p. 98) and the impact of environmental noise on hearing (p. 99).

7. Examine the olfactory sensory modality and discuss the processes involved in the sensation of smell (pp. 100-103). Consider the factors (e.g., age, individual differences, culture) that affect the sense of smell (p. 102). Discuss whether pheromones affect human behavior (pp. 102-3).

8. Consider the sensation of taste (pp. 103-4). Distinguish between types of taste and individual differences in taste sensitivity (p. 104).

9. Discuss the sensation of touch and what distinguishes this sensation from others (pp. 104-5). Distinguish between active and passive touch (p. 105). Consider the four basic types of sensation involved in touch (p. 105).

10. Examine the factors that affect the sensation of temperature (pp. 106-7).

11. Consider the sensation of pain (p. 107) and distinguish between gate-control theory (pp. 107-8) and psychological control (p. 108) as ways of decreasing pain awareness.

12. Consider the sensory systems involved in coordination (kinesthetic and vestibular) (pp. 108-9).

13. Discuss how sensory adaptation and selective attention enable the human sensory systems to respond to only particular types of information without confusion (p. 109).

14. Explain the process of perceptual organization (pp. 110-11). Define the concept of figure and ground (p. 111) and list and explain the five Gestalt "laws" of grouping (pp. 111-12).

15. Discuss the two types of perceptual constancy (pp. 112-13). Define size and shape constancy and discuss factors that affect these tendencies (pp. 112-13).

16. Consider the factors involved in depth perception; namely, binocular depth cues and monocular depth cues (pp. 113-16). Discuss whether depth perception is inborn or learned from experience (pp. 116-17).

17. Define the concept of perceptual set and examine how prior experiences and expectations can influence perception (pp. 117-18).

18. Provide examples of perceptual illusions and explain how such illusions may stem from overuse of "normal" perceptual rules (pp. 118-19).

19. Define extrasensory perception (p. 121). Examine the evidence both for (pp. 121-22) and against (pp. 122-23) ESP.

Key Terms

The following key terms and concepts are featured in this chapter and are important for you to know. Write out definitions of each term and check your answers with the definitions in the text on the pages listed.

Sensation (p. 82)
Transduction (p. 82)
Perception (p. 82)
Psychophysics (p. 84)
Absolute threshold (p. 84)
Signal-detection theory (p. 85)
Just noticeable difference (JND) (p. 86)
Weber's law (p. 86)
Cornea (p. 88)
Iris (p. 88)
Pupil (p. 88)
Lens (p. 88)
Accommodation (p. 88)
Retina (p. 88)
Rods (p. 89)
Cones (p. 89)

Fovea (p. 89)
Dark adaptation (p. 90)
Light adaptation (p. 90)
Optic nerve (p. 90)
Blind spot (p. 90)
Visual cortex (p. 91)
Feature detectors (p. 92)
Trichromatic theory (p. 93)
Afterimages (p. 93)
Opponent-process theory (p. 93)
Audition (p. 95)
White noise (p. 95)
Auditory localization (p. 97)
Conduction deafness (p. 98)
Nerve deafness (p. 98)
Olfactory system (p. 100)

Test Questions

Multiple-Choice Questions

Circle the correct choice for each question and compare your answers with those at the end of the Study Guide chapter.

1. The process in which raw physical energy is absorbed by sensory receptors is called
   A. sensation.
   B. perception.
   C. transduction.
   D. extrasensory perception.

2. The process in which energy that has been absorbed by sensory receptors is converted into neural signals that are then sent to the brain is called
   A. sensation.
   B. perception.
   C. transduction.
   D. extrasensory perception.

3. Joey has volunteered for a psychology experiment. His task is to gaze at a dark screen and indicate to the researcher whether or not he sees a point of light. The researcher is attempting to assess Joey's
   A. perceptual threshold.
   B. stimulus gate.
   C. absolute threshold.
   D. intensity point.

4. Psychophysics researchers define the _____ as the point at which a stimulus (like light or a sound) can be detected 50 percent of the time.
   A. JND
   B. difference threshold
   C. sensory adaptation
   D. absolute threshold

5. The difference threshold or just noticeable difference is defined as the smallest change in stimulation that people can detect _____ percent of the time.
   A. 25
   B. 50
   C. 75
   D. 100

6. Sofia is in her garden gathering flowers for a bouquet. She selects a bright red rose. What wavelengths are producing the color that she sees when she looks at the rose?
   A. short wavelengths
   B. medium wavelengths
   C. long wavelengths
   D. all of the above

7. Purity is to saturation as wavelength is to _____.
   A. color
   B. richness
   C. brightness
   D. strength

8. The _____ is a small, round hole in the center of the eye through which light passes.
   A. cornea
   B. iris
   C. pupil
   D. lens

9. Deb has brown eyes, Julie has hazel eyes, Pam has blue eyes, and Sonja has green eyes. Which part of the eye causes these differences in eye color?
   A. cornea
   B. lens
   C. retina
   D. iris

10. The lens of the eye becomes rounded for focusing on nearby objects and flatter for focusing on distant objects. This process is known as
    A. retination.
    B. vision.
    C. light adaptation.
    D. accommodation.

11. Of the following children, whose pupils are the least dilated (the most contracted)?
    A. Paul, who is playing with a toy in complete darkness
    B. Jen, who is playing under the bed with a flashlight
    C. Matthew, who is playing outside under a shady tree
    D. Brian, who is playing outside in direct sunlight

12. Suppose that you came across a creature who could only see in black and white and whose vision was best at night. What would you guess about the retina of that creature?
    A. it contains only cones
    B. it contains only rods
    C. it contains a mixture of cones and rods
    D. it contains neither cones nor rods

13. Suppose that you came across another creature who could only see in color and whose vision was best during the day. What would you guess about the retina of that creature?
    A. it contains only cones
    B. it contains only rods
    C. it contains a mixture of cones and rods
    D. it contains neither cones nor rods

14. Which of the following "feature detectors" are present in the visual cortex?
    A. simple cells
    B. complex cells
    C. hypercomplex cells
    D. all of the above

15. The existence of _____ was a problem for the trichromatic theory of color vision.
    A. the color yellow
    B. the color white
    C. afterimages
    D. all of the above.

16. Frequency is to pitch as amplitude is to _____.
    A. loudness
    B. timbre
    C. tonal quality
    D. white noise

17. The hammer, anvil, and stirrup are part of _____.
    A. the outer ear
    B. the middle ear
    C. the inner ear
    D. a jockey's riding gear

18. Hearing involves which of the following substances?
    A. air
    B. fluid
    C. hair
    D. all of the above

19. While walking to school, you think you hear someone calling your name. Without thinking, you turn to your right and glance across the street—and you see someone from your class waving at you. Your ability to turn in the direction of the sound of your name reflects
    A. sensory adaptation.
    B. cochlear ability.
    C. auditory localization.
    D. conduction.

20. Among humans, olfactory sensitivity (the "sense of smell") peaks in _____.
    A. adolescence
    B. young adulthood
    C. middle age
    D. old age

21. Kara's dog Boris frequently urinates on the fence surrounding her yard. Other dogs now avoid the yard and the fence. Boris's "marking" behavior and the subsequent avoidance behavior of the other dogs may reflect the activity of _____:
    A. territoriality
    B. pheromones
    C. olfactory sensitivity
    D. gustation

22. The flavor of a food substance is determined by
    A. taste.
    B. odor.
    C. temperature.
    D. all of the above.

23. The largest organ in the human body is
    A. skin.
    B. the brain.
    C. the optic nerve.
    D. the heart.

24. Kate and Abby are playing with their pet parrot. The parrot rubs her head against Kate's arm, while Abby strokes the parrot's back. Kate is experiencing _____ touch, and Abby is experiencing _____ touch.
    A. passive; passive
    B. active; active
    C. passive; active
    D. active; passive

25. The sense of touch consists of which of the following types of sensations?
    A. pressure
    B. warmth
    C. pain
    D. all of the above

26. When you first bought your new watch, the watchband felt constricting and binding. Now, however, you hardly notice that the watch is on your wrist. This change in your sensitivity is known as
    A. selective attention.
    B. sensory adaptation.
    C. synesthesia.
    D. sensory decline.

27. Judy is taking an art class. Her assignment for this week is to paint a picture of a flower using individual "dots" of color. When she is finished, she asks you to evaluate her work. Although up close you can see each separate dot of paint, from a distance you perceive a unified picture of a beautiful flower. This example illustrates the Gestalt principle of
A. proximity.   C. closure.
B. continuity.   D. common fate.

28. A plane is descending from the sky for a landing. Joe, who has never seen a plane before, looks up in the sky and exclaims, "Look at that object! It's growing bigger and bigger!" Joe is demonstrating a lack of _____.
A. size constancy   C. closure
B. figure-and-ground   D. peripheral vision

29. Monocular depth cues enable us to do which of the following?
A. perceive depth with one eye closed
B. perceive depth at long distances
C. "see" a three-dimensional image on an artist's canvas
D. all of the above

30. Every night, a possum comes into Mallory's yard and climbs up the tree outside her window. One night, her neighbor's cat climbs the tree. However, instead of recognizing the cat, Mallory glances out and "sees" the possum. Mallory's error is the result of
A. monocular cues.   C. perceptual set.
B. binocular depth cues. D. perceptual illusions.

True-False Questions

Indicate which of the following statements are true or false, and compare your answers with those at the end of the chapter.

T F   1. Current psychological theory suggests that sensation and perception are best conceptualized as separate and distinct processes.

T F   2. The opponent-process theory of color vision can explain color blindness.

T F   3. It is not currently possible to regenerate damaged auditory hair cells in humans.

T F   4. Smell is the only sensation that is routed to the cortex through the thalamus.

T F   5. The number of taste buds on the human tongue increases as we age.

T F   6. Pain is an objective, purely physical experience.

T F   7. As a general rule, information received by one sensory system does not cross over to another.

T F   8. The phrase "figure and ground" illustrates the first principle of perceptual organization.

T F   9. The ability to perceive depth is partially dependent on experience.

T F   10. Research provides compelling evidence for the existence of ESP.

Key Concepts Matching Exercises

Exercise #1: The Heat Grill

The pipe on the left has warm water running through it. To experience the sensation "very hot" upon grasping both pipes at once, the other pipe must contain _____.

A. hot water
B. cold water
C. warm water
D. no water

Exercise #2: Vision

Match the key concepts on the left with the definitions on the right.

_____ 1. Color   A. Light passes through this small, round hole in the eye

_____ 2. Brightness   B. Determined by a light wave's amplitude

_____ 3. Saturation   C. Clear window that bends and focuses light within the eye

_____ 4. Iris   D. Light-sensitive receptor cell

_____ 5. Pupil   E. Clear structure that changes its shape to bring an image into focus

_____ 6. Cornea   F. Determined by a light wave's length

_____ 7. Lens   G. Neural pathway that carries visual information to the brain

_____ 8. Retina   H. Ring-shaped structure that provides eye color

_____ 9. Rod   I. Center of the retina

_____10. Cone   J. Determined by light waves' purity

_____11. Fovea   K. Color-sensitive receptor cell

_____12. Optic nerve   L. Cell layer that lines the inside surface of the eyeball

Exercise #3: Hearing

Match the key concepts on the left with the definitions on the right.

_____ 1. Pitch   A. Determined by the complexity of a sound wave

_____ 2. White noise   B. The ability to tell from which direction a sound comes

_____ 3. Loudness   C. Soft inner-ear membrane

_____ 4. Timbre   D. The combination of all possible sound waves causes this phenomenon

_____ 5. Outer ear   E. Caused by damage to the inner ear

_____ 6. Oval window   F. Animals can wiggle this structure to maximize sound reception

_____ 7. Middle ear   G. Determined by the frequency of a sound wave

_____ 8. Auditory localization   H. Consists of the hammer, anvil, and stirrup

_____ 9. Conduction deafness   I. The amplitude of a sound wave causes this experience

_____10. Nerve deafness   J. Caused by damage to the eardrum or middle ear

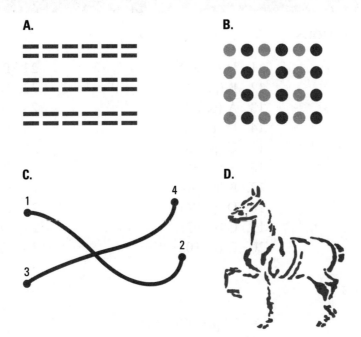

These figures represent which laws of grouping?

_____ 1. Similarity

_____ 2. Continuity

_____ 3. Closure

_____ 4. Proximity

Essay Questions

Write out answers to the following brief essay questions. Compare your responses with the sample answers at the end of the Study Guide chapter.

1. Define sensation and perception. Is it possible to have sensation without perception? What about perception without sensation? Answer both questions, using relevant examples cited in the text or from other sources.

2. What are pheromones and how do they affect behavior? Is there such a thing as a human pheromone?

3. Last week, Teresa fell and broke her foot. Although her doctor prescribed painkillers, she does not want to use them. Knowing that you are taking an introductory psychology course, she turns to you for advice. What two psychological approaches or methods can you suggest that Teresa use in order to reduce her pain? Be specific in your recommendations to her.

4. What is a sensory "crossover"? Is this a common experience?

5. "Depth perception is an innate skill that all humans have at birth." Agree or disagree with this statement.

Test Solutions

Multiple-Choice Solutions

1. A (p. 82)	11. D (p. 88)	21. B (p. 102)
2. C (p. 82)	12. B (p. 89)	22. D (p. 104)
3. C (p. 84)	13. A (p. 89)	23. A (p. 105)
4. D (p. 84)	14. D (p. 92)	24. C (p. 105)
5. B (p. 86)	15. C (p. 93)	25. D (p. 105)
6. C (p. 87)	16. A (p. 96)	26. B (p. 109)
7. A (p. 87)	17. B (p. 96)	27. C (p. 111)
8. C (p. 88)	18. D (p. 96)	28. A (p. 112)
9. D (p. 88)	19. C (p. 97)	29. D (p. 115)
10. D (p. 88)	20. C (p. 102)	30. C (p. 117)

True-False Solutions

1. F (p. 82)	6. F (p. 107)
2. T (p. 94)	7. T (p. 109)
3. T (p. 98)	8. T (p. 111)
4. F (p. 101)	9. T (p. 116)
5. F (p. 104)	10. F (pp. 122-23)

Key Concepts Matching Solutions

Exercise #1	*Exercise #2*	*Exercise #3*	*Exercise #4*
1. B	1. F	1. G	1. B
	2. B	2. D	2. C
	3. J	3. I	3. D
	4. H	4. A	4. A
	5. A	5. F	
	6. C	6. C	
	7. E	7. H	
	8. L	8. B	
	9. D	9. J	
	10. K	10. E	
	11. I		
	12. G		

Essay Solutions

1. In the process of sensation, raw physical energy from the environment (e.g., lightwaves) is absorbed by our different sensory systems (e.g., receptor cells in the eyes) and then converted into neural signals that are sent to the brain. In perception, these neural signals are selected, organized, and interpreted (e.g., we "see" someone we know) (p. 82).

   Yes, it is possible to have sensation without perception. For example, your text discusses the work of neurologist Oliver Sacks (1995), who presents a case study of a man (Virgil) who had been blind since he was a young child. When this man's sight was restored through surgical procedures, he could detect light, forms, movement, and color (he could sense), but he was unable to organize and interpret this information (no perception). He "saw," but didn't know what he saw! (pp. 82-3).

There is an ongoing debate about whether it is possible to have perception without sensation (ESP). Some people (parapsychologists) believe that there are three types of extrasensory ability (telepathy, clairvoyance, and precognition). Some early evidence suggested that ESP may be possible (Rhine's work in the 1930s, discussed by your textbook author). However, much of the so-called "evidence" is anecdotal in nature; aside from these colorful stories, there is little truly compelling research evidence for ESP (pp. 121-23).

2. Pheromones are chemicals secreted by animals to transmit signals (for example, a readiness to reproduce) to others (usually of the same species). Pheromones are implicated in the reproductive activity of bees, dogs, ants, and so on. However, there does not appear to be a human pheromone. Studies do indicate that humans can recognize other people by their body odor, but there is no hard evidence that we secrete a sexual attractant that influences the mating behavior of other humans (pp. 102-3).

3. The first approach you might tell Teresa about is the "gate-control" theory of pain. According to this theory, the nervous system can only process a limited number of sensory signals at one time. When the system is full, the spinal cord shuts a neural "gate" that blocks the passage of additional signals to the brain. The implication is that Teresa can stop or alleviate some of the pain caused by her broken foot by stimulating other areas of her body and creating competing sensations (she could, for example, have a deep massage, or rub her other foot very hard). The second approach is to block the pain from conscious awareness by practicing psychological control—basically, you could tell Teresa to "just not think about it." Although this can backfire (research suggests that the more we try to suppress a particular thought, the more readily it actually pops into our minds), Teresa could use a procedure called "focused self-distraction." This involves focusing on a specific aspect of the environment or of experience (for example, "What will I do tonight when I get home from school?") and thereby distracting oneself from the pain (pp. 107-8).

4. Sensory crossovers happen when information that is received from one sensory system crosses over and is experienced by another sensory modality. For example, people with synesthesia ("joining the senses") might report that bright lights sound "loud;" thus, visual sensory information has crossed over and been experienced as auditory. This is, however, a rare condition. As a general rule, our sensory systems do not cross, and each system operates independently of the other (p. 109).

5. Well, there is still a debate about this question! Research with infants using the "visual cliff" (a class-covered table top with a shallow drop on one end and a cliff on the other) suggests that depth perception is evident at very young ages. Infants will crawl across the clear table top toward their parents at the shallow end, but they will not cross to the steep end; this suggests that they perceive the difference in depth. This suggests that depth perception might be innate; however, critics argue that perceptual learning begins at birth, and so by six months of age an infant has already had lots of perceptual practice. Cross-cultural research provides additional evidence that learning plays a large role in perception; your text presents a case study of a Pygmy who "saw" distant buffalo as insects when he was taken from his dense forest home to an open plain. His life experiences in the forest had been with objects densely packed together—objects that appeared small *were* small, in his experience. In sum, depth perception may be innate, but it is highly influenced by experience (pp. 116-17).

Multimedia Study Resources

The Mind Matters™ unit called "Sensation" presents a review of sensory transduction, sensory coding, and sensory adaptation; the unit called "Perception" reviews perceptual constancy and perceptual illusions. There is a brief quiz on these topics at the end of each unit.

Several activities and articles in Chapter 3 (Sensation and Perception) of The Psychology Place™ supplement the material covered in your textbook. "Investigating Depth Perception" is a learning activity that allows you to explore how your brain interprets depth cues in order to accurately perceive three-dimensional objects. In Research News, a report entitled "Auditory Perceptual Deficits in Language-Impaired Children" examines how children with specific language impairments demonstrate an altered form of auditory perception. Finally, Best of the Web provides a direct link to "Color Vision Demonstrations," a freeware, PC-based program with a collection of color vision demonstrations (www.uni-mannheim.de/fakul/psycho/irtel/cvd.html).

4 Consciousness

Chapter Overview

This chapter examines the state of awareness that psychologists call consciousness, or all the thoughts, sensations, and feelings of which we are aware at any given moment in time. First, the author examines three important attentional processes that influence consciousness: (1) Selective attention, a filtering process in which individuals selectively focus on one stimuli among many; (2) divided attention, the ability to apportion our consciousness among many competing stimuli; and (3) influence without awareness, or the process by which we are influenced by information outside the realm of our conscious awareness. The next part of the chapter explores sleep, including the sleep-wake cycle, the stages of sleep, and theories about the function or purpose of this particular state of consciousness. The content and interpretation of dreams are discussed, as are a variety of sleep disturbances (e.g., insomnia, hypersomnia, parasomnias). The third section of the chapter examines yet another state of consciousness, the one that is caused by a set of attention-focusing procedures called hypnosis. The author examines why the use of hypnosis has engendered controversy, describes the stages involved in hypnosis (i.e., induction and suggestion), and examines the myths and realities about hypnotic effects. Then, the chapter explores how human consciousness is affected by different types of drugs, including sedatives, stimulants, hallucinogens, and opiates. This chapter ends with an examination of whether or not people can exert control over the contents of conscious awareness.

Chapter Outline

I. *What's Your Prediction?* Do Subliminal Self-Help Tapes Work?

II. Attentional Processes

    A. Selective Attention

    B. Divided Attention

Learning Objectives

By the time you have read and reviewed this chapter, you should be able to:

1. Define consciousness and describe the three processes that influence this state of awareness (pp. 131-34).

2. Explain the concept of selective attention and give examples of selective attention in different sensory modalities (p. 131).

3. Describe the phenomenon of divided attention and discuss how the distinction between effortful and automatic processing explains this occurrence (pp. 132-33).

4. Consider whether it is possible to experience influence without consciousness (p. 134). Explain how mere exposure, priming, prosopagnosia, and blindsight may influence preferences and behavior below the threshold of conscious awareness (pp. 134-35).

5. Discuss evidence about the consequences of subliminal persuasion (p. 136).

6. Explain the difference between biological rhythms and circadian rhythms (pp. 137-38). Discuss the human sleep-wake cycle and whether it is determined by endogenous (internal) or environmental (outside patterns of lightness and darkness) forces (pp. 138-39).

7. Consider the relation between the sleep-wake cycle, night work (and other disruptions of the cycle), and health (pp. 140-41).

8. List the stages of sleep and identify the EEG patterns associated with each stage (p. 143).

9. Distinguish between REM and NREM sleep (pp. 143-44).

10. Consider two theories about why humans sleep (pp. 145-46).

11. Explain the nature of dreams (e.g., is it biologically adaptive to dream?) and discuss the content of dreams (pp. 146-47). Consider the factors that influence the content of dreams (pp. 147-48).

12. Distinguish between the Freudian theory of dream interpretation and the activation-synthesis approach to understanding dreams (pp. 148-150).

13. List and describe the major sleep disturbances, including insomnia, hypersomnia, and parasomnias (pp. 150-53).

14. Define hypnosis and explain the stages involved in hypnosis (pp. 155-56). Discuss the concept of hypnotic responsiveness (p. 156).

15. Discuss research on the effects of hypnosis (e.g., coercion, pain relief, posthypnotic suggestion, memory enhancement) (pp. 156-58).

16. Consider how eyewitness memory is affected by hypnosis (p. 159).

17. Compare the special-process and social cognitive theories of hypnosis (pp. 158-161).

18. Explain how psychoactive drugs alter consciousness (p. 161). Explain the concepts of physical and psychological dependence (pp. 161-62).

19. Discuss the physical and psychological effects of sedatives, stimulants, hallucinogens, and opiates (pp. 163-67).

20. Discuss whether it is possible to control consciousness, and consider methods used to focus attention (e.g., meditation) (pp. 167-68).

Key Terms

The following key terms and concepts are featured in this chapter and are important for you to know. Write out definitions of each term and check your answers with the definitions in the text on the pages listed.

Consciousness (p. 131)
Attention (p. 131)
Cocktail-party phenomenon (p. 131)
Selective attention (p. 131)
Divided attention (p. 133)
Stroop test (p. 133)
Subliminal messages (p. 134)
Priming (p. 134)
Prosopagnosia (p. 135)
Blindsight (p. 135)
Biological rhythms (p. 137)
Circadian rhythm (p. 137)
Microsleeps (p. 141)
REM sleep (p. 144)
NREM sleep (p. 144)
Lucid dreaming (p. 148)
Manifest content (p. 148)
Latent content (p. 148)

Activation-synthesis theory (p. 149)
Insomnia (p. 150)
Narcolepsy (p. 152)
Sleep apnea (p. 152)
REM sleep behavior disorder (RBD) (p. 153)
Hypnosis (p. 155)
Hypnotic susceptibility (p. 156)
Posthypnotic suggestion (p. 157)
Posthypnotic amnesia (p. 158)
Hypermnesia (p. 158)
Dissociation (p. 158)
Psychoactive drug (p. 161)
Physical dependence (p. 161)
Psychological dependence (p. 162)
Sedatives (p. 163)
Stimulants (p. 165)
Hallucinogens (p. 165)
Opiates (p. 166)

Multiple-Choice Questions

Circle the correct choice for each question and compare your answers with those at the end of the Study Guide chapter.

1. Most psychologists define consciousness as the awareness of one's _____.
   A. sensations
   B. feelings
   C. thoughts
   D. all of the above

2. Doreen is watching her roommate compete in a large karate exhibition. Despite the many other competitors and the noisy crowd of spectators who keep walking in front of her, Doreen is able to focus on her roommate. Her ability to do so illustrates
   A. selective attention.
   B. divided attention.
   C. unconscious motivation.
   D. subliminal perception.

3. People are able to exhibit divided attention among competing tasks when at least one of the tasks involves _____.
   A. effortful processing
   B. automatic processing
   C. the Stroop test
   D. selective awareness

4. Suppose someone asked you to remember where you went for vacation last year. According to Freud's view of levels of awareness, your memory came from
   A. conscious awareness.
   B. the preconscious.
   C. the unconscious.
   D. all of the above.

5. Although Bernie doesn't remember seeing any of the pictures a researcher flashed on a screen in front of him, he likes certain ones more than others. This could be an example of
   A. selective attention.
   B. priming.
   C. mere exposure.
   D. divided attention.

6. A condition known as _____ impairs people's ability to consciously recognize familiar faces, including their own.
   A. mere exposure
   B. blindsight
   C. hindsight
   D. prosopagnosia

7. Charlene is consciously blind. However, she is able to locate and reach for her coat when getting ready to go out, and she is able to "track" her dog as he walks across the room toward her. Charlene probably has a condition known as _____.
   A. hindsight
   B. blindsight
   C. second sight
   D. pseudosight

8. Research suggests which of the following conclusions about subliminal messages?
   A. they affect simple judgments and actions
   B. they have a long-term impact
   C. they affect complex social behaviors
   D. all of the above

9. The changing of the seasons, the 28-day lunar cycle, the 24-hour day, and the 90-minute activity-rest cycle are examples of _____.
   A. circadian rhythms
   B. natural rhythms
   C. biological rhythms
   D. physiological clocks

10. Studies on people who live in environmentally controlled isolation chambers reveal which of the following?
    A. the majority naturally settle into a short day
    B. the majority naturally settle into a longer sleep-wake cycle
    C. the majority have difficulty readjusting their biological clocks upon emergence
    D. the majority experience physical illness and mental strain

11. Which one of the following individuals is most likely to experience jet lag?
    A. Sidney, who is flying east across two time zones
    B. Tammy, who is flying west across one time zone
    C. Cindy Sue, who is flying east within one time zone
    D. Bonnie, who is flying west within one time zone

12. Humans are _____ creatures.
    A. triurnal
    B. mono-urnal
    C. diurnal
    D. piurnal

13. While driving home late one night, you find yourself nodding off at the wheel for brief (two- to three-second) periods of time. These episodes are called
    A. micronaps.
    B. microsleeps.
    C. macrosleeps.
    D. cat naps.

14. As your classmate continues to drone on endlessly about his summer plans, your breathing slows, your muscles relax, and you start to feel drowsy. An EEG recording of your brain-wave activity will show _____ waves.
    A. delta
    B. zeta
    C. alpha
    D. beta

15. _____ is to alert as delta is to deeply asleep.
    A. Theta
    B. Alpha
    C. Spindle
    D. Beta

16. Sleep spindles are typical of which stage of sleep?
    A. Stage 1
    B. Stage 2
    C. Stage 3
    D. REM sleep

17. Most dreams occur during _____ sleep.
    A. stage 1
    B. stage 2
    C. NREM
    D. REM

18. The circadian theory of sleep explains the need for sleep by focusing on which of the following?
    A. eating patterns
    B. predation patterns
    C. cross-species comparisons of sleep patterns
    D. all of the above

19. Who will spend the least amount of sleep time in REM sleep?
    A. Carlo, a premature infant
    B. Ashleigh, a nonpremature infant
    C. Alex, a three year old
    D. Mackenzie, a ten year old

20. Dev is dreaming. Although asleep, he has the strange sensation of realizing that he is in a dream. His experience is known as
    A. circadian dreaming.
    B. nondreaming.
    C. lucid dreaming.
    D. hallucinatory dreaming.

21. A friend recounts a dream she once had in which she was taken to see the king and queen and given a knighthood for her bravery. Having just read your introductory psychology chapter on consciousness, you explain to her that she was "really" dreaming about her parents and their feelings about her decision to go to graduate school. Your analysis of this dream is based on _____.
    A. random guesswork
    B. activation-synthesis theory
    C. Freudian dream interpretation
    D. clinical neuropsychology

22. According to activation-synthesis theory, dreams come from _____ and they represent _____.
    A. the brainstem; random neural impulses
    B. the unconscious; drive fulfilment
    C. the cortex; unconscious impulses
    D. manifest content; latent content

23. Insomnia may be a consequence of which of the following?
    A. stress
    B. beliefs about sleep requirements
    C. old age
    D. all of the above

24. Jacqueline has no problem falling asleep at night. However, once she is asleep, she stops breathing for brief periods of time until she awakens, choking and gasping for air. Jacqueline may have a condition called
    A. narcolepsy.
    B. sleep apnea.
    C. NREM sleep disruption.
    D. REM sleep behavior disorder.

25. Hypnosis results in which of the following?
    A. heightened suggestibility
    B. enhanced memory for actual events
    C. heightened sensitivity to pain
    D. all of the above

26. People who are highly susceptible to hypnosis tend to also be
    A. more obedient.
    B. highly dependent.
    C. imaginative.
    D. unskilled at memory tasks.

27. While jogging along his normal exercise path, Guillermo finds himself daydreaming about his plans for the future. Later, when Bobbi asks him what he thought of the new trees that the city planted, he realizes that he didn't even notice them. What has Guillermo experienced?
   A. hallucination
   B. dissociation
   C. posthypnotic suggestion
   D. induction

28. Social cognitive theories of hypnosis argue that the effects of hypnosis stem from
   A. dissociation.
   B. induction.
   C. special process.
   D. social influence.

29. Which of the following drugs is capable of altering consciousness?
   A. cocaine
   B. amphetamines
   C. LSD
   D. all of the above

30. Maggie has ingested heroin, Joel has had a few beers, RuthAnn has taken a dose of LSD, and Ed has snorted some cocaine. Who will experience the most dramatic change in consciousness?
   A. Maggie
   B. Joel
   C. RuthAnn
   D. Ed

True-False Questions

Indicate which of the following statements are true or false, and compare your answers with those at the end of the chapter.

T   F   1. Current psychological theory suggests that subliminal messages have a strong and lasting effect on human behavior.

T   F   2. It is not possible to divide attention between competing tasks.

T   F   3. For the mere exposure effect to occur, people must be aware of their prior exposures to a stimulus.

T   F   4. It is possible to "prime" some aspects of human behavior.

T   F   5. The circadian rhythm is determined solely by endogenous factors.

T   F   6. Prolonged late-night activity results in diminished productivity and reaction time.

T   F   7. There is little compelling evidence that humans need to sleep.

T   F   8. The essential ingredient of hypnotic induction is a focusing of attention.

T   F   9. You cannot be hypnotized against your will.

T   F   10. Psychoactive drugs can become psychologically or physically addictive.

Key Concepts Matching Exercises

Exercise #1: The Stages of Sleep

Match each EEG pattern with the appropriate stage of sleep.

Non-REM

_____ 1.   Stage 1

_____ 2.   Stage 2

_____ 3.   Stage 3

_____ 4.   Stage 4

Exercise #2: Consciousness and Sleep

Match the key terms on the left with the definitions on the right.

_____ 1. Consciousness

_____ 2. Selective attention

_____ 3. Divided attention

_____ 4. Circadian rhythm

_____ 5. REM sleep

_____ 6. Lucid dreaming

_____ 7. Latent content

_____ 8. Manifest content

_____ 9. Narcolepsy

_____10. Sleep apnea

_____11. Stage 4 sleep

A. 24-hour biological cycle

B. Semiconscious dream state

C. Sudden "attacks" of REM sleep

D. The ability to focus on one stimulus and ignore others

E. The conscious or surface content of a dream

F. The "deepest" sleep stage

G. Most dreams occur during this stage of sleep

H. Cessation of breathing during sleep

I. What you are currently sensing, thinking, and feeling

J. The ability to distribute attention among different activities

K. The "hidden" meaning of a dream

Essay Questions

Write out answers to the following brief essay questions. Compare your responses with the sample answers at the end of the Study Guide chapter.

1. What is selective attention and how does it affect consciousness? Give an example of selective attention in two different sensory modalities.

2. Is the circadian rhythm of the human sleep-wake cycle controlled by endogenous factors alone? Consider evidence from isolation studies in your answer.

3. Why do humans sleep? Consider two theories about the purpose or function of sleep.

4. Discuss whether REM sleep is biologically adaptive. Consider three sources of evidence when constructing your answer.

5. Is hypnosis an "altered" state of consciousness? Compare the special-process and social-cognitive response to this question.

Test Solutions

Multiple-Choice Solutions

1. D (p. 131)	11. A (p. 139)	21. C (p. 148)
2. A (p. 131)	12. C (p. 140)	22. A (p. 149)
3. B (p. 133)	13. B (p. 141)	23. D (p. 150)
4. B (p. 134)	14. C (p. 143)	24. B (p. 152)
5. C (p. 134)	15. D (pp. 142-43)	25. A (p. 159)
6. D (p. 135)	16. B (p. 143)	26. C (p. 156)
7. B (p. 135)	17. D (p. 144)	27. B (p. 160)
8. A (p. 136)	18. D (p. 145)	28. D (p. 160)
9. C (p. 137)	19. D (p. 147)	29. D (p. 162)
10. B (p. 138)	20. C (p. 148)	30. C (p. 165)

True-False Solutions

1. F (p. 129)	6. T (p. 140)
2. F (p. 133)	7. F (p. 145)
3. F (p. 134)	8. T (p. 155)
4. T (p. 135)	9. T (p. 156)
5. F (p. 138)	10. T (p. 161)

Key Concepts Matching Solutions

Exercise #1

1. B
2. D
3. A
4. C

Exercise #2

1. I
2. D
3. J
4. A
5. G
6. B
7. K
8. E
9. C
10. H
11. F

Essay Solutions

1. Selective attention is the process in which people are able to focus on a single stimulus and ignore other, competing stimuli. This affects the information that is included or excluded from consciousness; through this process, we become aware of one stimulus but then we lose conscious awareness of the other stimuli (p. 131).

   You could draw your examples from any sensory modality. For example, in the auditory modality (hearing), research indicates that people who are presented with two messages at the same time (this is called a dichotic listening task) are able to "shadow" one of the messages with great accuracy; however, they lose track of the other message. The same phenomenon may happen in the visual system. For instance, people who watch two videotapes, one superimposed on the other, are able to follow the action and events of one videotape but they become unable to focus on and remember the events of the other (p. 131).

2. No, the human sleep-wake cycle is not controlled solely by endogenous (internal) factors, although we do have a "timing device" in our brains in the form of the hypothalamus and the pineal gland; these structures take in information about light from the optic nerve and then work to either facilitate or retard feelings of sleepiness (pp. 138-39).

   Evidence from isolation studies suggests that the human sleep-wake cycle is at least partly determined by outside patterns of lightness and darkness. Your text presents the story of a woman who volunteered to live in a cave that was sealed off from any environmental cues (e.g., sunlight, outside noises, temperature changes, clocks). Over the course of her 131-day stay in the cave, her "day" had extended to 48-hours; she slept and woke up later and later. However, when reexposed to sunlight, she readjusted her biological clock (p. 138).

3. There are two theories about why humans seem to need sleep. The first is restoration theory, which states that sleep is a time for the body to rest and repair or restore itself from the exertions of the day. This theory accounts for the feeling of rejuvenation most people feel after a night's sleep and is supported by research on sleep deprivation using animals (in which rats placed in stressful situations and deprived of sleep became ill and ultimately

died) (p. 145). [Also recall the information in Chapter 3 (Behavioral Neuroscience) about how the autonomic nervous system regulates the internal body environment; when we are resting, our parasympathetic system is engaged in conserving energy and getting us ready for the next time we need to be active.]

The second major theory of sleep is the circadian explanation, which focuses on the adaptive purpose of sleep. According to this theory, sleep is an evolved mechanism that enables us (and all other species) to conserve energy and minimize our exposure to predators. Humans sleep at night because such behavior is adaptive; our eyes are not equipped to see well in the dark, and so it makes evolutionary "sense" for us to be quiet and protected during times of darkness (p. 145).

4. Most researchers now believe that REM sleep is biologically adaptive. There are three sources of evidence in support of this belief. First, there is evidence that suggests that REM sleep is necessary for brain maturation; that is, the brain is incredibly active during REM sleep, and REM sleep therefore may be a way for the brain to "test drive" itself. Indeed, infants (whose brains are still developing) spend more time in REM sleep than older children and adults, and premature infants spend even more time in REM sleep. Cross-species comparisons provide the second source of evidence for the biological benefits of REM sleep—all mammals and most birds experience REM sleep, which suggests that cognitive complexity and cortex development go hand in hand with REM sleep. Finally, when people are deprived of REM sleep one night, they experience a "rebound effect" by spending more time in REM sleep the next night (as if the brain is trying to make up for lost REM time) (p. 147).

5. Psychologists do not agree on the answer to this question. Special-process theorists argue that hypnosis is in fact a unique state of consciousness in which one part of the mind dissociates or operates independently of another. Theorists who follow this approach point to evidence from pain-tolerance studies in which participants immersed their hands in ice water and rated their level of pain. Those who were hypnotized to "feel no pain" reported less pain than nonhypnotized individuals. However, when they were told to press a key with their free hand if "some part" of them was in pain, they did so; this suggests that they experienced a division of consciousness, with one part feeling pain that the other part did not (pp. 158, 160).

Social-cognitive theories argue that hypnosis does not result from a division of consciousness or an altered state of consciousness but rather from social influence processes. For example, it is possible that hypnosis effects are the result of a desire to comply with experimenter suggestion. Research indicates that the same pain tolerance effects outlined above can result simply from instilling sufficient motivation in participants (p. 160).

At this point, both theories may explain the phenomenon—perhaps highly motivated people experience hypnosis as a dissociative state (pp. 160-61).

Multimedia Study Resources

Several activities and articles in Chapter 5 (States of Consciousness) of The Psychology Place™ supplement the material covered in your textbook. "Investigating Dreams" is a learning activity that allows you to review major dream theories and then provides you with materials and instructions for recording and interpreting your own dreams. A related article in Scientific American magazine ("The Meaning of Dreams") presents a new theory of dream interpretation. You might also wish to explore the Op Ed Forum, which considers the question, "Are We Chronically Sleep-Deprived?"

5 Learning

Chapter Overview

This chapter explores the processes involved in three types of learning. Your textbook author begins by defining learning and examining the difference between learned behavior and instinctive behaviors (fixed action patterns). Next, the chapter examines a basic form of learning called classical conditioning. The fundamental principles of this type of learning (e.g., acquisition, extinction, generalization, and discrimination) then are discussed, as are recent advances in classical conditioning theory. This foray into classical conditioning ends with an examination of the practical applications of this type of learning for the human experience. The second part of Chapter 5 is devoted to operant conditioning; in turn, the law of effect, the basic principles of reinforcement and punishment, the impact of schedules of reinforcement on behavior, and the practical applications of operant conditioning are discussed. This section ends with an examination of recent developments in the arena of operant conditioning, including research on the ways in which biological predispositions constrain or interfere with the shaping of a new behavior, and the manner in which cognitive perspectives have been incorporated into operant conditioning theory. The third section of the chapter concerns observational learning. Classic studies in observational learning are presented, and the process involved in this form of learning (attention, retention, reproduction, motivation) is discussed.

Chapter Outline

I. *What's Your Prediction?* Can People Learn Without Realizing It?

II. Classical Conditioning

    A. Pavlov's Discovery

    B. Basic Principles
        1. Acquisition
        2. Extinction

By the time you have read and reviewed this chapter, you should be able to:

1. Distinguish between learning and fixed action patterns (p. 174). List four different types of learning that humans exhibit (p. 175).

2. Outline the process of classical conditioning (pp. 177-178).

3. Discuss four basic principles of classical conditioning, including the acquisition (p. 178) and extinction (p. 179) of a classically conditioned response, and the process of stimulus generalization (p. 180) and discrimination (p. 180).

4. Discuss how research on biological preparedness and cognitive representations has changed the early Pavlovian stimulus-response approach to conditioning (pp. 181-83).

5. Consider practical applications of classical conditioning, including how this form of learning may be applied to understanding the development of negative (e.g., phobias) and positive preferences (pp. 183-84), the formation of social attitudes (pp. 184-86), aspects of social behavior (p. 186), and the immune system (p. 185).

6. Explain the types of behaviors that are influenced by operant as opposed to classical conditioning (p. 187).

7. Discuss how Thorndike's law of effect served as the basis for operant conditioning (p. 187).

8. Define operant conditioning and explain the difference between operant conditioning and classical conditioning (pp. 187-88).

9. Distinguish between reinforcement and punishment (pp. 188-89) and a positive and negative stimulus (p. 189). Be able to provide examples of positive and negative reinforcement and punishment (p. 189).

10. Explain the process of shaping and how it can be used to alter behavior (pp. 189-90).

11. Discuss how a shaped behavior can be extinguished (p. 190).

12. Identify four schedules of reinforcement and how each one affects human behavior (pp. 191-93).

13. Discuss the consequences of punishment and the circumstances in which punishment is most effective (p. 193).

14. Consider the process involved in stimulus control (p. 194).

15. Discuss the concept of self-control and how it relates to operant conditioning (pp. 194-95).

16. Describe the practical applications of operant conditioning (pp. 195-97).

17. Consider how operant conditioning has been changed by research on biological predispositions and cognitive processes (pp. 198-201).

18. Define observational learning (p. 201).

19. Consider how aggressive and cooperative behavior can be learned via observation (p. 202).

20. Discuss the four steps involved in observational learning (pp. 202-203).

Key Terms

The following key terms and concepts are featured in this chapter and are important for you to know. Write out definitions of each term and check your answers with the definitions in the text on the pages listed.

Ethologists (p. 174)
Fixed action patterns (p. 174)
Learning (p. 174)
Habituation (p. 175)
Classical conditioning (p. 177)
Unconditioned response (UR) (p. 177)
Unconditioned stimulus (US) (p. 177)
Conditioned stimulus (CS) (p. 178)
Conditioned response (CR) (p. 178)
Acquisition (p. 178)
Extinction (p. 179)
Spontaneous recovery (p. 179)

Stimulus generalization (p. 180)
Discrimination (p. 180)
Law of effect (p. 187)
Skinner box (p. 187)
Operant conditioning (p. 187)
Reinforcement (p. 188)
Punishment (p. 189)
Shaping (p. 189)
Partial-reinforcement effect (p. 192)
Discriminative stimulus (p. 194)
Latent learning (p. 199)
Observational learning (p. 201)

Test Questions

Multiple-Choice Questions

Circle the correct choice for each question and compare your answers with those at the end of the Study Guide chapter.

1. The basic building block for all learning is _____.
   A. association
   B. habituation
   C. the law of effect
   D. instinct

2. Which of the following are examples of instinctive behavior?
   A. a honeybee builds a hive out of wax
   B. a dog sits up and "speaks" for a treat
   C. a child learns how to ride a tricycle
   D. all of the above

3. Learned behavior is defined as
   A. relatively permanent.
   B. the result of experience.
   C. changed behavior.
   D. all of the above.

4. The simplest form of learning is
   A. operant conditioning.
   B. classical conditioning.
   C. habituation.
   D. observational learning.

5. I recently adopted a baby crow who had fallen from her nest. When I first tried to feed her, she backed away from my hand and crouched in the corner of the box. Now, however, she appears much calmer and she does not back away when I approach her. The baby crow has become _____.
   A. associated
   B. habituated
   C. weaned
   D. bored

6. You have volunteered for a psychology experiment. During the study, the experimenter presses a buzzer and then shoots a puff of air into your eyes, making you blink. After a few trials, you blink as soon as you hear the sound of the buzzer. In this example, the buzzer is the _____, and the puff of air is the _____.
   A. unconditioned stimulus; conditioned stimulus
   B. conditioned stimulus; unconditioned stimulus
   C. unconditioned response; conditioned response
   D. conditioned response; unconditioned response

7. The type of learning demonstrated in the previous question is _____.
   A. habituation
   B. classical conditioning
   C. operant conditioning
   D. observational learning

8. Research on classical conditioning suggests that a response is acquired quickest when the conditioned stimulus (e.g., a buzzer) occurs _____ the unconditioned stimulus (e.g., puff of air, meat powder).
   A. immediately after
   B. at the same time as
   C. immediately before
   D. three hours before

9. Hank the cat always gets his dinner right after the clock chimes 5:00. As a result, he begins to salivate as soon as the clock chimes five times. His owner recently switched jobs and she is no longer able to feed him at 5:00; instead, she feeds him at 5:30. Now, Hank does not drool when the clock chimes at 5:00. Hank's response has been _____.
   A. extinguished
   B. generalized
   C. discriminated
   D. acquired

10. Last year, little Heather got to play with her neighbor's poodle. Now, she smiles and approaches all dogs, even those that are larger than poodles. Heather's behavior illustrates
    A. acquisition.
    B. discrimination.
    C. generalization.
    D. extinction.

11. Your textbook discusses a research study in which rats were exposed to radiation right after they tasted sweetened water, saw a flash of light, and heard a loud clicking noise. These rats then became nauseous due to the radiation. What did they learn to avoid?
    A. the light
    B. the noise
    C. the water
    D. all of the above

12. Birds have extremely good eyesight; they respond more to the appearance of their food than to its taste or smell. If you were to place birds in the same situation as that outlined in Question 11 (i.e., have them taste sweetened water, see a flash of light, and hear a loud noise right before exposing them to radiation and making them nauseous), what would you expect them to avoid in the future? Think about this one!
    A. the light
    B. the noise
    C. the water
    D. all of the above

13. Research now suggests that people all over the world share many of the same fears. These results provide evidence that some learning is _____.
    A. behaviorally modified   C. due to experience
    B. biologically programmed   D. culture-specific

14. Research on the applications of classical conditioning suggests that humans can be conditioned to learn
    A. fears and preferences.
    B. negative attitudes.
    C. positive attitudes.
    D. all of the above.

15. The "law of effect" suggests that
    A. behaviors that produce a negative outcome are more likely to recur.
    B. behaviors that produce a positive outcome are more likely to recur.
    C. behaviors that produce a neutral outcome are more likely to recur.
    D. all of the above.

16. In what ways does operant conditioning differ from classical conditioning?
    A. Operant conditioning involves reflexive behavior, whereas classical conditioning involves voluntary behavior.
    B. Operant conditioning produces positive outcomes, whereas classical conditioning produces negative outcomes.
    C. Operant conditioning happens quickly, whereas classical conditioning happens over time.
    D. None of the above.

17. Reinforcement _____ the likelihood of a response; punishment _____ the likelihood of a response.
    A. increases; increases   C. increases; decreases
    B. decreases; decreases   D. decreases; increases

18. Parents praise their daughter every time she studies and brings home a good grade. Now, she spends even more time studying and is earning even higher grades. The praise she receives from her parents is a _____.
    A. positive punisher   C. negative punisher
    B. positive reinforcer   D. negative reinforcer

19. The same parents allow their daughter to skip her chores when she gets an "A" on a test or paper. The removal of chores serves as a _____.
    A. positive punisher   C. negative punisher
    B. positive reinforcer   D. negative reinforcer

20. Over time, you have trained your pet rat to crawl though a tunnel, run up a ladder, and walk across a bridge in order to receive a treat. The procedure you followed to train the rat is called
    A. shaping.
    B. approximate learning.
    C. reinforcement.
    D. bribery.

21. Both Brian and Matthew receive treats for doing their chores. Brian knows that he will receive a treat if he does his chores five days in a row. However, Matthew does not know exactly how often he will have to do his chores in order to get a treat. Brian is on a _____ schedule, whereas Matthew is on a _____ schedule.
    A. variable-ratio; fixed-ratio
    B. variable-interval; fixed-interval
    C. fixed-ratio; variable-ratio
    D. continuous; partial

22. A conditioned response is more resistant to extinction when it is reinforced on a(n) _____.
    A. partial basis
    B. continuous basis
    C. ratio schedule
    D. interval schedule

23. Punishment is most effective when it is
    A. immediate.
    B. consistent.
    C. used in conjunction with positive reinforcement.
    D. all of the above

24. What are some consequences associated with using punishment to decrease an unwanted behavior?
    A. Punished behavior is not necessarily extinguished.
    B. Punishment can result in negative emotions.
    C. Punishment does not replace the unwanted behavior with a more desired one.
    D. All of the above

25. A man has learned that his partner will engage in conversation and answer questions when the television is off but not when it is on. He now only converses with his partner when the television is off. The television is a
    A. positive reinforcer.
    B. discriminative stimulus.
    C. generalizer.
    D. punisher.

26. Principles of operant conditioning have been used successfully in which of the following settings?
    A. workplace
    B. health care system
    C. classroom
    D. all of the above

27. Try as you might, you cannot seem to teach your Vietnamese pot-bellied pig to pick up the morning paper and carry it to you. Wilbur has learned to approach the paper and touch it, but instead of picking it up he pushes it around on the ground with his snout. What does Wilbur's behavior demonstrate?
    A. willful disobedience
    B. classical conditioning
    C. instinctive drift
    D. operant conditioning

28. Reinforcement will strengthen behavior in a person who has a(n) _____ locus of control.
    A. internal   C. hidden
    B. external   D. latent

29. At the beach one day, you see a lifeguard administer CPR to another person. In order for you to learn this behavior by observation, you must
    A. remember the lifeguard's behavior.
    B. have the ability to administer CPR.
    C. be motivated to administer CPR.
    D. all of the above

30. Which one of the following statements is accurate?
    A. Observational learning only occurs among primates.
    B. Complex new behaviors can be learned via observation.
    C. The ability to imitate a model's behavior develops during late childhood.
    D. Observational learning can account for aggressive but not helping behavior.

True-False Questions

Indicate which of the following statements are true or false, and compare your answers with those at the end of the chapter.

T   F   1. We may be biologically predisposed to learn some associations more easily than others.

T   F   2. Attitudes and preferences cannot be classically conditioned.

T   F   3. Classical conditioning provides the best explanation for the learning of simple reflexive behaviors.

T   F   4. Continuously reinforced responses are the most difficult to extinguish.

T   F   5. Inconsistent punishment is the most effective way to suppress an unwanted behavior.

T   F   6. Biological predispositions may interfere with the shaping of a new behavior.

T   F   7. Research on latent learning suggests that operant conditioning may occur without direct reinforcement.

T   F   8. Perceptions, expectations, and beliefs appear to have no significant effect on the operant conditioning of a response.

T   F   9. Observational learning of complex behavior may occur in many types of animals.

T   F   10. Observational learning can occur in infants.

Key Concepts Matching Exercises

Exercise #1: The Conditioning of Ivan

You have decided to train your cat, Ivan the Terrible, to drool when you ring a little bell. Outline the steps involved in your classical conditioning program, inserting the correct letter into each box.

Before conditioning

During conditioning

After conditioning

A. Bell

B. Reflexive (unconditioned) drooling

C. Meat powder

D. Conditioned drooling

E. Dry mouth (no drooling)

Exercise #2: Classical Conditioning and Time

Which of the following ways of pairing a conditioned stimulus (CS) and an unconditioned stimulus (US) is the most effective at producing learning?

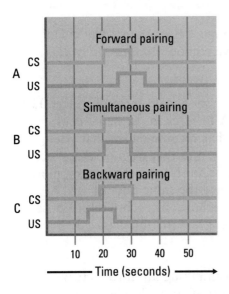

_____ 1. This is the most effective way to classically condition a response.

Exercise #3: Schedules of Reinforcement

Match each reinforcement schedule with the response pattern it produces.

_____ 1. This pattern is produced by a variable-ratio schedule.

_____ 2. This pattern is produced by a fixed-interval schedule.

_____ 3. This pattern is produced by a variable-interval schedule.

_____ 4. This pattern is produced by a fixed-ratio schedule.

Essay Questions

Write out answers to the following brief essay questions. Compare your responses with the sample answers at the end of the Study Guide chapter.

1. Is classical conditioning a mindless, automatic process? Compare the original Pavlovian view of classical conditioning with the more recent cognitive reconceptualization of this form of learning.

2. A family friend is about to undergo chemotherapy treatment for a mild form of cancer. His doctors disagree over the best treatment program. Doctor A believes in the benefits of establishing and following a regular treatment routine. She has recommended that your friend arrive at the same hospital each week on the same day, and that chemotherapy occur at the same time in the same room and with the same technician. Doctor B prefers a more varied treatment regimen. She suggests that your friend receive the same dose of chemotherapy, but in different hospitals and with different technicians each week. Whose advice should your friend follow? Base your answer on recent research on classical conditioning and the immune system.

3. André's roommate never picks up her clothes. André has been taking an introductory psychology course, and as he is reading about operant conditioning he decides to use positive reinforcement to change his roommate's behavior. Define positive reinforcement and give an example of how André might use operant conditioning in this situation. (Hint: What must first happen for reinforcement to work?)

4. Becky's dog Abigail eats the legs off chairs. Becky is running out of usable chairs and she wants this behavior to stop. She is thinking of using punishment to change Abigail's behavior. Should she? Define punishment and discuss when it is most effective. Consider the possible consequences of punishment.

5. Outline and describe (using an example) the four steps involved in observational learning. In what way does operant conditioning play a role in observational learning?

Test Solutions

Multiple-Choice Solutions

1. A (p. 176)	11. C (p. 181)	21. C (p. 192)
2. A (p. 174)	12. A (p. 181)	22. A (p. 192)
3. D (p. 174)	13. B (pp. 181-82)	23. D (p. 193)
4. C (p. 175)	14. D (pp. 183-85)	24. D (p. 193)
5. B (p. 175)	15. B (p. 187)	25. B (p. 194)
6. B (p. 178)	16. D (p. 188)	26. D (p. 196)
7. B (p. 177)	17. C (pp. 188-89)	27. C (p. 198)
8. C (p. 179)	18. B (p. 189)	28. A (p. 200)
9. A (p. 179)	19. D (p. 189)	29. D (p. 202)
10. C (p. 180)	20. A (p. 189)	30. B (p. 201)

True-False Solutions

1. T (p. 181)
2. F (pp. 184-85)
3. T (p. 187)
4. F (p. 192)
5. F (p. 193)
6. T (p. 198)
7. T (p. 199)
8. F (pp. 199-201)
9. T (p. 201)
10. T (p. 201)

Key Concepts Matching Solutions

Exercise #1

1. C
2. B
3. A
4. E
5. A, C
6. B
7. A
8. D

Exercise #2

1. A

Exercise #3

1. B
2. C
3. D
4. A

Essay Solutions

1. The original Pavlovian conceptualization of classical conditioning stated that classical conditioning occurs whenever a neutral stimulus (like the sound of a tone) is paired with an unconditioned stimulus (like food). This was assumed to be a rather mindless process; the dog or cat or person does not need to think in order to acquire the conditioned response (drooling). However, more recent work (particularly by Rescorla, as noted in your text) suggests that the organism is much more active, from a cognitive perspective, than the earlier model states. Specifically, the dog or cat or person might drool after hearing the sound of a tone because prior experience has led him or her to expect food. Here, the organism is much more than a simple recipient of classical conditioning principles; the tone has come to take on psychological significance (in this case, the expectation that food will shortly be presented) which in turn affects behavior (drooling) (pp. 182-83).

2. Assuming that your friend receives the same quality of care and the same chemotherapy dose in both treatment programs, he or she should probably follow the advice of Doctor B (the varied program). Recent research suggests that classical conditioning processes can actually weaken the immune system—something your friend cannot afford. For example, chemotherapy drugs (US) cause two responses—inhibition of new cancer cell growth and inhibition of immune cell growth (UR). It's possible that cues in the surrounding environment (like a particular treatment room or a particular technician who administers the chemotherapy) become associated with the chemotherapy drugs (US) and thus serve as powerful conditioned stimuli (CS). The consequence, of course, is that these environmental settings can actually result in the CR (immune cell inhibition). Thus, it would be best for your friend to undergo treatment in varied settings; this might prevent his or her immune system from "learning" to weaken in response to a particular situational cue (p. 185).

3. Positive reinforcement involves presenting a stimulus in order to increase the likelihood of a particular response (p. 189). There are a number of positive stimuli that might work in this

situation. For example, André might smile and thank his roommate every time she engages in the desired behavior; alternately, he might loan his roommate a CD, or bake her cookies or type a paper for her. The problem with using positive reinforcement in this situation is that André can only reinforce a behavior that actually occurs—and we know that his roommate does *not* pick up her clothes. Thus, André must rely upon shaping, a process in which he will gradually guide his roommate toward the desired response by reinforcing responses that come closer and closer to it. For example, André could smile and thank his roommate (or give her food or whatever) every time she hangs her coat up, or every time she throws her clothing down in the general vicinity of the laundry basket or closet. After a while, André might only reinforce his roommate for leaving clothing three feet from the laundry basket/closet, then one foot from the basket/closet, and so on (pp. 189-90).

4. Punishment is anything that decreases the likelihood of a behavior (p. 189). It's a coin toss as to whether Becky should or should not use punishment to stop her dog's behavior. On the one hand, punishment that is strong, immediate, consistent, and inescapable does appear to suppress unwanted responses. However, punishment can have unwanted side effects. For example, punishment may temporarily inhibit a behavior but not extinguish that behavior. That is, Abigail may stop chewing on the chairs in Becky's presence, but continue to do so when Becky is not in the house (she may also stop her chewing behavior in Becky's house, but then destroy the chairs in other people's houses). In addition, punishment only teaches an individual what *not* to do; it does not teach that individual what *to* do. Abigail may learn not to chew chairs, but she will not learn which objects are acceptable to chew (like toys or bones). Third, punishment may backfire if the attention is rewarding—perhaps when Becky scolds her, Abigail gets the attention that she wants. Finally, punishment may cause fear, anger, and aggressive responses—perhaps Abigail will learn to fear Becky rather than learning not to chew, or perhaps she will bite Becky out of anger or mistrust or fear (p. 193). In sum, Becky might try punishment (immediate, consistent, etc.) that is coupled with positive reinforcement for desired behaviors.

5. Observational learning involves four related steps. First, to learn by observation, we must pay attention to the model's behavior and to the consequences of that behavior. For example, Child A might see Child B help Child C go down a slide at the park, and then see Child B receive praise for her actions. Second, we must remember what we originally observed. In order for Child A to learn from the behavior or Child B, he or she must think about and remember that behavior and its consequences. Third, we must have the ability to actually reproduce the modeled behavior. Child A may attend to and remember Child B's helpful behavior, but physically be unable to climb a ladder and help another child down a slide. Fourth, we must be motivated to engage in the modeled behavior. Child A could be able physically to help another child go down a slide, but be too tired to do so or involved in another, more interesting activity (pp. 202-3).

Operant conditioning plays a role in the last step of observational learning—motivation. Specifically, our motivation to engage in a modeled behavior is not only affected by the consequences we've seen the model receive (vicarious reinforcement and punishment), but also by our own direct personal experience with reinforcement and punishment (p. 203). For example, if Child A has been reinforced in the past for helping other children on the swing set, he or she may be motivated to model a different form of helping behavior.

Multimedia Study Resources

The Mind Matters™ unit called "Learning and Memory" presents a review of classical and operant conditioning. There is a brief quiz on these topics at the end of the unit.

Several activities and articles in Chapter 6 (Basic Principles of Learning) of The Psychology Place™ supplement the material covered in your textbook. For example, "Principles of Learning in the Real World" is a learning activity in which you interact with Buster (a dog) and Dexter (a rat) in order to experience the development of a conditioned response and the processes of reinforcement and punishment. In Research News, you may read about recent research on classical conditioning, including how this type of learning is implicated in defense, reproduction, immune system function, drug addiction, and a host of other human behaviors ("Beyond Pavlov's Dogs"). This section also contains an article on reinforcement and creativity ("Should Creativity Be Rewarded?").

6 Memory

Chapter Overview

This chapter explores the structures and processes of human memory from an information-processing perspective. The first structure that is examined is the sensory register, the initial step in the information-processing system. Both iconic and echoic memories are examined. The chapter then turns to the second information-processing step; namely, short-term or working memory. Your author explores the capacity and duration limits of short-term memory, as well as the functions of this active workspace. The final type of memory that is examined is long-term memory, an enduring storage area that can hold vast amounts of information. In this section of the chapter, the author explains the process involved in storing information in long-term memory (i.e., encoding), discusses the manner in which this information is stored (i.e., semantic networks), and outlines the different types of long-term memories that can exist (i.e., procedural, declarative). The process involved in retrieving long-term memories is discussed, and the techniques used to assess both explicit and implicit memories are presented. The section on long-term memory ends with a discussion of forgetting (why we forget and ways to prevent information from being lost from the system) and memory reconstruction (e.g., how we create false or illusory memories). The chapter itself ends with a consideration of autobiographical memory, including the types of events or information that are best recalled, and the ways in which we censor or alter our memories in order to preserve and enhance self-esteem.

Chapter Outline

Learning Objectives

By the time you have read and reviewed this chapter, you should be able to:

1. Define the concept of memory (p. 211) and explain the information-processing model of human memory (p. 211). Consider the parallel processing alternative to the information-processing model of memory (p. 212).

2. Discuss the sensory register (pp. 212-14). Distinguish between iconic and echoic memory (pp. 213-14). Explain the purpose of sensory memories (in other words, what do they do for us?) (p. 214).

3. Explain the different types of encoding that can move information from sensory into short-term memory (p. 214).

4. Consider how attention limits the capacity of short-term memory (p. 214-15). Discuss the actual capacity of short-term memory and how chunking can add to the efficiency of short-term memory (pp. 215-16).

5. Discuss the duration of short-term memory (i.e., the length of time information can exist in short-term memory before it is lost) (p. 217). Consider how maintenance rehearsal affects short-term memory (pp. 217-18).

6. Explore the functions of short-term memory (pp. 218-19).

7. Define long-term memory (p. 221) and explain how information is transferred (encoded) into long-term memory (pp. 221-22).

8. Discuss long-term memory storage, including its format (semantic versus visual; p. 223), content (procedural versus declarative; semantic networks; pp. 224-25), and neural bases (anatomical structures and biochemical processes; pp. 226-29).

9. Distinguish between explicit and implicit memories (p. 229), and consider the techniques to assess these types of memory (pp. 230-31).

10. Consider the factors that affect the retrieval of long-term explicit memories (i.e., encoding specificity, context, state of mind; pp. 231-32).

11. Consider implicit memory in amnesia patients (p. 233), and explain the consequences of retention without awareness (i.e., false-fame effect, illusion of truth, eyewitness transference, unintentional plagiarism; pp. 234-36).

12. Explain the forgetting curve and what it demonstrates about memory failure (pp. 236-37).

13. Consider the four processes that can produce forgetting or memory failure: Encoding (lack of), decay, interference, and repression (pp. 238-42).

14. Define the concept of mnemonics and discuss eight techniques that we can use to increase our ability to retain information (pp. 240-41).

15. Consider the reconstructive nature of memory (p. 242). Explain how schemas may distort memory (pp. 242-43). Define the misinformation effect (pp. 243-44). Examine evidence that misinformation may alter a witness's memories (p. 244).

16. Discuss the factors that may impair or influence eyewitness memory for events (i.e., emotional arousal, race, lineup composition, lineup instructions) and consider the impact of eyewitness confidence on juror judgments (pp. 245-46).

17. Discuss the creation of illusory (false) memories and consider the differences, if any, between illusory and true recollections (pp. 244-247).

18. Define autobiographical memory (p. 247). Explain which aspects of our past we tend to remember (e.g., flashbulb memories; pp. 247-49). Explore the ways in which memory is shaped and altered by the self-concept (e.g., hindsight bias; pp. 249-50).

Key Terms

The following key terms and concepts are featured in this chapter and are important for you to know. Write out definitions of each term and check your answers with the definitions in the text on the pages listed.

Memory (p. 211)
Information-processing model (p. 211)
Sensory memory (p. 211)
Short-term memory (p. 211)
Long-term memory (p. 211)
Iconic memory (p. 213)
Echoic memory (p. 213)
Maintenance rehearsal (p. 217)
Working memory (p. 218)
Serial-position curve (p. 219)
Elaborative rehearsal (p. 221)
Procedural memory (p. 224)
Declarative memory (p. 224)
Semantic network (p. 224)
Hippocampus (p. 226)
Anterograde amnesia (p. 227)

Retrograde amnesia (p. 227)
Explicit memory (p. 229)
Implicit memory (p. 229)
Free recall (p. 230)
Recognition (p. 230)
Encoding specificity (p. 231)
Forgetting curve (p. 236)
Proactive interference (p. 242)
Retroactive interference (p. 242)
Schemas (p. 242)
Misinformation effect (pp. 243-44)
Autobiographical memory (p. 247)
Flashbulb memories (p. 248)
Childhood amnesia (p. 249)
Hindsight bias (p. 250)

Test Questions

Multiple-Choice Questions

Circle the correct choice for each question and compare your answers with those at the end of the Study Guide chapter.

1. Vicki is a cognitive psychologist. She is preparing to give an invited address at the American Psychological Association's annual conference. Most likely, her topic will be
   A. "Human Memory: The Faithful Workbench."
   B. "Human Memory: A Library Filled With Books."
   C. "Human Memory: The Extraordinary Computer."
   D. "Human Memory: A Busy Switchboard."

2. According to the information-processing model of human memory, a stimulus (for example, a sound) that registers on our senses will be remembered only if it
   A. catches our attention.
   B. is encoded in the brain.
   C. is retrieved for later use.
   D. All of the above.

3. The process whereby information is received from the environment and transferred to storage sites in the brain is known as
   A. encoding.   C. sensation.
   B. brain transfer.   D. saving.

4. According to the information-processing model, memory works in a(n) _____ fashion. According to the parallel-processing model, memory works in a(n) _____ fashion.
   A. linear; sequential
   B. passive; active
   C. sequential; simultaneous
   D. perpendicular; parallel

5. Lawrence is reading a chapter in his psychology text. As he reads, he recalls the sounds of the words themselves. This type of encoding is called
   A. semantic   C. echoic.
   B. visual.   D. acoustic.

6. "The magical number seven, plus or minus two" refers to the capacity of which type of memory?
   A. sensory   C. long-term
   B. short-term   D. autobiographical

7. Chunking allows people to
   A. increase the capacity of short-term memory to 20 individual pieces of information.
   B. improve their powers of concentration.
   C. enhance the duration of information in short-term memory.
   D. none of the above.

8. Upon meeting someone for the first time, Hildie silently repeats the person's name over and over to herself in order to really "learn" it. She is using _____ to encode this information.
   A. maintenance rehearsal
   B. working memory
   C. serial-positioning
   D. elaborative rehearsal

9. Short-term memory contains which of the following?
   A. central executive processor
   B. auditory storage-and-rehearsal system
   C. visual/spatial storage-and-rehearsal system
   D. all of the above

10. Roger's short-term memory system has an unlimited capacity. What is he likely to experience?
    A. increased intelligence
    B. constant distraction
    C. schizophrenia
    D. extreme emotional reactions

11. The term "working memory" refers to the fact that short-term memory
    A. is the hardest working of the memory systems.
    B. is a passive workplace where information is held.
    C. supplies the workforce that enables the human memory system to function.
    D. is an active mental workspace where information is processed.

12. Maintenance rehearsal can be used to maintain an item in short-term memory for how long a period of time?
    A. Seven seconds
    B. Five to nine seconds
    C. Indefinite
    D. No time

13. Alejandro met a lot of new people at the dorm party last night, and he tried to memorize the names of each one. This morning, try as he might, he can only remember the names of the first few people he met. This illustrates
    A. the recency effect.
    B. the primacy effect.
    C. the serial-position effect.
    D. the short-term fallacy.

14. Susanna also met a lot of new people at the dorm party last night, but she can only remember the names of those she met toward the end of the evening. This illustrates
    A. the recency effect.
    B. the primacy effect.
    C. the serial-position effect.
    D. the short-term fallacy.

15. Four students are trying to learn a list of words. Doreen repeats the words over and over to herself; Anne counts the number of letters in each word; Heather pronounces the words to see if they rhyme with her name; and Lauren thinks about the meaning of each word and tries to fit it into a sentence. Which student will be most successful at transferring the words into long-term memory?
    A. Doreen
    B. Anne
    C. Heather
    D. Lauren

16. _____ involves thinking about material that one wants to learn in a more meaningful way and associating it with other knowledge that is already stored in memory.
    A. Elaborative rehearsal
    B. Rote repetition
    C. Maintenance rehearsal
    D. Encoding rehearsal

17. Participants in a psychology study are asked to sit in front of a computer screen and look at ten trait words (for example, "shy," "intelligent," "friendly"). Participant A is asked to judge the length of each word; Participant B is asked to judge whether the words begin with a consonant or a vowel; Participant C is asked to judge whether the words rhyme with certain other words; and Participant D is asked to judge whether the words are self-descriptive. Who will have the best recall?
    A. Participant A   C. Participant C
    B. Participant B   D. Participant D

18. Research indicates that long-term memory is better when
    A. information is processed at a "deep" level.
    B. information is "overlearned."
    C. information is learned over a period of time rather than all at once.
    D. all of the above.

19. Our stored knowledge of learned habits and skills is called _____ memory.
    A. declarative   C. procedural
    B. episodic   D. semantic

20. Research suggests that the _____ is essential for the formation of new long-term memories.
    A. hypothalamus   C. frontal lobes
    B. hippocampus   D. temporal lobes

21. As part of a research project, Joleen attempted to learn a set of nonsense syllables. Which of the following would provide evidence that she in fact did store the syllables in memory?
    A. She can recall the nonsense syllables when asked to do so by the experimenter.
    B. She can correctly select the original syllables out of a larger list of syllables.
    C. It takes her less time to relearn the same syllables.
    D. All of the above.

22. Four people learn a list of words in a lecture hall. Later, each is asked to recall the original items. According to research on encoding specificity, who should have the best recall?
    A. the person who recalls the words in his or her own room
    B. the person who recalls the words in a different classroom
    C. the person who recalls the words in the same lecture hall
    D. the person who recalls the words outside under a tree

23. Lorelei was a participant in the study mentioned in Question 22. When she learned the list of words, she was in a particularly good mood. Research on state-dependent memory suggests that she will be able to recall the most words when she is
    A. in a particularly bad mood.
    B. in a particularly good mood.
    C. in a neutral mood.
    D. drunk.

24. People with _____ may show signs of long-term retention of visual information without awareness.
    A. schizophrenia   C. prosopagnosia
    B. alcoholism   D. depression

25. Dean and some other students are brainstorming ideas for a class project. Later, when describing some of the ideas he himself generated, Dean "remembers" an idea that was actually generated by another student. This demonstrates
   A. cryptomnesia.
   B. eyewitness transfer.
   C. illusion of truth.
   D. blatant dishonesty.

26. An inability to recall information may be caused by which of the following?
   A. a failure to encode the information
   B. the passage of time
   C. interference by other information
   D. all of the above

27. Xena has arrived for a study session. The teaching assistant asks her to wait for the rest of the group in small, cluttered "office." Almost immediately, however, she is taken to another room. When asked to remember the "office," which items is she likely to recall seeing?
   A. a desk that was actually present
   B. books that were not actually present
   C. a television that was not actually present
   D. A and B

28. Research on autobiographical memory suggests that we are most likely to remember
   A. events from the distant past.
   B. events that represent "transitional firsts."
   C. routine events.
   D. events that happened before we were 3 or 4 years old.

29. When he was younger, Antonio received an outstanding citizen award for rescuing three people from a burning building. Although over 20 years have passed, his memory for that occasion is as vivid and detailed as if he is still standing on that platform, hearing the mayor speak his name, and seeing the crowd of cheering people. Antonio's memory would be described as a(n)
   A. amnesiac memory.
   B. egocentric memory.
   C. flashbulb memory.
   D. hindsight memory.

30. Peggy has never really liked eating fruit or vegetables (she prefers fast food, the greasier the better). On the way to work one day, she hears an announcement on the radio from the American Medical Association about the importance of including fruits and vegetables in one's daily diet. When subsequently discussing her eating habits with a work colleague, Peggy recalls eating more fruit and vegetables (and less fast food) in the past month than she really did. What does this demonstrate?
   A. hindsight bias
   B. egocentric memory
   C. prosopagnosia
   D. memory transference

True-False Questions

Indicate which of the following statements are true or false, and compare your answers with those at the end of the chapter.

T   F   1. Sensory memory stores all stimuli that register on the senses.

T   F   2. With practice, the capacity of short-term memory can be expanded to hold an infinite number of items.

T   F   3. Chunking allows us to make more efficient use of our short-term memory capacity.

T　F　4. Short-term memory has a limited capacity but an unlimited duration.

T　F　5. Maintenance rehearsal is one way to prevent information loss in working memory.

T　F　6. The majority of modern memory researchers conceptualize short-term memory as a passive storage depot where information is held.

T　F　7. Multiple mechanisms are needed to explain the serial-position curve.

T　F　8. Certain types of information are encoded in long-term memory without conscious control.

T　F　9. Recent work on the engram reveals that it is chemically possible to transfer the memory of one organism into another.

T　F　10. Memory without awareness occurs in all humans.

Key Concepts Matching Exercises

Exercise #1: An Information-Processing Model of Human Memory

Indicate the structures and processes involved in memory by inserting the correct letter into each box.

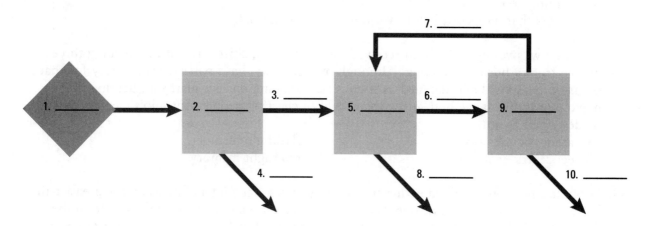

A. Short-term memory

B. Encoding

C. Sensory memory

D. Retrieval failure

E. Attention

F. Encoding failure

G. Long-term memory

H. Stimulus input

I. Attentional failure

J. Retrieval

Exercise #2: Memory

Match the key terms on the left with the definitions on the right.

_____ 1. Sensory memory

_____ 2. Short-term memory

_____ 3. Long-term memory

_____ 4. Iconic memory

_____ 5. Echoic memory

_____ 6. Maintenance rehearsal

_____ 7. Elaborative rehearsal

_____ 8. Procedural memory

_____ 9. Declarative memory

_____10. Proactive interference

_____11. Retroactive interference

_____12. Mnemonics

_____13. Flashbulb memory

_____14. Hindsight bias

A. "I can't remember my old phone number; I keep thinking of the new one."

B. "I remember it like it was yesterday, it's so clear and vivid in my mind."

C. "I learned to ski when I was five. I remember how excited I got when I first saw snow."

D. "This contains all of the information I've learned and all the memories I've formed."

E. "To really learn this information, I'll think about its meaning and how it relates to my own life."

F. "This records information from all of my sensory systems."

G. "I before E except after C;" "30 days has September, April, June, and November."

H. "This is a brief memory for the sounds that I hear."

I. "I can't remember my new password. I keep thinking of the old one."

J. "When putting on skis, one must first insert the toe and heel of one foot."

K. "I just knew it would turn out this way."

L. "This is my working memory."

M. "To learn this information, I'll just repeat it over and over again."

N. "This is a brief memory for the visual images that I see."

Essay Questions

Write out answers to the following brief essay questions. Compare your responses with the sample answers at the end of the Study Guide chapter.

1. The sensory memory system is capable of storing information for only a brief period of time. What is the point of forming memories that are lost almost immediately?

2. What is the serial-position effect? What explains this effect?

3. While walking to the university one day, Eric witnessed a man driving a car run through a stop sign. Later that day, his friend Sandy asks him about the incident. Eric remembers the event, but he can't seem to recall the man's face or the color of the car. What four factors might explain Eric's memory failure?

4. Knowing that you are studying memory, a friend approaches you and asks for help in learning material for a big history exam. What techniques might you suggest that your friend follow or use in order to prevent forgetting the material?

5. Your text presents a quotation by Vaillant (1977) in which he noted that "maturation makes liars of us all." Explain what he means, using research on autobiographical memory.

Multiple-Choice Solutions

1. C (p. 211)	11. D (p. 218)	21. D (pp. 229-30)
2. D (p. 211)	12. A (p. 218)	22. C (p. 231)
3. A (p. 211)	13. B (p. 219)	23. B (p. 232)
4. C (p. 212)	14. A (p. 219)	24. C (p. 233)
5. D (p. 214)	15. D (p. 221)	25. A (p. 235)
6. B (p. 215)	16. A (p. 221)	26. D (p. 238)
7. D (p. 216)	17. D (p. 222)	27. D (p. 243)
8. A (p. 217)	18. D (p. 222)	28. B (p. 247)
9. D (p. 218)	19. C (p. 224)	29. C (p. 248)
10. B (p. 218)	20. B (p. 227)	30. A (p. 250)

True-False Solutions

1. T (p. 211)	6. F (p. 218)
2. F (p. 215)	7. T (pp. 219-20)
3. T (p. 216)	8. T (p. 222)
4. F (p. 217)	9. F (p. 226)
5. T (p. 217)	10. T (p. 234)

Key Concepts Matching Solutions

Exercise #1

1. H
2. C
3. E
4. I
5. A
6. B
7. J
8. F
9. G
10. D

Exercise #2

1. F
2. L
3. D
4. N
5. H
6. M
7. E
8. J
9. C
10. I
11. A
12. G
13. B
14. K

Essay Solutions

1. Although it might seem pointless to create sensory memories that fade almost immediately, such memories actually serve an incredibly important purpose. Specifically, these memories provide continuity between our perceptions of an event or stimulus. For example, the visual icon preserves an image of what we are seeing in memory, so that when we blink we do not experience a disturbance of that image. Without iconic memory, we would "see" the image as a series of disjointed snapshots rather than as a continuous, flowing film. The same purpose is provided by echoic and other forms of sensory memory (p. 214).

2. The serial-position effect is the tendency for information that is presented earlier (this is called the primacy effect) and later (this is called the recency effect) to be better remembered than information that is presented in the middle. For example, if you received a list of words or met a series of people, you would probably remember the words or people first encountered (primacy) and those last encountered (recency); words and people sandwiched in the middle would not be recalled as well (p. 219).

   Different factors may be responsible for primacy and recency. For example, primacy appears to be a function of time spent rehearsing. That is, we begin rehearsing the first items, and can give them our undivided attention. However, we are less able to give attention (and devote time) to subsequent items. As noted by your author, the recency effect is harder to explain. It used to be thought that the last items were better remembered because they were still fresh in short-term storage when the recall test began; so, essentially, all the person had to do was "dump" whatever information was currently in short-term memory (and this information was the most recent, naturally). However, subsequent research indicates that this information may be better recalled not because it is still active in short-term memory, but because it is more distinctive (pp. 219-20).

3. Four factors might account for Eric's memory failure. The first two have to do with the possibility that the information is simply not in long-term memory. For example, it is possible that Eric saw the event, but he never actually encoded the information about the man's face and the car's color—he is unable to retrieve the information because it is not there and it never was there (this is called encoding failure). It is also possible that Eric did encode the information, but the memory for the man's face and car's color eroded with the passage of time (this is called decay). The next two factors that might explain Eric's memory failure have to do with the possibility that the memory exists but cannot be retrieved. For example, it is possible that other information is interfering with Eric's ability to retrieve the relevant details (perhaps he saw another person run a stop sign last week, and this old information is proactively interfering with the retrieval of the new information; or perhaps he saw another person run a stop sign right after the first man did, and this newer information is retroactively interfering with the first information). Finally, Eric may have encoded the information, but be unable to remember it due to a form of motivated forgetting called repression (perhaps the sight of the man running the stop sign brought back traumatic memories of a traffic accident Eric once saw, and so he "forgets" what he's seen as a way of keeping that other painful memory out of awareness) (pp. 238-42).

4. There are several methods you could suggest to your friend to help him or her prevent forgetting the material. For example, your friend could increase his or her practice time; could think actively and deeply about the material; could organize and learn the material hierarchically; could make use of verbal mnemonics (e.g., rhymes, acronyms); could use the method of loci; could use the peg-word method; could attempt to reduce the likelihood of interference (e.g., by studying right before sleeping to minimize subsequent distracting information); and could attempt to reinstate the context in which learning occurred (i.e., make sure that the learning and testing context or situation are the same) (pp. 240-41).

5. This quotation refers to the revisionist nature of our autobiographical memories. That is, it seems common for people to "remember" the past in a self-serving and self-esteem-enhancing way. For example, we tend to exaggerate our own role in past events (we see ourselves as central players rather than in bit parts). We also demonstrate something called the hindsight bias, which is the tendency to believe after an event occurs that we actually knew all along what was going to happen ("I just knew it would turn out this way;" "I've always said that she would go far in life"). This hindsight bias can cause us to revise our personal histories in ways that reflect favorably on us. For example, if we come to believe that exercise is good for our health, we may "remember" that we were more athletic in high school and college than we really were. We also update the past in ways that enhance our self-concept or self-esteem. Your text discusses a study in which college students were asked to recall their high school grades; when the researchers checked the accuracy of these grade reports, they found a tendency to overinflate rather than to underinflate grades (p. 250).

Multimedia Study Resources

Several activities and articles in Chapter 7 (Memory) of The Psychology Place™ supplement the material covered in your textbook. "Test Your Memory" is a learning activity that allows you to witness an event (in the form of a series of photographs) and then test your memory for the events you observed. After you take the memory quiz, you will be provided with your results and you'll be able to compare them to the results from other people who completed the same activity. A related article in *Scientific American* magazine, "Creating False Memories", explores how suggestion and imagination work together to create "memories" of events that did not actually occur. Finally, Research News presents an article that summarizes the debate with respect to recovered memories of child abuse ("The Repressed Memory Debate").

7 Thought and Language

Chapter Overview

This chapter examines the way people think and communicate. The first section focuses on thinking. Specifically, this section opens with an examination of the basic building blocks of thought, called concepts, and explores the ways in which we make use of these mental groupings when thinking and making judgments. Next, the mental activities or steps involved in problem-solving are described (i.e., defining and representing the problem, generating and evaluating possible solutions), as are the biases or "blind spots" that prevent effective problem-solving. The section on cognition then presents an overview of the rules of formal logic and a discussion of decision making in formal logic tasks, and ends with an examination of the biases that influence decision making and impede rational thought (e.g., heuristics, anchoring effects, overconfidence). The second section of the chapter focuses on language, beginning with a discussion of the characteristics of human language (i.e., semanticity, generativity, displacement). The chapter then moves into a consideration of whether the capacity for language is uniquely human or whether animals can also learn and use language for communication purposes. The final section of Chapter 7 explores the interrelationship between thought and language, starting with a discussion of the linguistic-relativity hypothesis (i.e., the notion that language influences thought) and some of the practical implications of linguistic relativity (i.e., the psychological impact of sexist language).

Chapter Outline

I. *What's Your Prediction?* Using Words to Shape Thoughts

II. Concepts

III. Solving Problems

    A. Representing the Problem
       1. Mental images
       2. Mental models

B. Generating Solutions
   1. Trial and error
   2. Algorithms and heuristics
   3. Insight

C. "Blind Spots" in Problem Solving
   1. Representation failures
   2. Functional fixedness
   3. Mental sets
   4. The confirmation bias
   5. Belief perseverance

IV. Making Judgments

   A. The Rules of Formal Logic
      1. Syllogistic reasoning
      2. Conditional reasoning

   B. Biases in Judgment
      1. The representativeness heuristic
      2. The availability heuristic
      3. Anchoring effects
      4. Framing effects
      5. Overconfidence

   C. *Debunking the Myths* ... That Cause Gamblers to Lose Money

   D. Can Heuristics Make Us Smart?

   E. *How To* ... Improve Your Critical Thinking Skills

V. Language

   A. Communication in the Animal World

   B. Characteristics of Human Language
      1. Semanticity
      2. Generativity
      3. Displacement

   C. Can Animals Learn Language?
      1. The talking parrot
      2. The bottle-nosed dolphins
      3. The great apes
      4. The controversy
         a. semanticity
         b. generativity
         c. displacement
         d. conclusion

Learning Objectives

By the time you have read and reviewed this chapter, you should be able to:

1. Define the term "concept" and explain how concepts are stored in memory (pp. 258-59). Explain the relation between a concept and a prototype (p. 259). Discuss how prototypes affect judgment and decision-making processes (p. 259).

2. List and describe the mental activities involved in the process of problem solving (p. 260).

3. Explain the different ways in which a problem may be represented mentally (i.e., words and concepts, mental images, mental models). Define mental images and mental models and explain how these representations affect problem solving (pp. 261-62-).

4. List and describe the four basic problem-solving processes that we can use to generate solutions (pp. 263-67).

5. Define the problem-solving strategy of trial-and-error, and consider the possible consequences of relying on this method (p. 263).

6. Explain what algorithms and heuristics are, and provide examples of how they may be used to solve problems (pp. 263-65). Define means-end analysis and analogies (p. 264).

7. Explain insight and consider the circumstances that may produce insight (pp. 265-66). Consider whether nonhuman animals can make use of insight (pp. 266-67).

8. Discuss the "blind spots" that compromise human problem solving, including representation failures (pp. 267-68), functional fixedness (p. 268), mental sets (p. 268), the confirmation bias (pp. 268-69) and belief perseverance (p. 269).

9. Describe the ways in which people solve logical problems (pp. 270-71).

10. Explain syllogistic reasoning and discuss how the format (concrete versus abstract) of syllogisms affects problem solving (p. 270).

11. Discuss the process involved in conditional reasoning and how the confirmation bias may affect conditional reasoning (pp. 270-71). Consider whether people can be trained in the logic of conditional reasoning (p. 271).

12. Define the representativeness heuristic and explain how it affects judgment and decision making (p. 272).

13. Define the availability heuristic and examine the consequences this heuristic can have on judgment and decision making (pp. 272, 275).

14. Consider how the illusion of control, misguided notions about probability, and biased explanations for outcomes can produce irrational thinking, particularly the "gambler's fallacy" (pp. 273-74).

15. Explain the anchoring effect and consider how this phenomenon may bias problem solving (p. 275).

16. Define the framing effect and its consequences for effective problem solving (pp. 275-76).

17. Discuss the overconfidence effect (p. 276).

18. Consider whether heuristics are "good enough" tools for problem-solving (pp. 276-77).

19. Define critical thinking and summarize the steps involved in critical thinking (p. 278).

20. Examine animal communication and compare it with human communication (pp. 278-79).

21. Describe and provide examples of the characteristics of human language, including semanticity (pp. 280-81), generativity (pp. 281-82), and displacement (pp. 282-83).

22. Discuss whether animals can learn language, using evidence from studies of birds, dolphins, and nonhuman primates (pp. 283-85). Consider whether this evidence meets the standards of semanticity, generativity, and displacement (pp. 285-86). Explain why the notion of animal language is controversial (pp. 286-87).

23. Explore the relationship between thought and language (pp. 288-91). In particular, explain the linguistic-relativity hypothesis (pp. 288-90). Consider how cultural differences in the use of words might (or might not) enable researchers to evaluate this hypothesis (pp. 289-90).

24. Discuss evidence that sexist language may affect cognition (e.g., the mental images that are triggered; subsequent beliefs about career options) (pp. 290-91).

Key Terms

The following key terms and concepts are featured in this chapter and are important for you to know. Write out definitions of each term and check your answers with the definitions in the text on the pages listed.

Concept (p. 258)
Prototypes (p. 259)
Images (p. 261)
Mental models (p. 262)
Trial and error (p. 263)
Algorithm (p. 263)
Heuristics (p. 263)
Means-end analysis (p. 264)
Analogy (p. 264)
Insight (p. 265)
Functional fixedness (p. 268)

Mental set (p. 268)
Confirmation bias (p. 268)
Belief perseverance (p. 269)
Syllogism (p. 270)
Representativeness heuristic (p. 272)
Availability heuristic (p. 272)
Illusion of control (p. 273)
Anchoring effect (p. 275)
Framing effect (p. 275)
Language (p. 277)
Critical thinking (p. 278)

Test Questions

Multiple-Choice Questions

Circle the correct choice for each question and compare your answers with those at the end of the Study Guide chapter.

1. _____ are mental groupings of people, places, ideas, or objects that share common properties.
   A. Classifications
   B. Concepts
   C. Protoconcepts
   D. Mental models

2. Research suggests that a robin is the "birdiest" bird; that is, it is the prototype of the concept bird. What does this mean?
   A. A robin is perceived to be a more typical example of the concept bird than other members of the concept.
   B. A robin has more of the concept's characteristic or defining features than other members of the concept.
   C. A robin will be more easily recognized as a member of the concept bird than other members of the concept.
   D. All of the above

3. As part of a class demonstration, Val and other students are shown a slide of a tilted container filled with water. Val, along with many of his classmates, assumes that the water surface is tilted in the same way as the container—when, in fact, the water surface remains horizontal to the ground. This error may be due to the use of _____.
   A. mental models
   B. intuition
   C. prototypes
   D. formal logic

4. The simplest (and sometimes least efficient) problem-solving strategy we can make use of is
   A. protologic.
   B. algorithms.
   C. trial and error.
   D. heuristics.

5. Jon and Linda enjoy word games, puzzles, and anagrams. Both are attempting to solve the following anagram: E H T E T. Jon tries all possible combinations by systematically varying the letters in each position. Linda tries the most familiar letter combinations (for example, she realizes that TH is a common combination in the English language). Both arrive at the solution (TEETH). Jon used a(n) _____, whereas Linda used a(n) _____.
   A. concept; prototype
   B. algorithm; heuristic
   C. means-end analysis; analogy
   D. insight; mental model

6. One important general heuristic involves breaking a larger problem (for example, writing a paper) into a series of subgoals (for example, obtaining references, which in turn means getting a library card). This heuristic is known as _____.
   A. analogy heuristic
   B. algorithm solution
   C. means-end analysis
   D. intuitive physics

7. Stephanie has been trying to solve a particular problem for the last 45 minutes, but to no avail. Frustrated, she decides to take a walk. When she returns and looks at the problem once more, the solution suddenly comes to her. Stephanie has experienced the _____.
   A. incubation effect
   B. insight effect
   C. discovery phenomenon
   D. mental leap experience

8. Connor is using tacks to hang posters on the wall of his dorm room. He has only one more small poster to hang, but when he reaches for a tack, he discovers that the box is empty. He really wants to hang all the posters now, so he decides to use a fork to attach the poster to the wall. Connor's use of the fork demonstrates the *absence* of _____.
   A. mental sets
   B. functional fixedness
   C. representation failure
   D. reasoning

9. The tendency to use a problem-solving strategy that has been effective in the past is called
   A. confirmation bias.
   B. mental model.
   C. mental set.
   D. functional fixedness.

10. Cathy is playing a game of hide-and-seek with her little nephew, Kevin. The first time they play, Cathy hides in the hall closet. Kevin finds her. The next time, Cathy hides in the bathroom. However, Kevin goes right back to the hall closet. Kevin's behavior demonstrates
    A. perseveration.
    B. representation failure.
    C. confirmation bias.
    D. mental set.

11. I have come to the conclusion that Dani is a friendly, outgoing, socially skilled person. When I talk with her, I only ask her about parties she's attended, new friends she's made, and fun activities she's done. I am demonstrating which problem-solving "blind spot?"
    A. syllogistic reasoning
    B. belief perseverance
    C. mental sets
    D. confirmation bias

12. As a class demonstration, Dr. Allbright tells her students the following story: "There is a group of 20 classics professors and 80 truck drivers. In that group, I randomly select a conservative man named Harold, who enjoys reading poetry and is shy, quiet, and thin. Is Harold a truck driver or a classics professor?" Most of her class guesses that Harold is a classics professor. Are they right?
    A. Yes, Harold resembles the typical classics professor.
    B. Yes, the probability is higher that a randomly selected man would be a classics professor than a truck driver.
    C. No, Harold resembles neither the typical classics professor nor the typical truck driver.
    D. No, they have ignored the base rate information given in the first sentence.

13. In the last question, the students fell prey to which bias in judgment?
    A. representativeness heuristic
    B. availability heuristic
    C. anchoring
    D. framing

14. A mental shortcut in which people estimate the likelihood of an event based on how easily they can bring instances of the event to mind is called the
    A. representativeness heuristic.
    B. availability heuristic.
    C. anchoring effect.
    D. framing phenomenon.

15. As noted by your textbook, people have a tendency to overestimate the likelihood of death by shark attack. This overestimation may be caused by
    A. the availability heuristic.
    B. the representativeness heuristic.
    C. anchoring.
    D. framing.

16. Two pills have been developed to treat flulike symptoms. Pill A is described as having a "95 percent success rate," and Pill B is described as having a "5 percent failure rate." Jordan, who has flu, decides that he would rather take Pill A. His decision reflects
    A. availability.
    B. overconfidence.
    C. framing.
    D. representativeness.

17. Gambling behavior may be the result of which cognitive phenomenon?
    A. the illusion of control
    B. lack of knowledge about probability
    C. biased explanations for outcomes (wins and losses)
    D. all of the above

18. The ability to solve problems and make decisions through a careful evaluation of the evidence is known as
    A. formal logic.
    B. syllogistic reasoning.
    C. linguistic relativity.
    D. critical thinking.

19. Nick and Nora are in the process of insuring their valuable art collection. They need to evaluate the claims made by various insurance companies. What is the first critical thinking step they should follow?
    A. Identify the assumptions that each company is making in its argument.
    B. Try to imagine alternative claims and arguments.
    C. Avoid being heavily influenced by big words and jargon.
    D. Adopt an attitude of healthy skepticism.

20. All languages share three universal properties. What are they?
    A. semanticity
    B. generativity
    C. displacement
    D. all of the above

21. The basic sounds of a language are
    A. semantics.
    B. phonemes.
    C. morphemes.
    D. syllables.

22. The fact that the sentence you are reading at this very moment is unique (i.e., has never been written before) demonstrates which property of language?
    A. generativity
    B. semantics
    C. displacement
    D. syntax

23. The rules of grammar that govern how words can be arranged in a sentence are known as
    A. phonemes.
    B. language.
    C. deep structure.
    D. syntax.

24. Which sentence illustrates the concept of displacement?
    A. "I see my neighbor's cat in the yard."
    B. "When I was a child, I had a cat."
    C. "The cat is being fed by my neighbor."
    D. "My neighbor is feeding the cat."

25. Attempts have been made to teach language to which types of animals?
    A. parrots
    B. primates
    C. dolphins
    D. all of the above

26. Research demonstrates that primates *conclusively* satisfy which of the following language criteria?
    A. semanticity
    B. generativity
    C. displacement
    D. all of the above

27. Which one of the following statements is accurate?
    A. Apes can develop the same size vocabulary as young children.
    B. Apes demonstrate a more complex syntax than young children.
    C. Apes can understand grammatical sentences.
    D. Apes cannot be taught words.

28. The linguistic-relativity hypothesis states that language _____.
    A. is caused by thought
    B. influences thought
    C. is a product of higher thinking processes
    D. and thought influence each other

29. Research on the impact of sexist language reveals which of the following?
    A. Sexist language does not influence the way we think about men and women.
    B. The use of generic masculine pronouns triggers images of women to the exclusion of men.
    C. The use of generic masculine terms is seen as exclusive, not inclusive, of women.
    D. All of the above.

30. Guidelines for nonsexist language suggest that we should replace the word "mankind" with the more inclusive term(s)
    A. people.
    B. humanity.
    C. human beings.
    D. All of the above.

True-False Questions

Indicate which of the following statements are true or false, and compare your answers with those at the end of the chapter.

T   F   1. People may rely on prototypes when making decisions.

T   F   2. The use of mental images to represent information is a rare (and purely human) ability.

T   F   3. People are quicker to understand new scientific concepts when these concepts are taught by analogy than when they are explained in literal terms.

T   F   4. Many of our beliefs are highly resistant to change.

T F 5. As a general rule, most people find syllogisms easier when they are stated concretely ("All robins are birds") rather than in an abstract format ("All As are Bs").

T F 6. People consistently underestimate the accuracy of their predictions.

T F 7. Speech is a necessary criterion for language.

T F 8. Today, most psychologists agree that language influences the way we think.

T F 9. Research suggests that sexist language has little impact on the way we think about the sexes.

T F 10. The way humans think and communicate is best understood as both rational and irrational, competent and flawed.

Key Concepts Matching Exercises

Exercise #1: Thought

Match the key terms on the left with the definitions on the right.

_____ 1. Concept	A. "He must be a lawyer; he just seems so lawyer-like."
_____ 2. Prototype	B. "I'll just keep plugging away and trying new combinations until I figure out the solution."
_____ 3. Mental model	C. All your knowledge about the group of objects called "dogs"
_____ 4. Trial and error	D. Intuitive theory about the way things work
_____ 5. Algorithm	E. "I'll just use the same strategy that worked last time."
_____ 6. Heuristic	F. The "doggiest" dog
_____ 7. Insight	G. "Experts are usually right"
_____ 8. Mental set	H. "Airplane travel just isn't safe. The news is filled with reports of crashes. Why, just last week there was that big one outside of Seattle..."
_____ 9. Belief perseverance	I. A systematic problem-solving strategy that is guaranteed to produce a solution
_____10. Representativeness heuristic	J. "Eureka! I figured it out! The solution just came to me out of nowhere!"
_____11. Availability heuristic	K. "If I wear my lucky shirt and blow on the dice gently, I can roll a winning hand."
_____12. Illusion of control	L. "I don't care what the research shows, I still believe that people are completely rational thinkers."

Exercise #2: Language

Match the key terms on the left with the definitions on the right.

_____ 1. Semanticity

_____ 2. Morphemes

_____ 3. Phonemes

_____ 4. Generativity

_____ 5. Syntax

_____ 6. Displacement

_____ 7. Linguistic-relativity
hypothesis

A. "I believe that honor and good name are important things we each should strive to attain."

B. "Wow! We can arrange the words in our language to produce an infinite variety of sentences."

C. The smallest unit of language that carries meaning

D. Rules of grammar

E. This language property accounts for the communication of meaning

F. "I speak, therefore I think."

G. These are the basic, distinct sounds of a spoken language.

Essay Questions

Write out answers to the following brief essay questions. Compare your responses with the sample answers at the end of the Study Guide chapter.

1. What is trial and error? Explain this problem-solving strategy, using a specific example from your own experience. What are the consequences (positive and negative) of using trial and error?

2. Your friend Stan is working on a creative writing project. Unfortunately, he cannot figure out how to put the idea he has for a particular paragraph into words. He's rewritten this paragraph several times, and is becoming increasingly frustrated. "If I could just have the insight into how to set this down into words!" he exclaims. Define the notion of insight, and explain to Stan what he might do in order to increase his chances of experiencing insight.

3. List and define the "blind spots" that can prevent effective problem solving.

4. Donelle frequently travels to Las Vegas. Although she loses more than she wins, she nonetheless keeps going back to try her luck at the casinos. Explain, from a cognitive perspective, why Donelle continues to gamble.

5. The intuitive view of the relationship between thought and language is that language is a tool for expressing thought (that is, thought causes language). What major alternative possibility was suggested by Whorf? Define the Whorfian alternative, and discuss evidence in favor of his hypothesis. What do most modern psychologists think about the relationship between thought and language?

Test Solutions

Multiple-Choice Solutions

1. B (p. 258)	11. D (p. 268)	21. B (p. 280)
2. D (p. 259)	12. D (p. 272)	22. A (p. 281)
3. A (p. 262)	13. A (p. 272)	23. D (p. 281)
4. C (p. 263)	14. B (p. 272)	24. B (p. 282)
5. B (p. 263)	15. A (p. 272)	25. D (pp. 283-84)
6. C (p. 264)	16. C (p. 275)	26. A (p. 285)
7. A (p. 266)	17. D (pp. 273-74)	27. C (p. 286)
8. B (p. 268)	18. D (p. 278)	28. B (p. 288)
9. C (p. 268)	19. D (p. 278)	29. C (p. 291)
10. D (p. 268)	20. D (p. 280)	30. D (p. 291)

True-False Solutions

1. T (pp. 259-60)	6. F (p. 276)
2. F (p. 261)	7. F (p. 285)
3. T (p. 265)	8. T (p. 288)
4. T (p. 269)	9. F (pp. 290-91)
5. T (p. 270)	10. T (pp. 291-92)

Key Concepts Matching Solutions

Exercise #1	*Exercise #2*
1. C	1. E
2. F	2. C
3. D	3. G
4. B	4. B
5. I	5. D
6. G	6. A
7. J	7. F
8. E	
9. L	
10. A	
11. H	
12. K	

Essay Solutions

1. Trial and error is the simplest problem-solving strategy, and it involves a "hit or miss" approach to a problem. Essentially, one would try a hodgepodge of potential solutions to a problem, in no particular order, and hope that one of these was correct. Any example from your own experience would be fine. For instance, I sometimes get an "error" message on the screen of my computer when running the SPSS statistical package. Often, I just go back to my command file and "tinker" with the commands; I might remove a comma, add a period, and so on. Then I try to rerun the analysis. I do this until the system accepts my command and runs the analysis completely (or I get too tired and frustrated and put it aside!). There are both positive and negative consequences to employing trial and error as your strategy. On the positive side, it's a simple strategy and it's often effective. However, on the negative side, it may not be the most efficient strategy. For example, if often takes a long time and sometimes fails completely (p. 263).

2. Insight is a problem-solving process in which the solution to a problem comes to mind all of a sudden, without conscious awareness. People who experience insight often do not realize that the solution is coming and cannot describe what they were thinking about at the time; it's almost as if the solution suddenly is just there. You might tell Stan that insight seems to be more likely when people do the following things: (1) They switch from one strategy to another (so maybe instead of writing things down, he could talk out loud for a while); (2) they reframe the problem (perhaps Stan should focus on the one basic point he wants to make, rather than the whole paragraph); (3) they remove a mental block (this is harder, maybe he could just free associate and write words and phrases down, instead of trying to create complete, entire sentences in a specified order); (4) they identify an analogy from prior experience; and (5) they take a break (walk away from) the problem (you might suggest that Stan go for a walk and stop consciously thinking about the problem) (pp. 265-66).

3. There are five "blind spots" that can prevent effective problem solving. First, there is something called representation failure; this is defined as incorrectly understanding or conceptualizing (representing) the problem. Functional fixedness may also prevent effective problem solving (this is the tendency to only think of objects in terms of their usual functions), as may mental sets (a mental set is the tendency to use the same problem-solving strategy that has worked in the past, even though you now are facing a new problem that may require a different strategy). Finally, the confirmation bias (the tendency to only look for evidence that confirms our existing beliefs) and belief perseverance (the tendency to maintain our initial beliefs even in the face of disconfirming evidence) may impede problem solving (pp. 267-69).

4. From a cognitive perspective, there are three basic explanations for Donelle's continued gambling behavior. First, she may harbor the belief that she can control chance events. This is known as the illusion of control. For example, Donelle may believe that certain activities that she does (throwing the dice in a certain way, using a particular slot machine) may influence what is in reality a game of pure chance. Second, Donelle's gambling behavior may stem from misguided or inaccurate notions about probability. She may believe, for example, that a slot machine that just produced a big payoff will be less likely to produce a second winning combination; she may assume that after a series of red numbers on the roulette wheel, it's "time" for a black number to come up. Finally, Donelle may form biased explanations for her wins and losses. She may take credit for her successes ("I knew I would win because I used my lucky numbers") and explain away her failures ("It was a bad day; we were all losing. That casino is run by thieves."); these explanations may cause her to continue to think that success is closer than it probably really is (pp. 273-74).

5. The Whorfian alternative, known as the linguistic-relativity hypothesis, states that our thoughts are relative to (a function of) our linguistic heritage; in other words, the language that we speak shapes the way we conceptualize and think about the world. Evidence for linguistic relativity was provided by cultural differences in the use of words to represent reality; for example, Whorf noted that Eskimos have several words for snow. He argued that these words enable them to perceive and think about snow in a different manner than English-speaking people (who have fewer words). However, this cross-cultural research is difficult to evaluate because people who speak different languages differ in other ways as well (thus, any differences in cognition may be the result of these other differences and not solely due to the language difference) (pp. 288-99).

Few modern psychologists believe in the linguistic-relativity hypothesis as it was originally stated (i.e., language determines thought). However, most do agree with a more moderate version of the hypothesis; namely, that language influences the way that we think, and that thought and language are closely interconnected processes (p. 288).

Multimedia Study Resources

Several activities and articles in Chapter 8 (Thinking and Intelligence) of The Psychology Place™ supplement the material covered in your textbook. For example, the Learning Activity called "Critical Thinking: I Know It's a Good Thing, But What Is It?" provides a tutorial that allows you to review the processes involved in critical thinking. This section also contains an interactive demonstration ("Understanding Mental Models") that explores how mental models work and how they sometimes contribute to faulty or illogical reasoning. In Research News, a report entitled "Babies, Phonetics, and Mastering Language" examines the innate human ability to develop language.

8 Motivation

Chapter Overview

The topic of this chapter is motivation. Your textbook author first defines the concept of motivation, and then explores the various theories that have been advanced to explain and account for motivated behavior. In turn, the chapter compares and contrasts general theories of motivation (i.e., instinct theories, drive theory, arousal theory, and incentive theory), as well as Maslow's hierarchy of needs explanation for motivation. Then, specific human motives are examined, beginning with basic motives (i.e., hunger, sex). First, the biological and psychological aspects of hunger and eating are discussed, as well as some consequences of the hunger motive (e.g., obesity, eating disorders). Then, a second basic motivation—sexual motivation—is explored. This section begins with an overview of information about sexual practices collected from survey data, and then discusses sex differences in sexual motives from both an evolutionary and social psychological perspective. The chapter then outlines the components of the human sexual-response cycle, and explores the topic of sexual orientation. The next section of the chapter focuses on social motives (i.e., belongingness, esteem). First, two distinct motives having to do with the need to belong are examined. Specifically, the personal and situational factors that influence the need for affiliation and the need for intimacy are discussed. Esteem motives, including the need for achievement and the need for power, similarly are examined. The chapter ends by considering the applied aspects of motivation, including the factors (e.g., perceived equity) that affect job performance and people's motivation to perform a particular task.

Chapter Outline

I. *What's Your Prediction?* What Does it Take to Motivate People at Work?

II. What Motivates Us?

    A. General Theories of Motivation
       1. Drive theory
       2. Arousal theory
       3. Incentive theory

Learning Objectives

By the time you have read and reviewed this chapter, you should be able to:

1. Define the concept of motivation and contrast the two major ways in which psychologists have approached this subject (p. 299).

2. Compare the four general theories of human motivation (i.e., instinct theory, drive theory, arousal theory, and incentive theory). Explain the basic tenets of, and the problems associated with, each of these theories (pp. 299-300).

3. Discuss Maslow's hierarchy of needs theory of human motivation. Explain the importance of the pyramid structure in terms of understanding human needs. Compare this approach with the general theories of motivation (pp. 300-1).

4. Examine the biological components of the basic motive of hunger. Discuss the role played by the stomach and the brain in regulating hunger (pp. 302-3).

5. Consider the importance of psychological factors in regulating hunger, including taste, smell, visual cues, and social influence (the presence of others) (pp. 303-4).

6. Discuss the consequences of the hunger motive, including obesity and eating disorders (pp. 304-8).

7. Explain the consequences of the sexual motive for the species and the individual (p. 308).

8. Summarize survey research on sexual practices, and discuss sex differences in sexual behavior (pp. 308-9).

9. Consider the evolutionary and social psychological explanation for sex differences in sexual motivation and behavior (pp. 310-11).

10. List and explain the stages of the human sexual-response cycle (p. 312).

11. Define sexual orientation and consider the prevalence (p. 312) and the biological and social origins (pp. 313-15) of homosexuality.

12. Define belongingness needs and the two types of belongingness motives (i.e., affiliation and intimacy) (pp. 316-17).

13. Explain the need for affiliation (p. 316). Consider individual differences in this motive as well as social factors that influence the need to affiliate (e.g., stress) (pp. 316-17).

14. Define the need for intimacy (p. 317). Explain how self-disclosure is related to the need for intimacy and consider gender differences in self-disclosure (pp. 317-18).

15. Define esteem needs and two types of esteem motives (i.e., achievement and power) (pp. 318-21).

16. Explain the need for achievement and consider ways to measure this motive (pp. 318-19). Explore the association among the need for achievement, actual behavior, and level of accomplishment, in individuals and in societies (p. 321).

17. Define the need for power and how it is related to leadership (pp. 321-22).

18. Consider how we can use fantasy play to motivate children's classroom achievement (p. 320).

19. Discuss how external rewards may be used to motivate people at work. Specifically, consider expectancy theory and how it has been used to explain and predict worker attendance, productivity, and other job-related activities (pp. 322-23).

20. Compare the concepts of intrinsic and extrinsic motivation (p. 323). Explain how external rewards can reduce intrinsic motivation (pp. 323-24).

21. Discuss how the interpretation placed on an external reward (e.g., money), as well as the perceived fairness of that reward, may influence motivation (p. 324).

22. Explain how equity theory accounts for work motivation and workplace behavior (pp. 324-325).

Key Terms

The following key terms and concepts are featured in this chapter and are important for you to know. Write out definitions of each term and check your answers with the definitions in the text on the pages listed.

Hawthorne effect (pp. 297-98)
Motivation (p. 299)
Instinct (p. 299)
Drive theory (pp. 299-300)
Arousal theory (p. 300)
Incentive theory (p. 300)
Hierarchy of needs (p. 300)
Obesity (p. 304)
Set point (p. 306)
Anorexia nervosa (p. 306)
Bulimia nervosa (p. 306)

Sexual-response cycle (p. 312)
Sexual orientation (p. 312)
Need for affiliation (p. 316)
Need for intimacy (p. 316)
Self-disclosure (p. 317)
Achievement motivation (p. 318)
Need for power (p. 321)
Intrinsic motivation (p. 323)
Extrinsic motivation (p. 323)
Equity theory (p. 324)

Test Questions

Multiple-Choice Questions

Circle the correct choice for each question and compare your answers with those at the end of the Study Guide chapter.

1. Which of the following are considered to be human needs or motives?
   A. hunger
   B. affiliation
   C. power
   D. all of the above

2. Dr. Dewey is an avid believer in the instinct theory of motivation. He is specifically interested in the aggression instinct. What is the title of his book most likely to be?
   A. "Aggression: The Drive to Reduce Tension"
   B. "Aggression: Hard-Wired by Evolution"
   C. "Aggression: How to Optimize Your Level"
   D. "Aggression: Expected Outcomes and You"

3. Dr. Lewis follows incentive theory. She, too, is interested in aggression. What is the title of her book most likely to be?
   A. "Aggression: The Drive to Reduce Tension"
   B. "Aggression: Hard-Wired by Evolution"
   C. "Aggression: How to Optimize Your Level"
   D. "Aggression: Expected Outcomes and You"

4. The drive theory of motivation has difficulty explaining
   A. why some people chronically overeat.
   B. why some people eat only when they feel hungry.
   C. why people seek out places to sleep when they feel tired.
   D. why people engage in sexual activity when they are aroused.

5. Rebecca prefers calm situations and risk-free activities, Elizabeth enjoys somewhat stimulating situations and moderately risky activities, and Thomas craves intense experiences and high-risk activities. The differences between these three individuals are best explained by the _____ theory of motivation.
   A. instinct   C. arousal
   B. drive   D. incentive

6. Drive theory suggests that humans are _____ into action by internal needs, whereas incentive theory suggests that humans are _____ into action by external goals.
   A. forced; pushed   C. pulled; pushed
   B. pushed; pulled   D. pushed; prodded

7. Tilly has met all of her basic, physiological needs. According to Maslow's hierarchy of needs, what need or needs will Tilly strive to fulfill next?
   A. needs for food and water
   B. needs for safety and financial security
   C. needs for affiliation and affection
   D. need for esteem

8. Which of the following biological structures or processes do *not* appear to have an important role in the regulation of hunger?
   A. the lateral hypothalamus
   B. the ventromedial hypothalamus
   C. the liver
   D. stomach contractions

9. The _____ hypothalamus seems to be the brain's "hunger center;" when it is stimulated, an animal will eat even when he or she is full.
   A. ventrical   C. ventromedial
   B. lateral   D. basal

10. Casey recently was involved in an accident in which part of his brain was destroyed. Now, he feels hungry all the time, and he eats larger and larger quantities of food. He has already doubled his body weight. Most likely, the brain area that was destroyed was the _____.
   A. brainstem   C. ventromedial hypothalamus
   B. lateral hypothalamus   D. cortex

11. Which of the following are considered external food cues?
    A. the time of day
    B. the smell of food
    C. the taste of food
    D. all of the above

12. Which of the following statements about set points is accurate?
    A. Obese people have higher set points than nonobese people.
    B. Set points fluctuate rapidly over the lifespan.
    C. Set points are determined by genetic factors.
    D. Anorexic people have higher set points than obese people.

13. Survey data on the sexual practices and attitudes of adult men and women indicate that
    A. sexual activity levels are at an all-time high.
    B. men hold more permissive attitudes toward casual sex than women.
    C. women are more likely than men to fantasize about sex with multiple partners.
    D. the vast majority of married couples prefer nontraditional sex.

14. According to the evolutionary perspective on sexual motivation, men should be more upset than women by _____ infidelity, and women should be more upset than men by _____ infidelity.
    A. emotional; sexual
    B. public; private
    C. sexual; emotional
    D. romantic; sexual

15. Which one of the following is *not* a stage of the human sexual response cycle?
    A. excitement   C. relaxation
    B. resolution   D. plateau

16. A person's preference for a sexual partner of a particular sex (male/female) is known as
    A. partner preference.   C. sexual motivation.
    B. sexual response.   D. sexual orientation.

17. Research on homosexuality suggests that it is caused by
    A. a disturbed family environment.
    B. overattachment to the same-sex parent.
    C. the onset of puberty at an early age.
    D. none of the above.

18. Research conducted by LeVay (1993) on the brains of homosexual and heterosexual individuals indicates that
    A. sexual orientation is associated with the size of the hypothalamic nucleus.
    B. the hypothalamus causes sexual orientation.
    C. there is a gene that determines sexual orientation.
    D. AIDS may cause homosexuality.

19. Dawn refers to herself as a "people person." She sends letters, makes phone calls, and arranges frequent get-togethers in order to maintain contact with her many old and new friends. Dawn probably has a _____.
    A. social disorder
    B. high need for affiliation
    C. low need for intimacy
    D. belongingness need

20. Flynn prefers to spend time with one close friend as opposed to a group of acquaintances. He particularly enjoys the deep affection and self-disclosure that characterize his close friendships. Flynn probably has a high need for
    A. intimacy.
    B. reciprocity.
    C. friendship.
    D. affiliation.

21. Research on sex differences in self-disclosure reveals that
    A. men disclose more to others than do women.
    B. women receive less self-disclosure from others than do men.
    C. men disclose less to others than do women.
    D. women and men are equally open in their communication styles.

22. The more that a couple engages in self-disclosure, the _____.
    A. more they will tend to like each other
    B. happier they will be in their relationship
    C. more likely they will be to remain in the relationship
    D. all of the above

23. Ever since he was a child, Pietro has been competitive—both with himself and with others. In college, he double-majored and took the most difficult classes in each area. At the office, he handles his firm's most difficult cases, and he works longer hours than any other partner. On the street where he lives, his yard is the neatest and his garden yields the most produce. This behavior demonstrates a high level of
    A. success.
    B. esteem.
    C. achievement motivation.
    D. need for power.

24. Columbine has a high need for achievement. Given this, what else might we expect from her?
    A. persistence
    B. hard work
    C. a desire for success
    D. all of the above

25. The need for power is the strong desire to _____ other people.
    A. gain prestige and influence over
    B. self-disclose to
    C. compete against
    D. affiliate with

26. According to expectancy theory, people are _____ decision makers who work hard when they expect that their efforts will improve their own performance and increase their rewards.
    A. selfish
    B. rational
    C. competitive
    D. irrational

27. William teaches high school because he enjoys working with young adults and he believes in the value of education. He finds the job challenging and always stimulating. Buddy teaches high school because he enjoys the summer vacation schedule and he wants to attain tenure and job security. William is _____ motivated; Buddy is _____ motivated.
    A. intrinsically; extrinsically
    B. extrinsically; intrinsically
    C. internally; expectantly
    D. extrinsically; extrinsically

28. Sheila wants to increase her workers' productivity by giving them bonuses (monetary incentives). These rewards are likely to have a positive effect if they
    A. are perceived as a means of controlling worker productivity.
    B. enhance extrinsic but not intrinsic motivation.
    C. are perceived as a source of information about performance quality.
    D. all of the above.

29. According to equity theory, people who feel that they are being underpaid for their work will experience _____ distress compared to those who feel that they are being overpaid for their work.
    A. slightly more   C. significantly more
    B. less   D. equal

30. Gerald feels that he is being underpaid for all the work he does. How can he relieve his distress at this situation and restore equity?
    A. He can work fewer hours and/or be less productive.
    B. He can seek to obtain a raise.
    C. He can convince himself that equity already exists.
    D. All of the above.

True-False Questions

Indicate which of the following statements are true or false, and compare your answers with those at the end of the chapter.

T   F   1. The "Hawthorne effect" refers to enhanced motivation under conditions of external (monetary) reward.

T   F   2. Modern psychologists have rejected instinct theories of motivation.

T   F   3. Drive theory is best able to explain biologically (as opposed to socially) driven behavior.

T   F   4. Research indicates that all people ascend Maslow's hierarchy of needs in the same order.

T   F   5. Eating and hunger are subject to both biological and social influences.

T   F   6. Sexual gratification is as necessary for the survival of the individual as it is for the survival of the species.

T   F   7. Stress can increase the need to affiliate.

T   F   8. The need for power is a special version of the need for achievement.

T   F   9. External reward for an enjoyable activity may decrease intrinsic interest in that activity.

T   F   10. Equity theory states that people who are underpaid will experience significantly more distress than people who are overpaid.

Key Concepts Matching Exercises

Exercise #1: Motivation

Match the key terms on the left with the definitions on the right.

_____ 1. Drive theory

_____ 2. Arousal theory

_____ 3. Incentive theory

_____ 4. Set point

_____ 5. Anorexia nervosa

_____ 6. Bulimia nervosa

_____ 7. Sexual orientation

_____ 8. Need for affiliation

_____ 9. Need for intimacy

_____10. Self-disclosure

_____11. Achievement motivation

_____12. Need for power

_____13. Intrinsic motivation

_____14. Extrinsic motivation

_____15. Equity

A. The need for close, intimate relationships characterized by open communication

B. "I must succeed. Give me the hardest tasks, and then stand back and watch me outperform all the others."

C. An eating disorder in which the individual limits food intake and becomes much thinner than normal

D. The need to establish and maintain social contacts

E. "I'm hungry. I'm irritable. I don't like feeling this way. I'm going to get some food."

F. An eating disorder that is characterized by repeated episodes of binge eating and purging

G. "I'll share my thoughts with you, and then you can share yours with me."

H. "I'll work the overtime because I love the job so much. I don't care if I get paid extra."

I. "No matter what I do, I seem to stay at the same weight."

J. "There were just too many people at that party. It was fun, but now I really need some down time."

K. The preference for a sex partner of a particular sex

L. "I'll work the overtime, but only if I get a bonus."

M. "It makes sense that Shawna makes more than I do; after all, she puts in more hours. We both get out what we put in."

N. The notion that people are motivated to obtain a valued outcome

O. "I must have more power, give me more, more more!"

This is Maslow's Hierarchy of Needs. Insert the correct labels into each level of the pyramid.

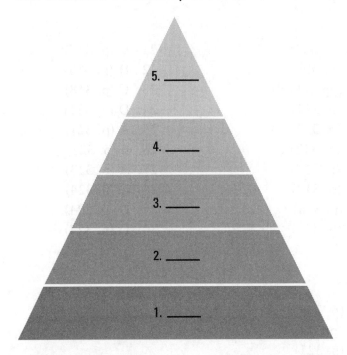

A. Self-fulfillment needs

B. Belongingness and love needs

C. Physiological needs

D. Esteem needs

E. Safety needs

Essay Questions

Write out answers to the following brief essay questions. Compare your responses with the sample answers at the end of the Study Guide chapter.

1. Chance likes to live up to his name by taking chances and engaging in daredevil activities like skydiving, parasailing, and bungee jumping. His friends joke that he never seems happy unless he's risking his life in some crazy stunt, and Chance himself says that "nothing beats the thrill you get when you're facing possible death—what a rush!" Explain Chance's risky behavior, from the perspective of drive theory, arousal theory, and incentive theory.

2. At a bakery one day, I happened to overhear a little girl ask her mother to buy some cookies. "But Mommy," she said, "my tummy is telling me that it's hungry!" Discuss the biological mechanisms underlying hunger. Is this little girl correct in her assumption that her stomach is sending "eat" messages to her brain? What evidence is there that hunger is also a psychological experience?

3. Describe the development of homosexuality according to Bem's "exotic becomes erotic" perspective.

4. Define the need for affiliation and contrast this motive with the need for intimacy. Examine personal (individual difference) and environmental factors that may influence the need for affiliation.

5. Alex needs to increase worker productivity. She has decided to implement a "pay-for-performance" program in which workers will receive a monetary reward for every extra client they bring in to the company. These rewards will be tracked, and a plaque will be awarded to the most productive employee at the end of each month. Knowing that you are a brilliant psychologist, Alex turns to you for some last minute advice about how to implement her program. What will you tell her?

Multiple-Choice Solutions

1. D (p. 299)	11. D (p. 304)	21. C (p. 317)
2. B (p. 299)	12. A (p. 306)	22. D (p. 318)
3. D (p. 300)	13. B (pp. 308-9)	23. C (p. 318)
4. A (p. 300)	14. C (p. 311)	24. D (p. 321)
5. C (p. 300)	15. C (p. 312)	25. A (p. 321)
6. B (p. 300)	16. D (p. 312)	26. B (p. 322)
7. B (pp. 300-1)	17. D (p. 313)	27. A (p. 323)
8. D (p. 302)	18. A (p. 314)	28. C (p. 324)
9. B (p. 303)	19. B (p. 316)	29. D (p. 324)
10. C (p. 303)	20. A (p. 317)	30. D (p. 324)

True-False Solutions

1. F (p. 298)	6. F (p. 308)
2. T (p. 299)	7. T (p. 317)
3. T (p. 300)	8. F (p. 321)
4. F (p. 301)	9. T (p. 323)
5. T (p. 303)	10. F (p. 324)

Key Concepts Matching Solutions

Exercise #1	*Exercise #2*
1. E	1. C
2. J	2. E
3. N	3. B
4. I	4. D
5. C	5. A
6. F	
7. K	
8. D	
9. A	
10. G	
11. B	
12. O	
13. H	
14. L	
15. M	

Essay Solutions

1. Well, Chance clearly likes to take risks and he seems to enjoy the rush of arousal associated with these daring activities. Drive theory would have a difficult time explaining Chance's behavior, since from that perspective we are motivated to reduce (and not increase) tension in order to return to a more pleasant, balanced state (p. 300). Arousal theory does a much better job of explaining his behavior. According to this perspective, human beings are motivated to achieve and maintain an optimum level of arousal, and this optimum level may be different for different individuals. Thus, Chance just has a higher optimum level of arousal, and he needs to engage in constant risky behaviors to maintain this level (p. 300). Incentive theory would posit a different process still; according to this perspective, human behavior is motivated by external goals or forces. Chance perhaps has been rewarded in the past for his behavior (he earns the respect and admiration of his friends, for example), and he has come to value this reward, which now serves as an incentive that motivates his continued risky behavior (p. 300).

2. Early researchers did believe exactly what the little girl believes; namely, that hunger was caused by sensations in the stomach. However, individuals who have had their stomachs removed for various reasons (and who therefore cannot experience stomach contractions or "hunger pangs") continue to feel hungry; therefore, the stomach alone cannot be responsible for hunger. Other biological mechanisms do appear to have a role in regulating hunger. For example, a complex biochemical system that includes the hypothalamus, nerves that run from the brainstem through the hypothalamus, and hormonal activities governed by the pancreas, liver, and intestines all appear to contribute to hunger (pp. 302-3).

   Hunger also is governed by psychological processes. For example, hunger may increase or decrease as a function of such external factors as the smell, taste, and sight of food (the little girl may feel that her stomach is "hungry" due to the smell of the freshly baked cookies, or their mouth-watering appearance). Perhaps the time of day signals to her that it's snack time, or she sees other people eating the cookies (p. 304).

3. Bem believes that homosexuality develops in a psychobiological, developmental process. First, he argues that genes influence the temperament with which an individual is born; some infants (and children) will have a more active, energetic, aggressive temperament than others (i.e., a more stereotypically "masculine" temperament). These children will be drawn toward male playmates and so-called "masculine" activities; others will prefer female playmates and so-called "feminine" activities. Children who prefer same-sex playmates and gender-typical activities are "gender-conformists;" those who prefer opposite-sex playmates and gender atypical activities are "gender-nonconformists." The next stage of development is more psychological. Specifically, gender-conforming children come to see the opposite-sex as different, unfamiliar, and arousing ("exotic"); gender-nonconforming children come to view the same-sex that way ("exotic"). During puberty, as adolescents physically and sexually mature, they become attracted to whichever group of potential partners (same- or opposite-sex) is the most exotic; Bem calls this the "exotic becomes erotic" process (pp. 314-315). Although interesting, there is currently little evidence to support this theory.

4. The need for affiliation is the desire to establish and maintain social contacts, whereas the need for intimacy is the desire for close, intimate relationships characterized by self-disclosure. Both are belongingness motives (p. 316). There are definitely individual differences in the need for affiliation; people with a higher need are more gregarious and will expend greater effort maintaining social contact (e.g., send letters, make phone calls) than those with a lower need. In addition, however, we seem to have a "sociostat" or social thermometer that regulates our need for affiliation; after spending much time with others, most of us prefer reduced contact (and vice versa) (p. 316).

Several environmental factors also influence affiliative needs. For example, people who are stressed are highly motivated to affiliate; we seek each other out in times of need in order to gain cognitive clarity (the information that others provide may help us cope with the situation). Others also provide emotional support, attention, and stimulation, and so we may seek them out when we feel a need for those experiences as well (p. 317).

5. First, you need to make sure that she is aware of the possible negative consequences of using monetary (and other) rewards as incentives for production. If her employees already enjoy bringing clients into the firm and find their jobs to be satisfying (in other words, they have high intrinsic motivation), then providing an external reward may actually inhibit productivity. The reward may alter their perceptions of the task of soliciting clients; it may come to be seen as "work" and not "fun" (p. 323).

   However, there are ways to present a monetary reward that increase the likelihood that it will be successful. Specifically, if Alex offers the payment in a way that her employees feel is manipulative and designed to control and bribe them (e.g., "I'll be watching you," "You'd better produce or else"), her efforts are probably doomed to failure. She should take great care to frame the reward as a source of information; for example, she might inform her employees that "these rewards are a way for you all to monitor your own progress and the quality of your performance." Also, the reward (and plaque) should be presented in a positive manner, as a tangible form of praise for a job well done (p. 324).

Multimedia Study Resources

Several activities and articles in Chapter 4 (Motivation and Emotion) of The Psychology Place™ supplement the material covered in your textbook. "Exploring Academic Dishonesty" is a learning activity that allows you to explore various topics related to dishonest behavior, including how to define cheating, the prevalence of cheating, attitudes toward academic dishonesty, and motivations for this type of behavior. In Research News, two reports explore the concepts of intrinsic and extrinsic motivation ("Giving Children Rewards: A Right Way and a Wrong Way," and "Should Creativity Be Rewarded?").

9 Emotion

Chapter Overview

This chapter focuses on emotion. First, the concept of emotion is defined, and then the chapter examines each of the three components that interact to produce emotional experiences. Specifically, the physiological or bodily sensations that are involved in emotion are examined, including the various brain centers (i.e., limbic system, cerebral cortex) and nervous systems (i.e., sympathetic, parasympathetic) that play an important role in emotion regulation. Cross-cultural research on the bodily symptoms associated with specific emotions also is examined. Next, the chapter turns to the expressive component of emotional experiences, beginning with an examination of the way in which our outward expressions of emotion can nonverbally communicate to others and to ourselves about how we feel. The question of whether some emotions and emotional expressions are "basic" or innate is examined, along with research that suggests that our own facial expressions, body posture, and vocal behavior can actually trigger an emotional experience (e.g., we smile, and then we feel happy). The cognitive component of emotion then is explored. The chapter presents Schachter's two-factor theory of emotion, and then discusses some implications of that theory for the intensification and also the diminishment of emotional experience (i.e., misattribution of arousal). The cognitive appraisals associated with various emotions are explored, as is the impact of counterfactual thinking (the tendency to imagine alternative outcomes that might have occurred but did not) on emotional experience. This section ends with a discussion of whether cognition is a necessary component of emotion. The chapter then segues into a consideration of different types of emotions and how a few basic human emotions can combine to produce the vast array of feelings we experience. The dynamics of emotion are explored, as are cultural differences in the types of events that trigger emotion and sex differences in emotional experience and expression. The chapter ends with a consideration of happiness and the conditions that produce a state of subjective well-being.

I. *What's Your Prediction?* Can Culture Influence Emotion?

II. The Physiological Component

    A. A Historical Perspective

    B. Brain Centers of Emotion

    C. Generalized Autonomic Arousal

    D. Specific Patterns of Arousal
       1. Culture and arousal patterns

    E. *Psychology and . . . Law* The Lie-Detector Test

III. The Expressive Component

    A. Nonverbal Communication
       1. Facial expression
       2. Body language

    B. Sensory Feedback

IV. The Cognitive Component

    A. Schachter's Two-Factor Theory of Emotion
       1. Misattribution

    B. Dimensions of Appraisal

    C. Counterfactual Thinking

    D. Is Cognition Necessary?

V. Human Emotion: Putting the Pieces Together

    A. Types of Emotions

    B. Dynamics of Emotion

    C. Are There Sex Differences in Emotion?

    D. *Through the Global Window . . .* Cultural Differences in Emotion

    E. Pleasure and the Pursuit of Happiness
       1. The Roots of Happiness

VI. The Big Picture

By the time you have read and reviewed this chapter, you should be able to:

1. Define the concept of emotion and describe the three components of emotional experience (p. 330).

2. Discuss the physiological component of emotion (pp. 331-336).

3. Compare and contrast the James-Lange and the Cannon-Bard theories of emotion (p. 331).

4. Discuss the role played by the brain (i.e., limbic system, cerebral cortex) and nervous system (i.e., parasympathetic, sympathetic systems) in the regulation of emotion (pp. 331-333).

5. Consider whether each emotion has its own specific pattern of physiological arousal or whether all emotions are accompanied by the same general state of arousal (p. 334). Discuss cross-cultural research on the bodily symptoms associated with various emotions (pp. 334, 336).

6. Explain what a polygraph is and how this instrument works (p. 335). Discuss whether the polygraph truly is a "lie detector" (pp. 335-36).

7. Consider the expressive component of emotion (p. 337). Discuss the two functions served by the behavioral expression of emotion (p. 337).

8. Explain how emotional states are communicated by facial expression and consider the adaptive significance of the ability to recognize emotion via facial expression (pp. 337-39). Discuss how other nonverbal behaviors (e.g., body language, eye contact, touch) may communicate emotion (pp. 339-40).

9. Define the facial-feedback hypothesis (p. 340). Explain how facial expression, body posture, and vocal behavior actually may trigger or cause an emotional experience (pp. 340-41).

10. Consider the cognitive component of emotion (p. 342). Define Schachter's two-factor theory of emotion (pp. 342-343).

11. Discuss the process whereby arousal produced by one source can be misattributed or transferred to another source (pp. 343-44).

12. Consider the association between cognitive appraisals and emotional reactions (p. 344). List and describe the cognitive dimensions of appraisal (i.e., pleasantness of the situation, attention, agency, certainty) that are most closely associated with emotion (pp. 344-45).

13. Define the concept of counterfactual thinking (p. 345). Discuss how counterfactual thinking may influence the experience of emotion (p. 345).

14. Consider the debate over whether cognition is a necessary component of emotion (pp. 345-47).

15. Explain how emotions can be classified and compared along the dimensions of pleasantness and intensity (p. 349).

16. Consider the dynamics of emotional experience (p. 349). Define the opponent-process theory of emotion (p. 350).

17. Discuss cultural differences in the types of antecedent events that cause various emotions, the folk theories of emotion and words used to describe emotional experiences, and the display rules that govern the expression of emotion (p. 351).

18. Consider sex differences in emotion (pp. 351-52).

19. Discuss different definitions of happiness and beliefs about its causes (p. 352). Summarize survey research on the prevalence of happiness (p. 353). Explain the causes and correlates of happiness (pp. 353-54). Discuss the determinants of subjective well-being according to social-comparison theory and adaptation-level theory (pp. 354-55). Consider the notion that people have "set" baseline levels of happiness (p. 356).

Key Terms

The following key terms and concepts are featured in this chapter and are important for you to know. Write out definitions of each term and check your answers with the definitions in the text on the pages listed.

Emotion (p. 330)
James-Lange theory (p. 331)
Cannon-Bard theory (p. 331)
Sympathetic nervous system (p. 332)
Parasympathetic nervous system (p. 333)
Polygraph (p. 335)
Facial electromyograph (EMG) (p. 339)

Facial-feedback hypothesis (p. 340)
Two-factor theory of emotion (p. 342)
Misattribution (of emotion) (p. 344)
Counterfactual thinking (p. 345)
Social-comparison theory (p. 354)
Adaptation-level theory (p. 355)

Test Questions

Multiple-Choice Questions

Circle the correct choice for each question and compare your answers with those at the end of the Study Guide chapter.

1. In general, psychologists agree that all emotions consist of which of the following components?
   A. internal physiological arousal
   B. expressive behavior
   C. cognitive appraisal
   D. All of the above

2. According to the James-Lange theory of emotions
   A. emotion triggers a physiological response.
   B. physiological and behavioral responses trigger emotion.
   C. emotion triggers a behavioral reaction.
   D. physiological responses trigger emotions, which in turn trigger behavioral responses.

3. Cannon and Bard criticized the James-Lange theory on the grounds that
   A. bodily sensations alone do not always produce emotion.
   B. specific emotions are not associated with specific physical changes.
   C. emotion is sometimes felt instantly, before the body has undergone any physical change.
   D. All of the above

4. The _____ regulates several emotions, including fear.
   A. limbic system
   B. brainstem
   C. sympathetic nervous system
   D. spinal cord

5. Anthony was born with a rare brain disorder that has caused damage to his amygdala. As part of his drama class, he and the other students are asked to use facial expressions to portray different emotions. Which emotion will Anthony have difficulty portraying?
   A. rage   C. fear
   B. joy   D. surprise

6. Joy and Dale have decided to go see the new romantic comedy playing at their local theater. Both find the lighthearted film to be humorous, sweet, and enjoyable. An EEG recording would reveal increased activity in what part of their brains?
   A. corpus callosum   C. right hemisphere
   B. left hemisphere   D. amygdala

7. Marika is outgoing and sociable. Her brother Eric is shy and withdrawn. Marika probably has a more active _____, whereas Eric probably has a more active _____.
   A. right hemisphere; left hemisphere
   B. left hemisphere; right hemisphere
   C. sympathetic system; parasympathetic system
   D. cortex; limbic system

8. During an emotional event, the _____ prepares the body for action. After an emotional event, the _____ returns the body to its premobilized state.
   A. cerebral cortex; limbic system
   B. left hemisphere; right hemisphere
   C. sympathetic system; parasympathetic system
   D. autonomic nervous system; cerebral cortex

9. The polygraph enables psychologists to _____.
   A. detect deception
   B. measure the expressive component of emotions
   C. assess brain activity
   D. record physiological arousal

10. The use of the polygraph is based on the assumption that people who are being deceptive experience _____.
    A. pupil dilation
    B. increased brain activity
    C. increased autonomic arousal
    D. decreased activity in the left hemisphere and increased activity in the right hemisphere

11. Recent cross-cultural research on the communication of emotion reveals that infants as young as _____ old are able to make facial expressions that signal joy, interest, sadness, and anger.
   A. 10 minutes
   B. 10 hours
   C. 10 weeks
   D. 10 months

12. According to the Darwinian or evolutionary perspective on emotions, people should be especially sensitive to signs of _____ from another person.
   A. happiness
   B. anger
   C. neutrality
   D. joy

13. Vincent and Don are listening to a political candidate speak about a highly controversial issue. Vincent is strongly interested in what the speaker has to say and pleasantly surprised by her knowledge of the opposing viewpoint. Don is bothered by the issue being discussed and angered at the candidate's portrayal of the opposing viewpoint. A facial EMG of Vincent would reveal increased activity in the _____; a facial EMG of Don would indicate increased activity in the _____.
   A. cheek muscles; forehead and brow area
   B. mouth area; cheek and eye area
   C. left half of the face; right half of the face
   D. right hemisphere; left hemisphere

14. Which of the following forms of nonverbal behavior can communicate emotion?
   A. eye contact
   B. body posture
   C. touch
   D. All of the above

15. Frequent gaze is interpreted as _____ among friends.
   A. a sign of power
   B. a sign of affection
   C. a sign of hostility
   D. a sign of fear

16. Which of the following statements about touch is *not* accurate?
   A. Men are more likely to touch women than women are to touch men.
   B. Higher status persons are less likely to touch lower status persons than vice versa.
   C. Physical touch is generally considered an expression of friendship or attraction.
   D. Older persons are more likely to touch younger persons than vice versa.

17. Touch may communicate
   A. intimacy.
   B. dominance.
   C. control.
   D. All of the above

18. According to the facial-feedback hypothesis, facial expressions activate emotion through a process of _____.
   A. self-perception
   B. social comparison
   C. cognitive appraisal
   D. misattribution

19. The two-factor theory of emotion states that we will feel a particular emotion
    A. whenever we become physiologically aroused.
    B. whenever those around us act in an emotional manner.
    C. when we are physiologically aroused and the situation provides us with an appropriate emotional label for our arousal.
    D. when we take drugs.

20. Four students participate in a psychology experiment. Student A and Student B are injected with a drug that causes physiological arousal. Student A is told to expect to feel symptoms of arousal; Student B is told nothing. Student C is injected with a harmless placebo drug that does not cause arousal, and Student D receives no injection at all. All students are then placed in a room with a confederate who begins to act in an extremely boisterous, happy, excitable manner. Which student is the most likely to experience an emotional response in this situation?
    A. Student A
    B. Student B
    C. Student C
    D. Student D

21. Jewel's roommate always leaves clothes lying around the apartment. Normally, Jewel is mildly annoyed by this behavior. One day, upon returning home after a particularly grueling soccer practice, she notices the clothes and experiences a surge of intense annoyance and anger at her roommate. What phenomenon explains her heightened emotional reaction?
    A. facial-feedback
    B. cognitive appraisal
    C. arousal misattribution
    D. sensory feedback

22. Research indicates that the various emotions we experience differ as a function of the cognitive appraisals we make on which dimensions?
    A. the pleasantness of the situation and/or experience
    B. our attention to the situation
    C. the clarity and predictability of the situation
    D. All of the above

23. Brett was recently involved in a car accident. "Gee," he thinks, "the repairs are going to be expensive, but it could have been so much worse. At least nobody was injured." Brett is engaging in _____.
    A. counterfactual thinking
    B. self-perception
    C. social comparison
    D. cognitive appraisal

24. Emotions that are considered "basic" are those that
    A. are accompanied by a distinct facial expression.
    B. are displayed by infants and young children.
    C. are experienced by people from diverse cultures.
    D. All of the above

25. Which of the following are considered to be "basic" emotions?
    A. surprise
    B. fear
    C. joy
    D. All of the above

26. The idea that every emotional experience triggers an opposite emotional experience is known as the _____ theory.
    A. opponent-process
    B. two-factor
    C. primary-state
    D. let-down

27. Research reveals striking cultural differences in the _____ of emotion.
    A. physiological components
    B. display rules
    C. expressive components
    D. facial expression

28. Which statement about sex differences in emotion is accurate?
    A. Women describe themselves as less emotional than men.
    B. Men and women have different autonomic reactions to emotion-triggering events.
    C. Women disclose their feelings to others more than do men.
    D. Men exhibit more facial signs of emotion than do women.

29. Survey data reveal that roughly _____ percent of the American population describe themselves as happy.
    A. 25
    B. 50
    C. 75
    D. 95

30. Research on happiness reveals that subjective well-being is *not* related to
    A. age.
    B. health.
    C. employment status.
    D. social relationships.

True-False Questions

Indicate which of the following statements are true or false, and compare your answers with those at the end of the chapter.

T   F   1. Emotions in general consist of a physiological, expressive, and cognitive component.

T   F   2. All emotions produce the same pattern of neural activity.

T   F   3. During an emotional event, the hypothalamus activates the sympathetic nervous system.

T   F   4. A liar cannot fake a truthful response on a polygraph test.

T   F   5. There are clear cross-cultural differences in the type and amount of autonomic arousal associated with various emotions.

T   F   6. Positive emotions are associated with characteristic activity in the cheek muscles.

T   F   7. Facial expressions, body posture, and vocal behavior can influence the experience of emotion.

T   F   8. Cognition appears to have little influence on emotional experience.

T   F   9. Some emotions are more "basic" than others.

T   F   10. There are clear differences in the types of emotions experienced by men versus women.

Key Concepts Matching Exercises

Exercise #1: Emotion

Match the key terms on the left with the definitions on the right.

_____ 1. James-Lange theory

A. "I feel kind of queasy and sick to my stomach. It can't be because I'm about to give a class presentation. No, it must be that sandwich I ate for lunch."

_____ 2. Cannon-Bard theory

B. "I'm so happy that I made that decision. The alternative could have been so much worse."

_____ 3. Facial-feedback hypothesis

C. "That huge spider just came right at me! I ran away as fast as I could. I can still feel my heart pounding—I'm really scared!"

_____ 4. Two-factor theory

D. "I'm feeling kind of tense and aroused. That guy over there looks scared. I must be feeling scared, too."

_____ 5. Misattribution

E. "When the big, hairy spider jumped out at me, my pulse began to race, my knees went weak, and I was overcome with terror—all at the same terrible moment."

_____ 6. Counterfactual thinking

F. "I'm smiling, so I must be having a good time."

Exercise #2: The Facial Expression of Emotion

Look at the photographs below and try to match each one with the listed emotions.

A. Sadness

B. Disgust

C. Anger

D. Surprise

E. Fear

F. Joy

Essay Questions

Write out answers to the following brief essay questions. Compare your responses with the sample answers at the end of the Study Guide chapter.

1. A prominent attorney calls you to ask for advice. It seems that her client has been accused of selling his company's computer software ideas to a rival development corporation. Her client wants to take a polygraph test to prove his innocence. What will you tell the attorney?

2. What evidence is there that the face communicates emotions in ways that are innate? In other words, are certain facial expressions inborn rather than learned?

3. Is cognition necessary for emotion?

4. Consider whether there are sex differences in emotion. If so, what factors might contribute to these differences?

5. Can money buy you happiness? Why or why not? Be sure to include a discussion of social-comparison theory and adaptation-level theory in your answer.

Multimedia Study Resources

Several activities and articles in Chapter 4 (Motivation and Emotion) of The Psychology Place™ supplement the material covered in your textbook. For example, the *Scientific American* magazine article called "Emotion, Memory, and the Brain" explores how an environmental stimulus (like a smell or a sound) can trigger something called an "emotion memory." A report presented in Research News discusses the evidence that psychologists use in order to classify a particular feeling as a distinct emotion ("Is Embarrassment a Distinct Emotion?").

Test Solutions

Multiple-Choice Solutions

1. D (p. 330)	11. C (p. 338)	21. C (p. 343)
2. B (p. 331)	12. B (p. 338)	22. D (p. 344)
3. D (p. 331)	13. A (p. 339)	23. A (p. 345)
4. A (p. 331)	14. D (pp. 339-40)	24. D (p. 348)
5. C (p. 331)	15. B (p. 340)	25. D (p. 348)
6. B (p. 332)	16. B (p. 340)	26. A (p. 350)
7. B (p. 332)	17. D (p. 340)	27. B (p. 351)
8. C (pp. 332-33)	18. A (p. 340)	28. C (pp. 351-52)
9. D (p. 335)	19. C (p. 342)	29. C (p. 353)
10. C (p. 333)	20. B (pp. 342-43)	30. A (p. 353)

True-False Solutions

1. T (p. 330)
2. F (p. 332)
3. T (p. 332)
4. F (p. 335)
5. F (p. 334)
6. T (p. 339)
7. T (pp. 340-41)
8. F (p. 342)
9. T (p. 348)
10. F (pp. 351-52)

Key Concepts Matching Solutions

Exercise #1

1. C
2. E
3. F
4. D
5. A
6. B

Exercise #2

1. C
2. E
3. B
4. D
5. F
6. A

Essay Solutions

1. Well, the first thing you will tell her is to make sure that she, her client, and the company realize that the polygraph is not a "lie-detector" in and of itself. All that the instrument does is to record physiological arousal. When combined with an oral examination, a naive subject, and a well-trained examiner, the test may in fact do a decent job of revealing deception or truth. However, there are some important considerations that the attorney (and her client) should keep in mind. First, it is possible for a truthful person to actually "fail" the test; that is, her client may be telling the truth, but his level of arousal may indicate that he is "lying." Second, the test can be "faked." People can inflate their arousal level (by tensing their muscles, biting their tongues, etc.) during the control question portion of the exam; this will give them a higher baseline of arousal, so that any arousal that they experience during the crime-relevant question portion will not appear unduly high. Therefore, perhaps her client should reconsider whether he wants to base his entire defense on a polygraph test! (pp. 335-56).

2. There is some solid evidence that some emotional expressions are unlearned or innate. First, cross-cultural research on facial expression and the nonverbal communication of emotion reveals that people from different cultures can reliably identify six emotions from facial expressions (i.e., joy, surprise, anger, fear, disgust, and sadness). This suggests that some emotions are universally recognized in the face. In addition, research with infants demonstrates that even humans who are too young to articulate particular feelings and who have not yet fully learned the emotional norms and display rules of their culture are able to make faces that are associated with basic emotions. For example, infants as young as 10 weeks old can make facial expressions that reliably signal joy, interest, sadness, and anger (pp. 337-38).

3. The debate continues to rage over whether cognition is necessary for emotion. On one hand, some researchers argue for the "primacy of affect." Zajonc, for example, suggests that people sometimes react with emotion instantly and without prior cognitive appraisal; we feel before we think. In support of his hypothesis, human infants demonstrate reflexive facial expressions of pain, joy, and so on to a stimulus before they have the neural capacity to actually make corresponding cognitive appraisals of the stimulus. In addition, animal

research suggests that certain emotions (e.g, fear) are triggered instantly and do not involve the cerebral cortex (which means that the response does not necessarily involve an initial processing of information). On the other side of the debate, some researchers argue for the "primacy of cognition." Lazarus, for example, agrees that emotions may occur without awareness, but he maintains that it is impossible to have emotion without some kind of thought (although that thought may be unconscious and effortless) (pp. 346-47).

4. There is little evidence that men and women differ in their actual feelings. That is, both sexes are equally capable of feeling anger, sadness, jealousy, happiness, surprise, and so on. Furthermore, the same events seem to trigger similar emotional responses in men and women (for example, the loss of a loved one produces sadness, and frustration produces anger, in both sexes). However, there are some reliable sex differences in emotion. First, women tend to describe themselves as more emotional than men describe themselves as being on self-report surveys. Second, men and women appear to differ in their public displays of emotion. Specifically, women tend to disclose their feelings to other people more than do men, and women also exhibit more emotion on their faces and more muscle activity on the facial EMG than do men (pp. 351-52).

Social factors appear to be implicated in these sex differences. For example, research reveals that girls more than boys are socialized at an early age to disclose their feelings, and parents also talk more about the emotional aspects of events and situations with their daughters than they do with their sons. Finally, in American culture, gender norms dictate that men more than women should hide their feelings and not publicly express emotions like fear and sorrow (p. 352).

5. To date, there is mixed evidence about the relationship between wealth (income) and subjective well-being. In general, research finds a strong positive correlation between a nation's wealth and the happiness of its people; that is, the wealthier a nation, the happier its members. However, within any given nation, there seem to be only modest correlations between income and subjective well-being (extremely wealthy people are only slightly happier than their less wealthy counterparts) (p. 353).

The finding that money does not seem to significantly and overwhelmingly contribute to happiness has been explained by two theories. Social-comparison theory suggests that our perceptions of wealth are not absolute but relative to a standard. That is, people do not simply focus on what they have in terms of wealth and possessions, but instead they compare themselves to others and then feel content or deprived depending on how they fare in this comparison. Thus, wealthy people may not be any happier than less wealthy people because they compare themselves to other highly affluent folks, and feel relatively deprived in comparison to those others. Adaptation-level theory posits that people also use their own recent past as a basis of comparison. Specifically, this theory argues that people become accustomed to a certain level of success—if they then experience an increase in salary, for example, they will also experience a heightened sense of subjective well-being. Over time, however, they will adapt to their new situation and raise their standard of comparison; for an increase in happiness, they will need to obtain even more income (pp. 354-56). In short, money does not necessarily produce happiness!

10 Infancy and Childhood

Chapter Overview

This chapter explores the biological, cognitive, and social aspects of development during infancy and early childhood. The opening section examines a basic question that continues to fascinate developmental psychologists. Called the "nature-nurture" debate, this classic philosophical question concerns whether human behavior is caused by genetic predispositions (nature) or life experiences (nurture). Your chapter introduces this debate and presents the various methods (e.g., twin-study method) that have been used to tease apart the relative contributions of nature and nurture in determining human development. The possibility that biological and environmental influences may interact to influence behavior and personality also is considered. Then, the major research strategies employed by developmental psychologists are examined (e.g., cross-sectional and longitudinal studies). The next section of your chapter focuses on the unborn child, including the major stages of prenatal development, the physical changes that occur during these stages, and the various factors (called teratogens) that can impede normal prenatal development. The chapter then turns to the topic of newborn babies—the research methods that can be used to examine their abilities, their innate reflexes, their sensory capacities (including their visual and auditory preferences, limitations, and abilities), and their sensitivity to number. The last section of this chapter focuses on various aspects of the development of the infant and young child. First, biological development is examined, including changes in the body and the brain and the coordination of motor skills. This is followed by a discussion of Piaget's theory of cognitive development and the ways in which children assimilate and accommodate new information into their understanding of the world. New advances in Piagetian theory and research methodology are presented, and the traditional Piagetian stage-theory is contrasted with the information-processing perspective. Then, the chapter considers the issue of children's memory and whether children are competent to provide eyewitness testimony. The section on cognitive development concludes with a discussion of the emergence of language and theories of language development. The chapter ends by considering social development, including parent-child attachment and peer relationships.

Chapter Outline

I. *What's Your Prediction?* Nature or Nurture?

II. Basic Developmental Questions

    A. The Nature-Nurture Debate
        1. Genetic influences
        2. Environmental influences
        3. Interactive influences

    B. Developmental-Research Strategies

III. The Unborn Child

    A. Genetic Building Blocks

    B. Prenatal Development

    C. *Psychology and . . . Health* Do Drugs Affect the Fetus?

    D. The Birth Experience

IV. The Remarkable Newborn

    A. Reflexes

    B. Sensory Capacities
        1. Vision and visual preferences
        2. Hearing and auditory preferences
        3. Taste and smell

    C. Sensitivity to Number

V. The Infant and Growing Child

    A. Biological Development
        1. Physical growth
        2. Motor skills

    B. Cognitive Development
        1. Piaget's theory
            a. Sensorimotor stage
            b. Preoperational stage
            c. Concrete operational stage
            d. Formal operational stage
            e. Piaget's legacy
        2. Information-processing perspectives

3. Emergence of language
   a. Developmental sequence
   b. Developmental theories

C. *Psychology and . . . Law* Are Child Witnesses Competent to Testify?

D. Social Development
   1. The parent-child relationship
      a. The first attachment
      b. Styles of attachment
      c. The day-care controversy
      d. Beyond attachment
   2. Peer relationships

E. *Through the Global Window* . . . Cultural Differences in Infant Care

VI. The Big Picture

Learning Objectives

By the time you have read and reviewed this chapter, you should be able to:

1. Define developmental psychology and discuss the topics of interest to developmental psychologists (p. 363).

2. Consider the nature-nurture debate (p. 363). Discuss two methods that have proven valuable in examining the relative impact of nature and nurture on human development (pp. 363-64).

3. Consider genetic influences on human behavior (pp. 364-65). Define the concept of heritability (p. 365). Explain how twin studies provide evidence for genetic influences in abilities and personality (pp. 365-66).

4. Consider environmental influences on human behavior (pp. 366-67). Define the concepts of shared and nonshared environments (p. 366). Explain how twin studies provide evidence for environmental influences in abilities and personality (p. 366).

5. Discuss the bioecological model of development (p. 367).

6. Compare cross-sectional and longitudinal research strategies (pp. 367-68).

7. Outline the three stages of prenatal development (pp. 369-370). Define teratogens and discuss how specific factors (e.g., drugs, alcohol, AIDS virus) can impede normal prenatal development (pp. 370-71, 372-73). Define fetal alcohol syndrome (p. 372).

8. Discuss the birth experience and the newborn's sensory experiences prior to and immediately following birth (p. 375).

9. Define habituation and recovery (p. 376). Consider the various research techniques used to study very young infants (p. 376).

10. Discuss the newborn infant's reflex capacities (p. 376). Consider the limitations and abilities that characterize the newborn infant's sensory systems (e.g., sight, sound, taste) (pp. 377-79). Consider whether infants are born with an innate sensitivity to numbers (pp. 379-80).

11. Explain the biological changes that occur during infancy and early childhood (pp. 381-83). Explain how the body and brain change during this period of development (p. 381). Consider the changes in motor skill that occur (pp. 382-83).

12. Explain Piaget's theory of cognitive development (pp. 384-88). Define the process of assimilation and accommodation (p. 384). Consider the major cognitive limitations and milestones that characterize the sensorimotor, preoperational, concrete operational, and formal operational stages of development (pp. 384-88).

13. Examine the contributions made by, and the criticisms of, Piagetian cognitive theory (pp. 388-89). Compare Piaget's theory with the information-processing theory of cognitive development (p. 389). Discuss the changes in memory that occur during early childhood (pp. 389-90).

14. Consider whether children are competent to provide eyewitness testimony (pp. 391-92). Explain the factors that can bias a child's memory report (p. 392).

15. Discuss the developmental sequence of language acquisition (pp. 392-93). Define the concept of telegraphic speech (p. 393).

16. Consider theories of language development (pp. 393-94).

17. Discuss social development in infancy and early childhood (pp. 394-401). Explain the difference between imprinting and attachment (pp. 394-95).

18. Consider the significance of the Harlow monkey studies for the study of attachment (pp. 395-96).

19. Explain the strange-situation test (p. 396). Consider the difference between a secure and an insecure attachment style (p. 396). Discuss the importance of the first attachment (pp. 396, 398).

20. Consider cultural differences in infant care (e.g., sleeping arrangements, physical contact) (p. 397).

21. Discuss the controversy over day-care versus home-care of children (pp. 398-99).

22. Explain the concept of horizontal relationships (p. 399). Discuss the peer relationship patterns of infants and young children (pp. 399-400). Consider the importance of friendship formation (pp. 400-1).

The following key terms and concepts are featured in this chapter and are important for you to know. Write out definitions of each term and check your answers with the definitions in the text on the pages listed.

Developmental psychology (p. 363)
Nature-nurture debate (p. 363)
Twin-study method (p. 364)
Adoption studies (p. 364)
Heritability (p. 365)
Cross-sectional studies (p. 367)
Longitudinal studies (p. 368)
Chromosomes (p. 368)
Deoxyribonucleic acid (DNA) (p. 368)
Genes (p. 368)
Zygote (p. 369)
Embryo (p. 369)
Fetus (p. 370)
Teratogens (p. 370)
Fetal alcohol syndrome (FAS) (p. 372)
Habituation (p. 376)
Recovery (p. 376)
Grasping reflex (p. 376)
Rooting reflex (p. 376)

Schemas (p. 384)
Assimilation (p. 384)
Accommodation (p. 384)
Sensorimotor stage (p. 384)
Object permanence (p. 385)
Separation anxiety (p. 385)
Preoperational stage (p. 386)
Egocentric (p. 386)
Conservation (p. 386)
Concrete operational stage (p. 387)
Formal operational stage (p. 388)
Babbling (p. 392)
Telegraphic speech (p. 393)
Imprinting (p. 394)
Critical period (p. 395)
Attachment (p. 395)
Strange-situation test (p. 396)
Secure attachment (p. 396)
Insecure attachment (p. 396)

Test Questions

Multiple-Choice Questions

Circle the correct choice for each question and compare your answers with those at the end of the Study Guide chapter.

1. A central concern for developmental psychology is
   A. how people grow and change across the lifespan.
   B. the genetic basis of personality.
   C. how human behavior is affected by the social environment.
   D. the treatment of abnormal behavior.

2. Dr. Nature is a biological psychologist interested in aggressive behavior in schoolage children. Which of the following research topics might reflect her orientation?
   A. peer influences on aggression
   B. genetic predispositions toward aggression
   C. aggressive behavior as a function of exposure to violent television
   D. cultural forces and aggression

3. Dr. Nurture works in the same department as Dr. Nature. He has just written a book. What might his book be titled?
    A. "Violent Television: Creating Aggressive Kids"
    B. "The Violence Gene: Making Aggressive Kids"
    C. "Aggression: Does it Run in the Family?"
    D. "Twin Studies of Aggressive Behavior"

4. In one of the twin studies mentioned in your text, the heritability estimates for personality characteristics averaged about 48 percent. This means that
    A. genetics control about 48 percent of human personality.
    B. about 48 percent of our personality is determined by our genetic makeup.
    C. personality in twins is caused by genetic factors.
    D. genetic factors account for about 48 percent of the variation in personality seen in that group of twins.

5. Sophia and Lauren are sisters. They have the same parents, attend the same school, and vacation at the same summer camp. They each have a different best friend, and Sophia is in charge of the indoor chores whereas Lauren takes care of the outside chores. Aspects of their *shared* environment are _____; their *nonshared* environment includes _____.
    A. parents, school, and chores; best friend and vacation
    B. best friend and chores; parents, school, and vacation
    C. parents, school, and vacation; best friend and chores
    D. best friend; parents

6. The bioecological model of development suggests that
    A. genetic predispositions determine personality.
    B. inherited traits cause us to develop in a particular direction.
    C. genetic predispositions and life experiences interact to influence development.
    D. life experiences determine development.

7. In order to examine whether age is related to reasoning ability, Dr. Mathers gives the SMK Reasoning Ability Test to a group of individuals ranging in age from 20 to 50 years old. He finds that the younger age groups outperform the older age groups. What kind of study is this?
    A. experimental   C. descriptive case study
    B. cross-sectional   D. longitudinal

8. What should Dr. Mathers be concerned about when he interprets his results?
    A. cohort effects
    B. the logistics of conducting this kind of study
    C. the lack of correlation
    D. All of the above

9. The first stage in prenatal development is called the _____ stage.
    A. embryonic   C. germinal
    B. zygotic   D. fetal

10. All major body structures form during the _____ stage of prenatal development.
    A. germinal   C. fetal
    B. embryonic   D. zygotic

11. Which substance can function as a teratogen?
    A. aspirin
    B. cocaine
    C. x-rays
    D. All of the above

12. At a pediatric clinic, you notice a young child who seems very small for her age. Her nose is flattened, her eyes are wide apart, and she seems to be slightly mentally retarded. This child may have
    A. cocaine abuse syndrome.
    B. fetal alcohol syndrome.
    C. x-ray exposure.
    D. nicotine syndrome.

13. Infants exposed to cocaine in utero tend to be _____ than non-cocaine-exposed infants.
    A. smaller
    B. less cognitively developed
    C. less socially developed
    D. All of the above

14. Why is the measurement of habituation and recovery important in conducting research on infants?
    A. It allows infants to vocally indicate their preferences for things.
    B. It allows researchers to communicate with very young infants.
    C. It allows infants to develop their sucking reflex skills.
    D. It allow researchers to determine when infants can make distinctions between different stimuli.

15. Which one of the following reflexes is innate?
    A. rooting
    B. sucking
    C. grasping
    D. All of the above

16. Newborn infants can do which of the following?
    A. distinguish between light and dark
    B. track slow movements with their eyes
    C. engage in rudimentary facial imitation
    D. All of the above

17. Which item is out of place here?
    A. information processing approach
    B. Jean Piaget
    C. stage theory
    D. cognitive development

18. Little Nancy is fascinated by the kitten playing on the floor nearby and does not take her eyes off him. When the kitten passes behind Nancy, however, she makes no attempt to turn around toward him. Nancy
    A. has a visual problem.
    B. lacks object permanence.
    C. is not yet in the sensorimotor stage.
    D. is mentally retarded.

19. The little girl who insists that her sister does *not* have a sister is demonstrating
    A. separation anxiety.
    B. egocentric thinking.
    C. conservation.
    D. formal operational thinking.

20. Three-year-old Miko is very upset. His dad gave him and his friend each a cookie. However, his friend's cookie broke in half. Miko is convinced that his friend now has more cookie than he himself does. His misunderstanding is due to
    A. the absence of object permanence.
    B. egocentric thinking.
    C. lack of conservation.
    D. abstract logic.

21. What have researchers concluded regarding Piaget's ideas about the sudden stair-step transitions from one cognitive stage to another?
    A. There is no evidence for separate stages of cognitive growth; rather, children show only a slow and gradual increase in abilities.
    B. There is only one leap in cognitive abilities and this seems to occur at puberty.
    C. Piaget's stage theory applies only in Western societies.
    D. There are periods of rapid cognitive change, but gradual gains occur within each period so that the development of one strategy overlaps with the reduction of an older strategy.

22. In general, research indicates that Piaget was incorrect in his estimates of the _____ of development, but correct in his estimates of the _____ of development.
    A. overall rate; sequential achievements
    B. sequential achievements; overall rate
    C. age periods; overall rate
    D. measurement; thought processes

23. According to the information processing perspective, the difference in the problem-solving abilities of a two year old and a five year old is due primarily to
    A. differences in social skills.
    B. differences in selective attention and memory.
    C. the differences in their language abilities.
    D. the increase in the ability to conserve and to reason abstractly.

24. Research on children's memory reveals that _____ can bias what a child remembers and reports.
    A. leading questions
    B. misinformation
    C. repetition of questions
    D. All of the above

25. Which of the following illustrates telegraphic speech?
    A. "Ball now please see want."
    B. "Ah bah bah."
    C. "Want ball.
    D. "I'd like to play with the ball now."

26. Harlow's monkey studies demonstrated which of the following?
    A. that babies prefer rewards (food) over "contact comfort"
    B. that babies prefer "contact comfort" over food
    C. that babies who are raised in isolation develop into normal adults
    D. All of the above

27. The very deep emotional bond that forms between infants and their caregivers is called
    A. attachment.
    B. imprinting.
    C. critical bonding.
    D. a horizontal relationship.

28. An infant cries when her father leaves the room, and also when a stranger is in the room. When the father returns, the baby is all smiles and hugs. This infant is
    A. imprinted on her father.
    B. insecurely attached to strangers.
    C. securely attached to her father.
    D. insecurely attached to her mother.

29. Desdemona brings her young son to the psychology lab. He cries when she attempts to leave the room, screams in the presence of a stranger, and stiffens up when Desdemona returns and tries to comfort him. This baby would be classified as
    A. securely attached.
    B. insecurely attached.
    C. securely imprinted.
    D. insecurely imprinted.

30. The key factor that seems to determine how day care affects young children is the
    _____.
    A. amount of time a child spends in day care
    B. quality of the time spent in day care
    C. type of parent-child attachment
    D. number of siblings in the home

True-False Questions

Indicate which of the following statements are true or false, and compare your answers with those at the end of the chapter.

T F 1. Most psychologists believe that both genetic and environmental forces interact to influence development.

T F 2. Cross-sectional studies allow researchers to measure behavioral and personality changes that occur as a function of age.

T F 3. In the womb, the unborn child is protected from all environmental influences.

T F 4. Binge drinking but not social drinking appears to be related to fetal alcohol syndrome.

T F 5. Research suggests that human infants are born with a special orientation toward the face.

T F 6. Newborns are able to distinguish between sweet and sour tastes.

T F 7. The process of myelination in the brain stops after the second year of life.

T F 8. Piaget's first three stages of cognitive development occur in children from different cultures at roughly the same time.

T F 9. There is a critical period for the development of attachment.

T F 10. Almost all horizontal relationships in childhood are between members of the same sex.

Key Concepts Matching Exercises

Exercise #1: Cognitive Development

Place the developmental milestones and concepts on the right into the correct Piagetian stage listed on the left. Note that more than one concept will "fit" into each stage!

_____ 1. Sensorimotor

_____ 2. Preoperational

_____ 3. Concrete operations

_____ 4. Formal operations

A. "A cup of water is still a cup of water, no matter what size container it's in."
B. Usually occurs during adolescence and adulthood
C. Stage marked by intuitive, prelogical thinking
D. "Out of sight, out of mind."
E. "If I close my eyes, you won't be able to see me."
F. Separation anxiety
G. Usually spans years two to six
H. Knowledge of the world is gained by touching, tasting, smelling, and manipulating objects
I. Verbal skills develop rapidly during this stage
J. Systematic hypothesis testing becomes possible during this stage.
K. This stage is marked by a lack of conservation
L. Research reveals cross-cultural differences in the development of this stage
M. This stage is marked by the development of logical reasoning
N. "What you see is what you get."
O. Egocentrism is a hallmark of this stage
P. Spans about ages six to twelve

Essay Questions

Write out answers to the following brief essay questions. Compare your responses with the sample answers at the end of the Study Guide chapter.

1. Explain the bioecological model of development. How does this model contribute to our understanding of the nature and nurture debate?

2. What are the two basic approaches for studying developmental processes? Compare and contrast these two approaches. What are the problems associated with each one?

3. What is a teratogen? Define this concept and discuss the impact of prenatal alcohol exposure.

4. Your text discusses some of the legacies and the criticisms of the classic Piagetian theory of cognitive development. What is one of the major legacies? What are the problems with Piagetian theory?

5. Horizontal relationships with peers become an important aspect of social development in childhood. Discuss the four types of children who have been identified based on the sociometric method. Why are these friendship patterns and peer evaluations important?

Multimedia Study Resources

Several activities and articles in Chapter 9 (Developmental Psychology I) of The Psychology Place™ supplement the material covered in your textbook. For example, Research News presents a report that explores whether attachment style—long assumed by researchers to be stable over the lifespan—can change ("Childhood Attachment Style: How Stable Over the Life Span?"). Another article challenges the assumption that the two-parent, heterosexual family is the "best" model for child rearing ("Is a Male Role Model Essential to Positive Child Development?"). Op Ed Forum presents different sides to the debate over whether parents or peers are the most important influence on children's development ("The Power of Parents").

Test Solutions

Multiple-Choice Solutions

1. A (p. 363)	11. D (p. 371)	21. D (p. 389)
2. B (p. 363)	12. B (p. 372)	22. A (p. 389)
3. A (p. 363)	13. D (p. 373)	23. B (p. 389)
4. D (p. 365)	14. D (p. 376)	24. D (p. 392)
5. C (p. 366)	15. D (p. 376)	25. C (p. 393)
6. C (p. 367)	16. D (pp. 377-78)	26. B (p. 395)
7. B (p. 367)	17. A (pp. 384, 389)	27. A (p. 395)
8. A (p. 368)	18. B (p. 385)	28. C (p. 396)
9. C (p. 369)	19. B (p. 386)	29. B (p. 396)
10. B (p. 369)	20. C (p. 386)	30. B (p. 399)

True-False Solutions

1. T (p. 363)	6. T (p. 379)
2. F (p. 368)	7. F (p. 381)
3. F (p. 370)	8. T (p. 388)
4. F (p. 372)	9. F (p. 395)
5. T (pp. 377-78)	10. T (p. 399)

Key Concepts Matching Solutions

Exercise #1

1. D, F, H
2. C, E, G, I, K, N, O
3. A, M, P
4. B, J, L

Essay Solutions

1. The bioecological model of development states that all infants come into this world genetically endowed with certain predispositions, but that these genetic predispositions are then acted upon by environmental factors (i.e., life experiences). Some of the life experiences will foster the expression of the genetic endowments, while others will inhibit their expression. For example, a child may be born predisposed to develop high intelligence, but then mature in an intellectually deprived home that ultimately prevents the expression of that intelligence. Thus, this model takes into account both nature (genetics) and nurture (life experiences), and suggests that both interact to produce personality and behavior (p. 367).

2. Cross-sectional studies involve examining people of different ages at the same point in time and then comparing their responses. For example, a researcher might measure the IQ of a number of people of varying ages and then see whether IQ and age are correlated. The major problem with this type of study (aside from the fact that it is correlational and therefore cannot be used to demonstrate causality) is that of cohort effects. A cohort effect occurs when there are preexisting differences between generations or age groups (called cohorts). A researcher who finds that older adults reason differently from younger adults might conclude that there are age differences in reasoning ability; but these differences might be due to the fact that one cohort spent less time in school than the other cohort (pp. 367-68).

   The second method is the longitudinal study, which involves following the same group of participants over time and testing them repeatedly. For example, a researcher might measure reasoning ability in the same group of people during their 10th year, 15th year, and 20th year of life. This strategy allows the researcher to measure change over time, something the cross-sectional study cannot do. However, on the downside, this strategy takes a great deal of time and requires long-term cooperation from participants (p. 368).

3. Teratogens are any substances or factors that prevent normal prenatal development. Almost any substance can function as a teratogen, including drugs, environmental agents (like pollution or X-rays), and viruses (p. 370). Alcohol is a particularly potent teratogen. Upon ingestion by the mother, alcohol passes through the placenta into the fetus's bloodstream, flows to the brain, and impairs breathing. Women who use alcohol regularly throughout their pregnancies are prone to have children with fetal alcohol syndrome (FAS), a pattern of physical and mental defects (p. 372).

4. Not only did Piaget propose the first major widely accepted theory of cognitive development, but he brought forth in his theory the notion that children mature in stages, and that a particular child may not be developmentally "ready" for reading, or writing, or arithmetic at a given time (p. 388).

   There have been several criticisms lobbied at classic Piagetian theory. The first concerns Piaget's interview method, which has since been refined. The original rather crude method caused Piaget to underestimate the overall rate of cognitive development (however, he does appear to have been correct about the sequence of development). The second major criticism concerns whether children actually progress in a series of steplike cognitive stages, or whether their development is more gradual, with one strategy overlapping and flowing into the next (pp. 388-89).

5. Teachers have identified four types of school-age children based on their "sociometric" status among peers (this method involves asking the children to rate themselves and to nominate the classmates they like the most and the least). Children can be classified as popular (sociable, skilled, and well liked), rejected (aggressive or withdrawn, lacking social skills, and disliked), controversial (sociable, often aggressive, liked and disliked), and neglected (less sociable and aggressive than average, seldom mentioned by peers). These peer ratings appear to have important correlates. For example, popular children have the most friends and thus have access to the benefit of these friendships. Rejected children seem to be the most at risk—they are more likely to be lonely, to drop out of school, and to have academic difficulties and social adjustment problems as adults. Thus, friendships seem to provide a child with certain developmental advantages (pp. 400-1).

11 Adolescence and Adulthood

Chapter Overview

This chapter continues to explore the field of developmental psychology by focusing on the biological, cognitive, and social changes that occur during adolescence, adulthood, and old age. The first part of the chapter concerns adolescence. The definition and changing views of adolescence are discussed, as are the various biological and physical events that mark this transitional developmental stage (e.g., puberty, menarche for girls, spermarche for boys). The cognitive changes—and corresponding alterations in moral reasoning—that occur during adolescence are discussed. Alternative theoretical conceptions of moral development during the lifespan also are presented. Aspects of social development then are examined, including changes in the parent-child relationship, the influence of peers, and sexuality. The next section of your chapter focuses on adulthood and old age, beginning with a consideration of the physical changes that mark adult development and the aging process. Cognitive development is examined (including age-related alterations in memory and forgetting and possible reasons for these changes), and the impact of Alzheimer's disease on cognitive and physical functioning is addressed. Your chapter then considers the topic of aging and intelligence, presenting research that indicates which forms of intelligence decline with age and which are relatively unaffected by the aging process. Next, Erikson's life-span theory of psychosocial development, the critical events or turning points of adulthood, life satisfaction, and other aspects of social development are discussed. The chapter ends with a consideration of the psychological aspects of coping with dying and death.

Chapter Outline

I. *What's Your Prediction?* How Old Do People Feel?

II. Adolescence

    A. Biological Development

B. Cognitive Development
  1. Moral reasoning
  2. Alternative conceptions
  3. Moral dilemmas in law

C. Social Development
  1. Parent relationships
  2. Peer influences
  3. Sexuality

D. Adolescence and Mental Health

E. *Debunking the Myth* ... That Adolescence Brings Inevitable Storm and Stress

III. Adulthood and Old Age

A. Biological Development
  1. The adult years
  2. Old age

B. Cognitive Development
  1. Memory and forgetting
    a. Alzheimer's disease
  2. Intelligence

C. *Psychology and* ... *Work* Patterns of Career Development

D. Social Development
  1. Ages and stages of adulthood
  2. Critical events of adulthood
  3. Life satisfaction
  4. Changing perspectives on time

E. Dying and Death

IV. The Big Picture

Learning Objectives

By the time you have read and reviewed this chapter, you should be able to:

1. Discuss the debate in developmental psychology over stability versus change (p. 408).

2. Define adolescence (p. 409). Consider the biological milestones associated with the transition to adolescence (pp. 410-12). Compare menarche and spermarche (pp. 410-12). Discuss factors that influence boys' and girls' reactions to puberty (pp. 410-12).

3. Consider the cognitive changes that occur during adolescence (p. 412). Consider how cognitive changes influence changes in moral reasoning (pp. 412-13).

4. Outline Kohlberg's theory of moral development (p. 414). Discuss three major criticisms of Kohlberg's theory and consider alternative theoretical conceptions to this theory (pp. 413-16).

5. Consider the social crises (e.g., identity crisis) that characterize adolescence (p. 417). Outline how the parent-child relationship changes during adolescence (pp. 417-419).

6. Discuss peer influences during adolescence (pp. 419-20).

7. Examine the changes in sexuality that mark adolescence (pp. 420-21). Consider ethnic and cultural differences in rates of sexual activity (p. 421). Explain why many teenagers do not use contraception (p. 421).

8. Consider adolescence and mental health. Is adolescence truly a time of "storm and stress" (pp. 421-23)?

9. Distinguish between the human life span and the average human life expectancy (p. 423). Describe the physical changes that mark adult development (pp. 424-25). Consider whether the body's aging process can be slowed down (pp. 425-26).

10. Discuss changes in memory and forgetting that occur as we age (p. 426). Discuss two possible reasons for age-related declines in memory (p. 427).

11. Define Alzheimer's disease (AD) and describe the cognitive effects of this progressive brain disorder (pp. 427-28).

12. Examine the relation between aging and changes in various types of intelligence (pp. 428-29).

13. Discuss changes in work productivity and performance that occur during adulthood (pp. 430-31).

14. List and describe the eight stages of Erikson's theory of social development, along with the ages and primary crisis associated with each stage (pp. 431-32).

15. Describe Levinson's four eras of adulthood (p. 432).

16. Examine the critical events of adulthood (pp. 433-34). Define the concept of social clock and explain its purpose (p. 434).

17. Describe the relation, if any, between life satisfaction and age (pp. 434-35). Consider whether adults experience a "midlife crisis" (pp. 434-35).

18. Consider the ways in which the both the perception and the management of time change as people age (p. 436).

19. List and describe the five stages of coping with death and dying (p. 436). Consider whether psychological factors (e.g., the "will to live") can influence the timing of a person's death (p. 437).

Key Terms

The following key terms and concepts are featured in this chapter and are important for you to know. Write out definitions of each term and check your answers with the definitions in the text on the pages listed.

Adolescence (p. 409)
Puberty (p. 410)
Menarche (p. 410)
Spermarche (p. 411)
Moral reasoning (p. 412)
Empathy (p. 415)
Identity crisis (p. 417)

Life span (p. 423)
Life expectancy (p. 423)
Menopause (p. 425)
Alzheimer's disease (AD) (p. 427)
Fluid intelligence (p. 428)
Crystallized intelligence (p. 428)
Social clock (p. 434)

Test Questions

Multiple-Choice Questions

Circle the correct choice for each question and compare your answers with those at the end of the Study Guide chapter.

1. Which of the following statements about the period of adolescence is accurate?
   A. Adolescence begins with a social event.
   B. Adolescence corresponds to the childhood years.
   C. Adolescence is characterized by few biological, social, and cognitive changes.
   D. The way in which psychologists have viewed adolescence has changed over time.

2. Adolescence begins with a(n) _____ event.
   A. biological
   B. emotional
   C. cognitive
   D. social

3. Menarche is to girls as _____ is to boys.
   A. womenarche
   B. puberty
   C. spermarche
   D. testarche

4. A major factor that influences a girl's reaction to puberty is _____.
   A. cultural views of menarche
   B. her own personality traits
   C. the timing of menarche
   D. A and C

5. In girls, early puberty often is associated with _____; in boys, early puberty tends to be related to _____.
   A. personal benefits; interpersonal benefits
   B. adjustment difficulties; social benefits
   C. interpersonal benefits; adjustment difficulties
   D. positive adjustment; negative adjustment

6. Older adolescents often are capable of thinking at the _____ stage of cognitive development.
   A. sensorimotor
   B. preoperational
   C. concrete operational
   D. formal operational

7. Michael believes that we should help others because "by helping others, you avoid dishonor and people will respect you and look up to you." Michael is at the _____ level of moral reasoning.
   A. preconventional
   B. conventional
   C. postconventional
   D. social conventional

8. Anita shoplifts and then sells the merchandise to support her family. The person who says she should be punished because it is against the law to steal is at the _____ moral level.
   A. preconventional
   B. conventional
   C. postconventional
   D. unconventional

9. Your text mentions the controversial topic of assisted suicide. Suppose that a physician decides that it is moral to help dying people to end their lives, even though this behavior violates the law. This physician could be classified as _____ in his/her moral reasoning.
   A. preconventional
   B. unconventional
   C. conventional
   D. postconventional

10. Nick is willing to let other students copy his old papers—but only if he is offered enough money. This exemplifies _____ moral reasoning.
    A. preconventional
    B. conventional
    C. postconventional
    D. unconventional

11. Which of the following represents a criticism of Kohlberg's theory of moral development?
    A. It is culturally biased.
    B. It is gender biased.
    C. Moral thinking may not be related to moral behavior.
    D. All of the above

12. Kohlberg's model of moral development has been considered culturally biased because
    A. only well-educated adults from complex urban societies demonstrate postconventional reasoning.
    B. Americans typically do not demonstrate postconventional reasoning.
    C. only individuals from fundamentalist Christian sects demonstrate postconventional reasoning.
    D. advanced education and social status lead to unconventional rather than postconventional reasoning.

13. Hoffman's theory of moral development assumes that morality in children is based upon the ability to experience _____.
    A. sympathy
    B. empathy
    C. pleasure
    D. distress

14. According to Erikson, the transitional period of adolescence is marked by a(n) _____ crisis.
    A. sexual
    B. cognitive
    C. identity
    D. moral

15. Karla is 13 years old. Research suggests that her relationship with her parents will change in what way as she goes through adolescence?
    A. increased tension over routine household matters
    B. increased time spent with family members
    C. increased conflict over explosive political issues
    D. All of the above

16. Which person in the most likely to conform to the influence of friends?
    A. Tommy, a second-grader
    B. Tammy, a sixth-grader
    C. Timmy, a ninth-grader
    D. Tuppence, a college student

17. Which of the following statements is accurate?
    A. American teenagers are less sexually active today than they were during the time of Kinsey's large-scale sex survey.
    B. American teenagers often do not use contraceptives the first time they engage in intercourse.
    C. Many American teenagers have extensive knowledge about human reproductive physiology.
    D. There are few cultural and ethnic differences in rates of sexual activity in teenagers.

18. Research suggests that adolescent risk-taking is a function of:
    A. rebelliousness.
    B. reacting to social situations that call for risk.
    C. increased opportunities to engage in "adult" behaviors.
    D. All of the above

19. Among humans, life expectancy is influenced by
    A. genetics.
    B. nutrition.
    C. personality factors.
    D. All of the above

20. The end of menstruation is called _____.
    A. fertile pause
    B. menopause
    C. womenopause
    D. fempause

21. Deborah is in her late fifties. Her ovaries have stopped producing estrogen and she is experiencing "hot flashes." Research suggests that she also may experience _____ during this period.
    A. headaches
    B. extreme emotional trauma
    C. irreversible decreases in her sexual activity level
    D. All of the above

22. There appear to be age-related declines in the ability to
    A. recognize names, faces, and other stimuli that have been previously encountered.
    B. recall names, faces, and other stimuli that have been previously encountered.
    C. recognize and recall names, faces, and other stimuli that have been previously encountered.
    D. recognize faces and recall names of previously encountered persons.

23. The effects of Alzheimer's disease include which of the following?
    A. the development of a viral infection
    B. a steady increase in phobic responses
    C. an overall loss of cognitive functions
    D. hyperactivity and compulsive behavior

24. Research suggests that _____ declines and _____ remains relatively stable across the life span.
    A. crystallized intelligence; fluid intelligence
    B. fluid intelligence; crystallized intelligence
    C. reasoning ability; mental speed
    D. mental speed; wisdom

25. According to Erikson's model of social development, the major crisis experienced by young adults is _____.
    A. identity vs. role confusion
    B. generativity vs. stagnation
    C. intimacy vs. isolation
    D. integrity vs. despair

26. An adult who is in his or her fifties must resolve the conflict between _____.
    A. initiative vs. doubt
    B. intimacy vs. isolation
    C. integrity vs. despair
    D. generativity vs. stagnation

27. Levison's theory of social development proposes that our lives alternate between periods of _____.
    A. generativity and stagnation
    B. stress between eras and calm within eras
    C. adolescent angst and midlife crises
    D. depression and elation

28. "It's time for you to settle down," Bill's mother is fond of telling him. "All of my friends' children are married and raising children of their own. Why don't you go out and meet someone nice. . ." These statements reflect the existence of
    A. a social clock.
    B. parent-child conflict.
    C. a social crisis.
    D. intimacy vs. isolation.

29. Which of the following statements about life satisfaction is accurate?
    A. Life satisfaction declines in the elderly years.
    B. Life satisfaction is lowest during the midlife years.
    C. The majority of adults are dissatisfied with their lives.
    D. None of the above

30. Which of the following stages are individuals likely to pass through as they cope with the knowledge of death?
    A. depression
    B. anger
    C. denial
    D. All of the above

True-False Questions

Indicate which of the following statements are true or false, and compare your answers with those at the end of the chapter.

T   F   1. Subjective age does not always match chronological age.

T   F   2. Many cultures have initiation rites to celebrate the passage from childhood to adulthood.

T   F   3. Early puberty generally has positive social consequences for boys and girls.

T   F   4. Kohlberg's model of moral development may be most applicable to complex, urban societies.

T   F   5. The early stages of adolescence are marked by higher levels of conformity to peer influence.

T   F   6. There are few cultural differences in rates of teenage sexual activity.

T   F   7. One of the hallmarks of adolescence is severe emotional distress.

T   F   8. Aging is both a biological and psychological process.

T   F   9. All types of intelligence decrease with age.

T   F   10. Life satisfaction generally does not decline with advancing age.

Key Concepts Matching Exercises

Exercise #1: Kohlberg's Theory of Moral Development

Place the motivations and statements listed below into the correct moral stage.

I. Preconventional Morality	II. Conventional Morality	III. Postconventional Morality
Stage 1: _____	Stage 3: _____	Stage 5: _____
Stage 2: _____	Stage 4: _____	Stage 6: _____

A. The motivation to fulfill one's duty to society and avoid feelings of guilt

B. "Stealing is bad. When you steal, you get in trouble."

C. "Stealing is bad. When you steal, you break the law, and we all should follow the law."

D. The motivation to avoid punishment

E. "I had to steal. I know it was against the law, but sometimes laws must be broken. By stealing, I was able to do what my conscience tells me is right."

F. The motivation to gain approval and avoid disapproval

G. "I would never steal. After all, I have a reputation to uphold. What would other people think if I were to be caught stealing?"

H. The motivation to uphold one's own ethical principles and values

I. The motivation to obtain rewards

J. "I help people because it's my duty to do so. I would feel so guilty if I saw someone in need and didn't stop to offer assistance."

K. "I help my brother because my parents praise me when I do."

L. The motivation to maintain and follow social principles

Exercise #2: Erikson's Stages of Social Development

Place each "crisis" into its corresponding stage of social development.

_____ 1. Infancy   A. Autonomy vs. shame and doubt

_____ 2. Toddler   B. Intimacy vs. isolation

_____ 3. Preschool   C. Trust vs. mistrust

_____ 4. Elementary school   D. Integrity vs. despair

_____ 5. Adolescence   E. Industry vs. inferiority

_____ 6. Young adulthood   F. Generativity vs. stagnation

_____ 7. Middle adulthood   G. Identity vs. role confusion

_____ 8. Late adulthood   H. Initiative vs. guilt

Exercise #3: Coping With Death and Dying

Match the statements on the right with the five stages in the coping process listed on the left.

_____ 1. Denial   A. "If I pull through this, I will exercise every day and I will never yell at my family again."

_____ 2. Anger   B. "Well, there's not much I can do about this now. I guess what has to be, will be."

_____ 3. Bargaining   C. "This is so unfair! Why do these things always happen to me? I could just scream!"

_____ 4. Depression   D. "It's all over. My life is meaningless. I just want to be left alone."

_____ 5. Acceptance   E. "This is not happening to me. The doctors must be wrong."

Essay Questions

Write out answers to the following brief essay questions. Compare your responses with the sample answers at the end of the Study Guide chapter.

1. Define puberty. How does early puberty affect boys and girls?

2. When four-year-old Lyle sees his little sister fall down and start to cry, he runs over to her and offers her his "blankie." His aunts disagree over the meaning of Lyle's behavior. Auntie Eleanor says, "Oh look, Lyle feels sorry for Becky. He wants to make her feel better and so he's giving her his blanket." Auntie Mildred disagrees. "Children are incapable of that sort of higher moral thinking. Lyle knows that we'll reward him if he behaves nicely to his sister." Who is right?

3. "Teenagers are the helpless mental-health victims of their own hormones." Agree or disagree with this statement.

4. "You're only as old as you feel." What do you think about this statement? Is there any evidence that the body's aging process can be slowed down?

5. A common stereotype of the elderly is that they are absentminded and perhaps senile. What changes occur in memory and forgetting as we age? What are two possible explanations for these age-related changes?

Several activities and articles in Chapter 10 (Developmental Psychology II) of The Psychology Place™ supplement the material covered in your textbook. For example, the *Scientific American* magazine article called "The Oldest Old" explores the finding that people in their late 90s are often healthier and more robust than men and women 20 years younger—perhaps traditional views of aging are in need of revision. A report presented in Research News examines how people handle the fear of death, and allows readers to measure their own anxiety over this final developmental milestone ("Fear of Death: Our Final Developmental Crisis"). And finally, an Op Ed Forum piece entitled "Who or What is to Blame for the Littleton Massacre" discusses the factors that are implicated in producing self-regulation (or its lack) in adolescents and young adults.

Test Solutions

Multiple-Choice Solutions

1. D (p. 409)	11. D (pp. 413-14)	21. A (p. 425)
2. A (p. 409)	12. A (p. 413)	22. B (p. 426)
3. C (p. 411)	13. B (p. 415)	23. C (p. 427)
4. D (pp. 410-11)	14. C (p. 417)	24. B (p. 429)
5. B (pp. 411-12)	15. A (p. 418)	25. C (p. 432)
6. D (p. 412)	16. C (p. 420)	26. D (p. 432)
7. B (pp. 413-14)	17. B (p. 422)	27. B (p. 432)
8. B (pp. 413-14)	18. D (p. 422)	28. A (p. 434)
9. D (pp. 413-14)	19. D (p. 423)	29. D (p. 435)
10. A (pp. 413-14)	20. B (p. 425)	30. D (p. 436)

True-False Solutions

1. T (p. 407)	6. F (p. 421)
2. T (p. 409)	7. F (p. 422)
3. F (p. 412)	8. T (p. 423)
4. T (p. 413)	9. F (p. 429)
5. T (p. 420)	10. T (p. 435)

Key Concepts Matching Solutions

Exercise #1	*Exercise #2*	*Exercise #3*
1. D, B	1. C	1. E
2. I, K	2. A	2. C
3. F, G	3. H	3. A
4. A, J	4. E	4. D
5. C, L	5. G	5. B
6. E, H	6. B	
	7. F	
	8. D	

Essay Solutions

1. Puberty is the "biological motor" of adolescence. Specifically, puberty is a biological, hormonally-driven event defined as the gradual onset of sexual maturation (p. 410). Early puberty appears to have different consequences for girls and boys. Specifically, girls who mature before their peers are usually less satisfied with their bodies and are more likely to diet and to develop eating disorders. They are also more likely to spend time with older peers, to have sex at an earlier age, to have lower grades, and to become involved in norm-breaking behaviors (e.g., drinking, stealing, fighting, cutting classes) (p. 411). In boys, however, early maturation is generally a positive experience that is associated with positive body image, self-confidence, and social benefits (e.g, popularity as a result of increased size and strength relative to peers) (p. 412).

2. Both of Lyle's aunts could be correct in their explanations of his behavior. Auntie Mildred is espousing the traditional Kohlberg view that young children resolve moral dilemmas in ways that reflect self-serving motives. Mildred views Lyle's act of kindness as motivated out of his desire to obtain rewards. According to Kohlberg's theory, then, Lyle is functioning within the preconventional level of moral development (p. 413). Auntie Eleanor holds a different view. She suggests (and other theorists would agree) that morality in children is a function of empathy—the ability to experience joy for others who are happy and distress for others who are in pain or sad. According to this perspective, Lyle's behavior was motivated by the distress he felt over viewing his sister's pain (p. 415). In sum, both aunts may be correct in their assessment of Lyle's behavior.

3. Although mood swings, conflict with parents, conformity to peers, questions of identity, and so on all characterize the teenage years, there is little accuracy in that statement. About 80 percent of teenagers do not develop serious emotional problems, and most teenagers are happy and reasonably well-adjusted (p. 422). Thus, a teenager who is severely disturbed, or who reports feeling lonely, depressed, and/or suicidal, should receive immediate care—because such feelings are not "typical" or "just part of a phase."

4. As noted in the first few pages of this chapter, many adults and older people feel younger than they actually are; that is, subjective age does not always match chronological age (p. 407). Biological data suggest that it is impossible, at this point, to reverse or stop the body's aging process. However, there is some fascinating research that indicates that it may be possible to at least slow down the aging process. For example, Ellen Langer and her colleagues (1989) designed an experiment in which one group of elderly men went on a retreat and "lived" in the year 1959 (e.g., they wrote autobiographical sketches of their lives during that year in the present tense, listened to music and watched movies circa 1950s, and so on). The second group of men went on a similar retreat, but they reminisced about the year 1959 from the vantage point of the present time. Both groups of men were rated as looking younger by independent judges; however, the first group was in better physical condition than the second. Thus, perhaps aging is, at least to some extent, "in our minds"! (pp. 425-26).

5. There are several age-related changes in cognitive function that occur. For example, older adults are less able than younger adults to free-recall previously learned information (although their recognition memory appears unimpaired). There is a similar age-related decline in performance on prospective memory tasks, where the goal is to remember to do something in the future (p. 426).

Two explanations have been proposed for these changes. The first is neurocognitive in nature and has to do with sensory acuity and neural speed. Specifically, as people age, their eyesight and hearing becomes increasingly impaired; this may influence their ability to perform a variety of cognitive tasks. In addition, as people age, they process and react to information more slowly; this neural speed loss impairs performance on a range of cognitive tasks (since it takes more time to process information, people have less time to actually rehearse that information). The second factor is psychological in nature; as people get older, they may lose faith in their cognitive abilities. People who succumb to negative beliefs about the elderly or about their own cognitive ability (or lack thereof) may not even try to remember or learn information (p. 427).

12 Intelligence

Chapter Overview

This chapter revolves around the topic of intelligence. The opening section explores definitions of intelligence and the various testing instruments that have been created to measure this construct (e.g., Stanford-Binet, Wechsler scales). The concept of IQ (and how to interpret an IQ score) is presented, and your author discusses the essential "ingredients" of an intelligence test (of any test, for that matter); namely, standardization, reliability, and validity. The question of bias in intelligence testing is then addressed, with a particular emphasis on culture and whether tests should be "culture-fair." The second major section of the chapter explores the nature of intelligence, beginning with an overview of the major theorists who consider intelligence to be a general underlying mental capacity (e.g., Spearman) and with empirical research that supports the notion of general intelligence. Then, multifactor models of intelligence are presented, including Thurstone's "primary mental abilities," Gardner's "multiple intelligences," and Sternberg's "triarchic theory." The chapter then turns to the great debates that have raged within the domain of intelligence theory and measurement. Specifically, your author explores the political controversy surrounding the issue of whether intelligence is determined by genetics or the environment (i.e., the nature and nurture debate) and the empirical research that speaks to this issue. Group differences in IQ scores (within the United States and across cultures), and research concerning the origin of these differences, are discussed. This section ends with a consideration of sex differences in tests of specific abilities (i.e., verbal, mathematical, spatial) and the various biological and environmental factors that might create the observed differences. The final part of the chapter explores the topic of education—in particular, the educational implications of IQ testing—beginning with an examination of individuals whose IQ scores place them in special educational categories (i.e., gifted, mentally retarded). This section concludes with a discussion of how IQ-based teacher expectancies, stereotype vulnerability, and ability grouping may influence the educational process.

Chapter Outline

V. Education

    A. Giftedness

    B. Mental Retardation

    C. The Self-Fulfilling Prophecy
       1. Teacher expectancies
       2. Stereotype vulnerability
       3. Ability grouping

VI. The Big Picture

Learning Objectives

By the time you have read and reviewed this chapter, you should be able to:

1. Define the concept of intelligence (pp. 444-45).

2. Compare different testing instruments used to measure intelligence, including the Stanford-Binet, Wechsler tests, and group tests (pp. 445-51).

3. Explain the concept of mental age and compare this concept to that of intelligence quotient (IQ) (pp. 446-47). Discuss why the notion of IQ is useful for children but less so for adults (p. 447).

4. Define the concept of aptitude (p. 450).

5. Consider whether intelligence tests are "accurate" (pp. 451-52). Explain the measurement concepts of standardization, reliability, and validity (pp. 451-52). Compare test-retest and split-half reliability (pp. 451-52). Explain the distinction between content and criterion validity (p. 452).

6. Discuss whether intelligence tests are culturally biased (pp. 452-54). Consider the possible reasons for race differences in IQ scores (p. 453). Explain the concept of a "culture-fair" test (p. 453).

7. Define the concept of "g," or general intelligence (p. 455). Discuss two sources of evidence that support the concept of general intelligence (pp. 455-56).

8. Contrast Spearman's notion of general intelligence with the theories of Thurstone, Gardner, and Sternberg (pp. 456-60).

9. Define the concept of multiple intelligences (p. 457). Discuss the converging lines of evidence that Gardner used to support this theory (p. 457). Contrast the seven major types of intelligence proposed by Gardner's theory (pp. 457-58).

10. Explain Sternberg's triarchic theory of intelligence (pp. 459-64). List and define the three types of intelligence proposed by this theory (p. 459-62). Consider ways to measure—and research conducted on—analytic, creative, and practical intelligence (pp. 462-64).

11. Explain why the debate about the biological and environmental basis of intelligence (nature and nurture) is so politically heated (pp. 465-66).

12. Summarize the research on the relative influence of genetics and environment on intelligence (pp. 466-68).

13. Explain the purpose of Head Start programs and how successful they are (pp. 468-70).

14. Consider racial and cultural differences in IQ score and research that has examined the origin of those differences (pp. 470-72).

15. Discuss sex differences in tests of specific abilities (i.e., verbal, mathematical, spatial) (pp. 473-74). Explain possible biological and environmental/social explanations for these differences (p. 474).

16. Consider the educational implications of labeling those individuals who obtain very high ("gifted") or very low ("retarded") IQ scores (p. 475).

17. Explore the notion of "giftedness," including how this has been defined and the results of longitudinal studies on gifted individuals (pp. 475-76).

18. Define the notion of mental retardation and discuss how it is diagnosed (p. 476). List and describe the four categories of mental retardation (p. 477).

19. Describe the phenomenon of the self-fulfilling prophecy (p. 477). Explain how IQ-based teacher expectancies can affect educational attainment in the classroom (pp. 477-78).

20. Describe how stereotype vulnerability can contribute to a self-fulfilling prophecy (pp. 478-79).

21. Examine the concept of ability grouping ("tracking") and how this might affect both the performance and the self-esteem of students (pp. 479-80).

Key Terms

The following key terms and concepts are featured in this chapter and are important for you to know. Write out definitions of each term and check your answers with the definitions in the text on the pages listed.

Intelligence (p. 444)
Mental age (p. 446)
Stanford-Binet (p. 446)
Intelligence quotient (IQ) (p. 447)
Wechsler Adult Intelligence Scale (WAIS) (p. 447)
Standardization (p. 451)
Reliability (p. 451)
Test-retest reliability (p. 451)
Split-half reliability (p. 452)
Validity (p. 452)
Content validity (p. 452)
Criterion validity (p. 452)

General intelligence (p. 455)
Factor analysis (p. 455)
Multiple intelligences (p. 457)
Prodigies (p. 457)
Idiot savants (p. 457)
Triarchic theory of intelligence (p. 460)
Creativity (p. 461)
Divergent thinking (p. 461)
Practical intelligence (p. 462)
Project Head Start (p. 466)
Mental retardation (p. 476)
Self-fulfilling prophecy (p. 477)

Multiple-Choice Questions

Circle the correct choice for each question and compare your answers with those at the end of the Study Guide chapter.

1. Most psychologists view the construct of intelligence as
    A. expertise on a particular academic subject.
    B. the capacity to learn from experience and adapt to one's environment.
    C. the ability to attain a high grade point average.
    D. professional success in one's chosen field.

2. The first psychologist to devise a "mental test" to measure intelligence was _____.
    A. Charles Darwin
    B. Alfred Binet
    C. Francis Galton
    D. Theopile Simon

3. Galton believed that a person's _____ provided an accurate index of his or her intelligence.
    A. verbal aptitude
    B. physical abilities
    C. cognitive abilities
    D. All of the above

4. The original intelligence test devised by Binet and Simon was developed in order to
    A. identify children needing special academic assistance.
    B. select men who were suited for military duty.
    C. predict worker productivity.
    D. determine the age at which children would reach their maximum academic potential.

5. The average eight-year-old child has a mental age of _____.
    A. 100   C. 8
    B. 1   D. 80

6. According to Terman's notion of intelligence quotient, people who are of "average" intelligence have an IQ of _____.
    A. 100   C. 1
    B. 10   D. 50

7. Suppose you were to take the Wechsler Adult Intelligence Scale (WAIS). What scores would you receive?
    A. a verbal score
    B. a nonverbal performance score
    C. an overall score
    D. All of the above

8. A weakness of the Wechsler intelligence scales is that they
    A. do not provide the participant with an overall intelligence score.
    B. are not practical for quick group assessments.
    C. provide only one overall intelligence measure.
    D. cannot be used to measure nonverbal skills.

9. The SAT and ACT are used to _____.
   A. predict college performance
   B. assess knowledge that has been acquired
   C. provide an objective reliability "check" of a student's current GPA
   D. All of the above

10. All intelligence tests should be _____.
    A. reliable
    B. valid
    C. standardized
    D. All of the above

11. Dr. Grable has developed a new intelligence test. She administers her test to a group of 200 college students in early September and again in November, and then compares the two sets of test scores. Dr. Grable is assessing the _____ of her test.
    A. criterion validity   C. test-retest reliability
    B. standardization   D. split-half reliability

12. If a test that is supposed to predict future college performance actually does so, then that test has high _____.
    A. criterion validity   C. content validity
    B. split-half validity   D. reliability

13. Which of the following statements about research on group differences in IQ scores is accurate?
    A. Test scores can be influenced by a person's racial and/or cultural background.
    B. Group differences are found on "culture-fair" test items.
    C. Test scores predict academic performance within a given culture, regardless of the race of the students.
    D. All of the above

14. Which of the following would be considered a "culture-fair" test?
    A. forming a pattern with blocks
    B. reciting a series of numbers
    C. putting together the pieces of a puzzle
    D. All of the above

15. Dr. Monroe administers several tests to a group of students, including tests of reasoning ability, mathematical skill, memory span, reading comprehension, and so on. He finds that the test scores correlate poorly with one another; in other words, students who do well on reading comprehension do not necessarily do well on memory span. This result pattern provides evidence *against*
    A. Sternberg's triarchic theory of intelligence.
    B. Gardner's theory of multiple intelligences.
    C. Spearman's general intelligence factor.
    D. The theory that environment contributes to intelligence.

16. Which of the following behavioral measures in infants is related to later IQ scores?
    A. rate of smiling
    B. ability to visually track moving objects
    C. responsiveness to changes in a stimulus
    D. age at which first word is spoken

17. Research generally reveals that people with high IQ scores respond _____ on perceptual and cognitive tasks.
    A. more quickly than average
    B. less quickly than average
    C. about average
    D. slowly

18. Which of the following theorists constructed multifactor models of human intelligence?
    A. Thurstone
    B. Guilford
    C. Sternberg
    D. All of the above

19. According to Gardner's theory of intelligence, which of the following reflect "intelligent" behavior?
    A. the ability to play an instrument
    B. the ability to run at high speeds and/or over great distances
    C. the ability to design a building
    D. All of the above

20. Caitlin can perform rapid-fire mental arithmetic and spends much of her time solving puzzles and equations. However, she is extremely awkward around other people and has a reputation for "always saying or doing the wrong thing at the wrong time." Gardner would say that Caitlin has a high amount of _____ intelligence and a low amount of _____ intelligence.
    A. intrapersonal; relational
    B. logical-mathematical; interpersonal
    C. spatial; linguistic
    D. general; specific

21. Sternberg argues that there are three kinds of intelligence. What are they?
    A. analytic; creative; practical
    B. general; specific; individual
    C. intrapersonal; interpersonal; extrapersonal
    D. verbal; mathematical; spatial

22. Academic intelligence is to "school smarts" as _____ intelligence is to "street smarts."
    A. social   C. practical
    B. interpersonal   D. creative

23. Many psychologists believe that practical intelligence consists of _____.
    A. social competence
    B. common sense
    C. emotional intelligence
    D. All of the above

24. Those who believe that intelligence is influenced by environmental factors would be in favor of
    A. mandatory sterilization of mentally retarded persons.
    B. monetary incentives to keep people who are low in intelligence from reproducing.
    C. intellectual enrichment programs for socially disadvantaged children.
    D. decreased educational opportunities for children with low IQ scores.

25. Studies designed to examine the relative influence of genetics and environment on intelligence generally find that
    A. identical twins are more similar than fraternal twins in IQ scores.
    B. biological siblings raised together are less similar in IQ scores than biological siblings raised apart.
    C. children's IQ scores resemble the scores of their adoptive parents more than they do the scores of their biological parents.
    D. All of the above

26. Research indicates that
    A. about 50 percent of our IQ is inherited.
    B. heredity accounts for about 50 percent of the population variation in intelligence.
    C. the environment plays little to no role in intelligence.
    D. All of the above

27. Which of the following environmental factors might influence intelligence?
    A. family configuration
    B. amount of time spent in school
    C. prenatal care
    D. All of the above

28. Which of the following statements about Head Start programs is accurate?
    A. Head Start programs are effective at raising IQ scores into the gifted range.
    B. The initial gain in IQ seen in Head Start children wears off over time.
    C. Head Start children are more likely to repeat classes.
    D. Head Start children are no more or less confident in the classroom than their peers.

29. Most gifted children grow up to be _____.
    A. well adjusted
    B. eccentric "nerds"
    C. unemployed and penniless
    D. successful in work but unsuccessful in their personal lives

30. Bill needs some supervision in his personal hygiene. He relates to others in a childlike and rather limited way, but has successfully mastered the skills needed for a part-time maintenance position in a local veterinary clinic. His IQ is 65. Bill would be classified as
    A. mildly retarded.
    B. moderately retarded.
    C. severely retarded.
    D. profoundly retarded.

True-False Questions

Indicate which of the following statements are true or false, and compare your answers with those at the end of the chapter.

T   F   1. There has been a worldwide decline in IQ scores over time.

T   F   2. Mental age increases at the same rate as chronological age.

T   F   3. The Wechsler tests are the most commonly used individually administered tests.

T   F   4. A valid test measures what it is supposed to measure.

T F   5. IQ test scores are highly predictive of professional (nonacademic) success.

T F   6. Group score differences are not found on "culture-fair" IQ test items.

T F   7. The legal system has unanimously ruled in favor of IQ tests used for placement purposes.

T F   8. The age at which babies smile and start babbling is not related to later IQ scores.

T F   9. Research provides evidence for both a general intelligence and specific abilities.

T F   10. Most experts agree that intelligence is influenced by genetic factors.

Key Concepts Matching Exercises

Exercise #1: Theorists

Match the terms, concepts, or contributions listed on the right with the correct theorist on the left

_____ 1. Galton

_____ 2. Binet & Simon

_____ 3. Terman

_____ 4. Wechsler

_____ 5. Spearman

_____ 6. Thurstone

_____ 7. Gardner

_____ 8. Sternberg

A. Created the concept of IQ
B. Proposed that we have multiple intelligences, including physical, musical, and interpersonal
C. Proposed the notion of general intelligence
D. Developed a test to measure "mental age"
E. Distinguished between analytic, creative and practical intelligence
F. First psychologist to develop a "mental test"
G. Argued that intelligence consists of seven primary mental abilities
H. Created the most widely used modern intelligence test

Exercise #2: Testing Concepts

Match the concepts on the left with the examples or definitions on the right.

_____ 1. Standardization

_____ 2. Test-retest reliability

_____ 3. Split-half reliability

_____ 4. Content validity

_____ 5. Criterion validity

A. When scores from one testing occasion are correlated with scores from a second testing occasion
B. When the content of the test items reflects what the test is supposed to measure
C. Enables psychologists to compare a person's score to existing norms
D. When the test scores accurately predict a particular outcome
E. When scores on one version of a test are correlated with scores on a second version

Essay Questions

Write out answers to the following brief essay questions. Compare your responses with the sample answers at the end of the Study Guide chapter.

1. What is academic aptitude? Can aptitude by changed?

2. Are IQ tests culturally biased or not? Consider both sides of the issue in your answer.

3. What is creative intelligence? What factors promote or are part of creativity?

4. Review the research on sex differences in specific abilities. What differences are there? Discuss possible reasons for the difference in spatial ability.

5. Your textbook author mentions an expression that has been used to describe gifted children: "Early ripe, early rot." Define the concept of "giftedness" and consider whether this expression provides an accurate description of gifted persons.

Multimedia Study Resources

Several activities and articles in Chapter 8 (Thinking and Intelligence) of The Psychology Place™ supplement the material covered in your textbook. In particular, three articles presented in Research News explore topics related to the concept of intelligence. "Another Explanation for Differences in Intellectual Performance" discusses the concept of stereotype threat, one possible explanation for group differences in performance on standardized tests. "Another Measure of Intelligence: Working Memory" considers whether working memory (short-term memory) is an accurate measure of verbal and nonverbal problem-solving skill. And finally, "The Growing Popularity of 'Emotional Intelligence'" introduces the concept of emotional intelligence and considers evidence for this variety of intelligence.

Test Solutions

Multiple-Choice Solutions

1. B (p. 445)	11. C (p. 451)	21. A (p. 459)
2. C (p. 445)	12. A (p. 452)	22. C (p. 460)
3. B (p. 445)	13. D (p. 453)	23. D (p. 464)
4. A (p. 445)	14. D (p. 453)	24. C (p. 465)
5. C (p. 446)	15. C (p. 455)	25. A (p. 467)
6. A (p. 447)	16. C (p. 455)	26. B (p. 467)
7. D (p. 448)	17. A (p. 455)	27. D (pp. 467-68)
8. B (p. 448)	18. D (pp. 456, 459)	28. B (p. 470)
9. A (p. 448)	19. D (pp. 457-58)	29. A (p. 475)
10. D (p. 551)	20. B (pp. 457-58)	30. A (p. 477)

True-False Solutions

1. F (pp. 443-44)
2. F (p. 447)
3. T (p. 448)
4. T (p. 452)
5. F (p. 452)

6. F (p. 453)
7. F (pp. 453-54)
8. T (p. 455)
9. T (p. 457)
10. T (p. 466)

Key Concepts Matching Solutions

Exercise #1

1. F
2. D
3. A
4. H
5. C
6. G
7. B
8. E

Exercise #2

1. C
2. A
3. E
4. B
5. D

Essay Solutions

1. Academic aptitude is defined as the potential for learning. To the extent that aptitude is influenced by innate potential, the answer to the second question would appear to be "no." However, many individuals believe that aptitude can be influenced or changed by specific experiences. For example, students routinely enroll in preparation courses for "aptitude" tests (e.g., SAT) in the hopes of increasing their test scores. However, research on the outcomes of these test preparation courses indicates that they are less effective than might be hoped (for instance, courses tend to increase scores by an average of 30 to 50 points on the 400-1600 point scale) (pp. 450-51).

2. As noted by your textbook author, there is evidence for both sides of the debate. Specifically, there is evidence for bias in that the question content of IQ tests does appear to favor the cultural and educational experiences of the dominant culture (in the United States, that culture is the white middle class). For example, to answer the question, "Who was Thomas Jefferson?", one needs to have an understanding of American (as opposed to another country's) cultural heritage. In addition, a person's own cultural/racial/ethnic background can guide his or her perception of the testing situation itself and affect his or her scores (p. 453).

   On the other side of the debate, there is evidence that group differences are found even on test items that are considered to be "culture-fair," which suggests that the differences are not due solely to a lack of knowledge of the dominant culture. In addition, intelligence and aptitude tests are valid predictors of academic performance within a particular culture; individuals who obtain lower scores, irrespective of their race/ethnicity, in fact do not do as well academically as those who obtain higher scores (p. 453).

3. According to Sternberg, creative intelligence involves insight—the ability to know what information is relevant or irrelevant, to find connections between old and new information

and problems, to combine facts that appear to be unrelated, and to see the "big picture." Creativity is the ability to find solutions and conceptualizations that are unique and novel (p. 461). Some psychologists believe that one critical factor in creativity is divergent thinking, which is the ability to think flexibly and to open the mind to a wide range of possible solutions (for example, divergent thinkers are able to come up with nontraditional uses for common objects like a brick). Other psychologists suggest that a second factor that influences or is associated with creativity is attitudinal or personality-related. Specifically, they argue that a creative individual has a personality (or adopts an attitude) that lends itself to adventure, risk, open-mindedness, curiosity, passionate involvement, and so on (pp. 461-62).

4. Researchers have examined sex differences in three different areas; namely, verbal abilities, mathematical abilities, and spatial abilities. To date, the research indicates that (1) on verbal tests, girls tend to outperform boys (but the gender gap is decreasing); (2) on mathematical tests, girls outperform boys in grade school, but boys and men outperform girls and women in later grades and college; (3) on spatial tests, males tend to outperform females, and this is the most robust sex difference (pp. 473-74).

Researchers point to both nature (biology) and nurture (environment) in attempting to explain the difference in spatial performance. On the biological side of the debate, some speculate that sex differences in spatial skill stem from prenatal exposure to testosterone, which presumably enhances the growth of the right hemisphere (the side of the brain associated with spatial ability). Since male fetuses are exposed to greater amounts of testosterone than female fetuses, this is hypothesized to explain the sex difference in test scores. On the environmental side, some theorists point to assumptions and stereotypes about males and females (e.g., the notion that math is a "boy" thing), to differential treatment by parents and teachers of boys and girls (e.g., girls might receive less encouragement to take math and science courses and to excel in spatial tasks), and to different childhood experiences (e.g., "masculine" toys, like action-oriented video games and construction sets, tend to demand spatial skills more than "feminine" toys). Both influences probably are at work (p. 474).

5. Giftedness has been defined in a variety of ways. For example, Terman (one of the first researchers to study gifted individuals over time) selected participants according to their IQ scores (over 135). Today, giftedness is viewed in broader terms. Some researchers propose that it is a combination of above-average intelligence, task commitment, and creativity, whereas others maintain that giftedness is specific to a particular domain (so one could be a gifted musician, but not necessarily gifted in other areas) (pp. 475-76).

The expression does not appear to an accurate description of gifted persons. Specifically, although there are of course examples of extremely bright children who become social misfits and eccentric outcasts, the largest longitudinal study of gifted children conducted to date (by Terman), revealed that most high IQ children developed into healthy, well-adjusted, successful adults (p. 475).

13 Social Influences

Chapter Overview

This chapter explores some of the major topics in the field of social psychology. The first topic, social perception, concerns how people form impressions of others and how they make attributions, or draw conclusions, about the causes of others' behavior. For example, your author considers how observers try to determine whether another person's behavior is caused by personal factors or by situational factors. Next, the text examines several of the biases that cloud our judgment and prevent us from viewing other people accurately (e.g., self-serving biases, primacy effect, behavioral confirmation). The chapter then focuses on interpersonal attraction and two of the basic factors that influence our feelings of liking for others; namely, similarity and physical attractiveness. Factors that influence (and often bias) social perception in the courtroom are also presented. The second part of the chapter considers the topic of social influence. Conformity and obedience, and the variables that act to increase or decrease these types of social influence, are examined. The chapter then turns to a discussion of attitudes and the process of attitude change (called persuasion). The two cognitive routes to persuasion are discussed, as are the various source, message, and audience factors that influence attitude change. This section concludes by considering the topic of self-persuasion (attitude change that is brought about by our own attitude-discrepant behavior). The next part of the chapter concerns group processes, including social facilitation, social loafing, and groupthink. The final section involves the topic of social relations, evenly divided between aggression and altruism (prosocial or helping behavior). Each social behavior is defined, theories about its origin are presented, and the factors that increase or decrease the likelihood of its occurrence are identified and discussed.

Chapter Outline

I. *What's Your Prediction?* How Far Can People Be Pushed?

II. Social Perception

    A. Making Attributions
        1. Attribution theory

2. The fundamental attribution error
3. Self-serving attributions

B. Forming Impressions
    1. Cognitive-confirmation biases
    2. Behavioral-confirmation biases

C. *Psychology and . . . Law* Biases in Jury Decision Making

D. Attraction
    1. Similarity and liking
    2. Physical attractiveness

III. Social Influence

A. Conformity
    1. The early classics
    2. Majority influence
    3. Minority influence
    4. Obedience to authority

B. Attitudes and Attitude Change
    1. Persuasive communications
        a. The source
        b. The message
        c. The audience
    2. Self-persuasion
        a. Cognitive-dissonance theory
        b. Alternative routes to self-persuasion

C. Group Processes
    1. Social facilitation
    2. Social loafing
    3. Groupthink

D. *Psychology and . . . Sports* The Trouble with Supportive Audiences

IV. Social Relations

A. Aggression
    1. Biological roots
    2. Aversive stimulation
    3. Situational cues
        a. Weapons
        b. Media violence
    4. Deindividuation

B. *Psychology and . . . the Environment* Population Density, Architecture, and Social Behavior

C. Altruism
   1. The altruism debate
   2. Bystander intervention

V. The Big Picture

Learning Objectives

By the time you have read and reviewed this chapter, you should be able to:

1. Define social psychology and consider the topics of interest to social psychologists (p. 487).

2. Explain the concept of social perception (p. 488).

3. Distinguish between personal and situational attributions (p. 488). Discuss Kelley's theory and how people make attributions based on consensus, distinctiveness, and consistency information (pp. 488-89).

4. Define and provide an example of the fundamental attribution error (p. 490). Consider Gilbert's cognitive explanation for why people fall prey to the fundamental attribution error (p. 491). Discuss just how "fundamental" this error is, using cross-cultural research to support your argument (p. 491).

5. Provide examples of and explain the purpose of self-serving attributions (p. 491).

6. Discuss the process of forming an impression of another person (p. 491). Consider the cognitive- and behavioral-confirmation biases that affect the process of impression formation (pp. 492-93).

7. Define the primacy effect and consider two reasons for the occurrence of this effect (p. 492).

8. Discuss the three-step process of behavioral confirmation or self-fulfilling prophecy (p. 493).

9. Discuss three sources of bias in the legal system (i.e., pretrial publicity, inadmissible evidence, and physical attractiveness of the defendant) (pp. 494-95).

10. Explain the relationship between similarity and interpersonal attraction (pp. 495-96). Define the mere-exposure effect (p. 496).

11. Consider the role that physical attractiveness plays in interpersonal attraction (pp. 496-99). Explain what is meant by the term "physical attractiveness" (p. 497). Discuss the origins of this bias for beauty (p. 498).

12. Define conformity (p. 500) and explain the method and results of Sherif's classic study of conformity (pp. 500-1). Distinguish between informational and normative social influence and consider the relation between these forms of social influence and conformity (p. 501).

13. Identify the situational factors (i.e., group size, presence of an ally, salience of social norms, culture) that increase or decrease majority influence (pp. 502-3).

14. Consider factors that affect minority influence (pp. 503-4).

15. Discuss Milgram's classic study on obedience—explain the procedure that he used and his results (pp. 504-5). Consider three factors (i.e., authority status, victim proximity, situation) that affect obedience (p. 505).

16. Define the concept of attitude and consider ways to change attitudes (p. 506). Compare the central and the peripheral route to persuasion (p. 506).

17. Discuss how persuasion is affected by features associated with the source, the message, and the audience (pp. 507-9).

18. Consider the ways in which attitude-inconsistent behavior may produce attitude change (pp. 509-11). Explain the concept of cognitive dissonance and how this state might lead to attitude change (pp. 509-11). Examine alternative routes to self-persuasion (p. 511).

19. Explain the phenomenon of social facilitation (p. 512) and compare the mere-presence, evaluation, and distraction explanations for this occurrence (p. 512).

20. Define social loafing, explain why it occurs, and examine the conditions that reduce social loafing (p. 514).

21. Define groupthink, describe the three behavioral symptoms of groupthink, and consider ways to prevent groupthink (pp. 514-15).

22. Explain the difference between density and crowding (p. 517). Examine the association between crowding and density and personal, cultural, and architectural factors (pp. 517-18).

23. Define aggression (p. 516) and consider the biological (pp. 516, 518) and situational (pp. 518-22) factors that influence aggression. Explain the frustration-aggression hypothesis (p. 519). Consider how weapons and media violence may influence aggressive behavior (pp. 520-21). Define the concept of deindividuation and explain how this state may promote aggressive behavior (pp. 521-22).

24. Define altruism (p. 522) and consider the altruism debate (pp. 523-24). Explain Batson's empathy-altruism hypothesis (pp. 523-24). Consider the bystander effect (p. 525) and analyze the intervention process (pp. 525-26). Identify the factors that predict when helping behavior is most likely to occur (p. 526).

Key Terms

The following key terms and concepts are featured in this chapter and are important for you to know. Write out definitions of each term and check your answers with the definitions in the text on the pages listed.

Social psychology (p. 487)
Social perception (p. 488)
Attribution theory (p. 488)
Fundamental attribution error (p. 490)
Primacy effect (p. 492)
Mere-exposure effect (p. 496)
Conformity (p. 500)
Informational influence (p. 501)
Normative influence (p. 501)
Attitude (p. 506)
Central route to persuasion (p. 506)
Peripheral route to persuasion (p. 506)

Cognitive dissonance (p. 509)
Social facilitation (p. 512)
Social loafing (p. 514)
Groupthink (p. 514)
Aggression (p. 516)
Frustration-aggression hypothesis (p. 519)
Deindividuation (p. 522)
Altruism (p. 522)
Empathy-altruism hypothesis (p. 523)
Bystander effect (p. 525)
Diffusion of responsibility (p. 526)

Multiple-Choice Questions

Circle the correct choice for each question and compare your answers with those at the end of the Study Guide chapter.

1. _____ is the study of how individuals come to understand and evaluate other people.
   A. Social cognition
   B. Social perception
   C. Self-perception
   D. Self-cognition

2. Your romantic partner forgot your birthday. She/he claims that work has been so busy that the big event just slipped her/his mind. You suspect that your partner was simply being lazy and irresponsible. You are making a _____ attribution for this unforgivable behavior; your partner is making a _____ attribution.
   A. situational; situational
   B. personal; situational
   C. personal; personal
   D. situational; personal

3. According to Kelley's attribution theory, people seek different types of information when explaining the behavior of others, including _____.
   A. consensus information
   B. consistency information
   C. distinctiveness information
   D. All of the above

4. When consensus and distinctiveness are _____ and consistency is _____, people tend to make stimulus attributions.
   A. high; low
   B. low; high
   C. high; high
   D. low; low

5. The fundamental attribution error is the tendency to overattribute a person's behavior to _____ causes and to underestimate the importance of _____ causes.
   A. personal; situational
   B. internal; personal
   C. stimulus; situational
   D. distinctive; consistent

6. During a research meeting, a professor praises a student at great length. Which of the following conclusions that you might draw illustrates the fundamental attribution error?
   A. "The professor behaved that way because she truly appreciates her students."
   B. "The professor behaved that way because the student sucked up to her."
   C. "The professor behaved that way because the student deserved praise."
   D. "The professor behaved that way because other professors told her to be nice to students."

7. You notice your friend Harold helping an elderly woman load groceries into her car. According to the two-step attribution process outlined by social psychologists Gilbert and Malone (1995), which of the following inferences will you <u>first</u> make when trying to understand the causes of Harold's behavior?
   A. "Harold helped the woman because he is a really kind person."
   B. "Harold helped the woman because he is really kind and also because the woman asked him for assistance."
   C. "Harold helped the woman because she asked him for assistance."
   D. "There is no way to tell why Harold helped the woman."

8. A _____ effect occurs when early information about a person has a stronger impact on perceivers' impressions than later information.
   A. recency
   B. primacy
   C. situational
   D. dispositional

9. The behavioral-confirmation cycle can be broken if
   A. the perceiver is motivated to form an accurate impression.
   B. the perceiver attends closely to his or her interaction with the target.
   C. the target becomes aware of the perceiver's expectations.
   D. All of the above

10. Nicole sees the same dog every day on her way to work. Although she initially paid little attention to him, she finds that she misses the dog when his owners move away. Nicole's feelings for the dog reflect the _____.
    A. bias for beauty
    B. fundamental attribution error
    C. mere exposure effect
    D. interpersonal attraction effect

11. According to Byrne and his colleagues, when we meet someone for the first time we focus on _____, and then later we take into account _____.
    A. similarity; similarity
    B. similarity; dissimilarity
    C. dissimilarity; similarity
    D. dissimilarity; dissimilarity

12. Based on research examining physical attractiveness, which one of the following men will be rated as most attractive?
    A. Brian, who has extremely unusual, distinctive features
    B. Trevor, who has average features
    C. Tom, who has features that resemble a famous celebrity
    D. Glen, who has childlike features

13. One explanation that has been proposed to explain the preference for physically attractive people is that
    A. it is rewarding to be in the company of beautiful others.
    B. we associate beauty with other desirable qualities.
    C. beautiful others also tend to be intelligent and well-adjusted.
    D. A and B

14. Possible sources of bias in the court system include
    A. jurors' exposure to pretrial publicity.
    B. jurors' exposure to inadmissible evidence.
    C. the physical attractiveness of the defendant.
    D. All of the above

15. Irena usually does not drink. However, when she is at a campus party, she notices that all her friends seem to be drinking. As a result, she begins to drink. Irena's behavior illustrates _____.
    A. conformity
    B. pressure
    C. dissonance
    D. obedience

16. North is debating between signing up for math or geology. His sister tells him, "Oh, take the math course. The professors in the math department are pretty good." North knows that his sister has taken both math and geology courses, and so he decides to follow her advice and sign up for math. North's decision is based upon _____.
    A. normative social influence
    B. informational social influence
    C. obedience
    D. social pressure

17. People sometimes conform to normative social influence because _____.
    A. they believe that others have information that they themselves lack
    B. they fear the social rejection that might follow nonconforming behavior
    C. they are high self-monitors
    D. they are immoral

18. People sometimes conform to informational social influence because _____.
    A. they are not certain that their own views are accurate
    B. past experience has shown them that nonconformity will be punished by other group members
    C. they believe that they can sway the opinions of group members later
    D. they fear social rejection

19. A factor that influences conformity is
    A. the size of the majority.
    B. whether the dissenter has an ally.
    C. the salience of group norms.
    D. All of the above

20. Which one of the following statements best describes the significance of the Milgram obedience experiments?
    A. Most people enjoy harming others.
    B. Social forces can strongly influence human behavior.
    C. Society is to blame for all criminal behavior.
    D. Only deviant or psychotic people aggress against others.

21. Ed is watching a commercial on television for a diet soda. He sees handsome men and beautiful women drinking the soda and having a fun time together. Ed decides to buy some of that diet soda the next time he goes shopping. Ed has been persuaded via the

    _____.
    A. central route   C. peripheral route
    B. attitude route   D. dissonance route

22. The _____ route to persuasion takes place when people think carefully about the content of the persuasive message.
    A. central   C. peripheral
    B. medium   D. cognitive

23. While shopping for toothpaste, Gwen sees a printed advertisement featuring Dr. Knowsalot, an expert in the area of dental hygiene. Gwen will be most persuaded by the message if she thinks that Dr. Knowsalot _____.
    A. has ulterior motives for giving this message
    B. is trustworthy
    C. is being deceptive
    D. received a nice, fat fee for doing this advertisement

24. Strong fear appeals are most effective when _____.
    A. they create extreme distress in the audience
    B. they create no distress in the audience
    C. they are accompanied by precise recommendations for actions to avoid the danger
    D. they are accompanied by additional fear-producing arguments and graphic images

25. A company has created an image-oriented clothing commercial featuring attractive people wearing expensive, designer clothing. Which person will be the most persuaded by this commercial?
    A. Mark, a high self-monitor
    B. Amy, a low self-monitor
    C. Saul, who has a high need for cognition
    D. B and C

26. Cognitive dissonance is a state of _____.
    A. physical illness
    B. mental disorder
    C. psychological tension
    D. brain activity

27. Research on the social facilitation effect demonstrates that higher arousal leads to _____ performance when tasks are difficult and _____ performance when tasks are easy or well-learned.
    A. decreased; increased
    B. increased; decreased
    C. decreased; decreased
    D. increased; increased

28. The decrease in individual effort that occurs when people engage in shared group activity is called _____.
    A. deindividuation
    B. social facilitation
    C. laziness
    D. social loafing

29. Which of the following factors are implicated in producing aggression?
    A. temperature
    B. the presence of a weapon
    C. media violence
    D. All of the above

30. John is walking to work one day when he sees an elderly man stumble and fall to the sidewalk. There are many other people present, but no one stops to help. John also does not stop. John's behavior may reflect _____.
    A. prosocial behavior
    B. aggression
    C. diffusion of responsibility
    D. egocentricity

True-False Questions

Indicate which of the following statements are true or false, and compare your answers with those at the end of the chapter.

T F   1. People often use "mental shortcuts" when forming impressions of others.

T F   2. The fundamental attribution error occurs mostly in Western cultures.

T F   3. Once people form an impression, they often interpret later information in light of that first impression.

T F   4. As a general rule, opposites attract.

T F   5. Credibility and likability are the keys to being a persuasive communicator.

T F   6. People are easier to persuade when they are in a good mood.

T F   7. Attitude-discrepant behavior can produce attitude change.

T F   8. On easy tasks, the presence of others does not affect our performance.

T F   9. Aggression is not subject to biological influences.

T F 10. Helping is more likely to occur when the bystander observes another person helping.

Key Concepts Matching Exercises

Exercise #1: Conformity

Stanley has agreed to participate in a psychology study in exchange for extra course credit. Upon arriving at the lab, he is seated in a room with other "participants" (actually trained confederates). He and the other participants are asked to indicate which of three comparison circles is identical in size to a standard circle—an easy task, to be certain. Specifically:

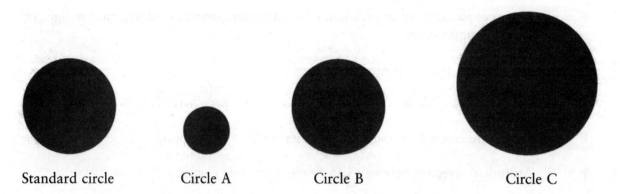

| Standard circle | Circle A | Circle B | Circle C |

The answer is clear—Circle B. To Stanley's surprise, however, the other participants provide the same patently incorrect answer—Circle A. Assume that the experimenter is interested in the influence of group size on conformity, and assume that Stanley has been randomly assigned to participate with a certain number of confederates. Research suggests that the pressure Stanley feels to conform, and his actual level of conformity, will increase dramatically as the number of confederates grows to _____, and then will level off.

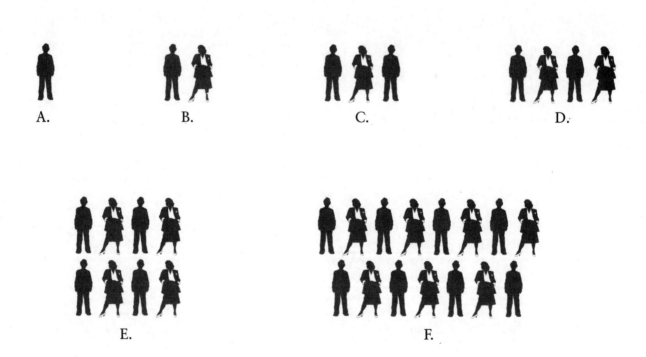

Exercise #2: Two Routes to Persuasion

Indicate which of the items listed on the right will induce attitude change via the central route or the peripheral route.

_____ 1. Central Route

_____ 2. Peripheral Route

A. Attractiveness of source
B. Quality of message arguments
C. Strength of message arguments
D. Emotional response by target audience
E. High involvement by target audience
F. High ability to think critically about message by target audience
G. Reaction of others to message

Exercise #3: The Helping Decision Tree

Latané and Darley provided a step-by-step analysis of the decision-making process that bystanders go through when faced with an emergency situation. Match the statements on the right with the appropriate step in that process.

_____ Step 1

_____ Step 2

_____ Step 3

_____ Step 4

_____ Step 5

A. "That's it, I've decided—I'm going to help that kid."
B. "Hey, what was that? I think I heard a scream."
C. "I wonder why no one else is helping? Maybe I should be the one to help."
D. "Here I come, kid—give me your hand and I'll pull you up!"
E. "Oh my gosh, that kid needs help!"

Essay Questions

Write out answers to the following brief essay questions. Compare your responses with the sample answers at the end of the Study Guide chapter.

1. Define and give an example of the fundamental attribution error. What might explain why this error occurs? Exactly how "fundamental" is the fundamental attribution error?

2. What is the primacy effect? What two reasons explain why this effect occurs?

3. Nancy recently joined the psychology club at her college. She disagrees with one of the club's policies, and wishes to change the majority support for this policy. What should she do to sway the majority?

4. Lena is the senior partner of a large computer company. Due to recent financial developments, she feels that the company needs to reallocate resources from one area to another. She also feels that the company may need to reduce the number of employees. Lena schedules a meeting with the other partners to discuss these possibilities. Define groupthink,

outline its behavioral features, and discuss three procedures Lena and the other partners can use to reduce the likelihood of groupthink.

5. Buddy is out walking his dog when he sees a woman on rollerblades lose her footing and fall to the ground. List the five decision-making points that Buddy must cognitively traverse in determining whether to help the fallen rollerblader. Assuming that other people are present, how might this affect whether Buddy helps the woman?

Multimedia Study Resources

Several activities and articles in Chapter 16 (Social Psychology: The Individual in Psychology) of The Psychology Place™ supplement the material covered in your textbook. For example, one Learning Activity allows you to examine gangs (e.g., how social psychologists define the concept of gang, what typically motivates individuals to join gangs, the association between gang membership and crime). In addition, a number of activities are provided, including the design of a program to reduce gang involvement. The Op Ed Forum provides the opportunity to consider whether capital punishment actually deters crime, or whether it increases it ("A Psychologist Looks at the Death Penalty").

Test Solutions

Multiple-Choice Solutions

1. B (p. 488)	11. C (p. 496)	21. C (p. 506)
2. B (p. 488)	12. B (p. 497)	22. A (p. 506)
3. D (pp. 488-89)	13. D (p. 498)	23. B (p. 507)
4. C (p. 489)	14. D (pp. 494-95)	24. C (p. 508)
5. A (p. 490)	15. A (p. 500)	25. A (p. 509)
6. A (p. 490)	16. B (p. 501)	26. C (pp. 509-10)
7. A (p. 491)	17. B (p. 501)	27. A (p. 512)
8. B (p. 492)	18. A (p. 501)	28. D (p. 514)
9. D (p. 493)	19. D (pp. 502-3)	29. D (pp. 519-21)
10. C (p. 496)	20. B (p. 505)	30. C (p. 526)

True-False Solutions

1. T (p. 489)	6. T (p. 508)
2. T (p. 491)	7. T (pp. 509-11)
3. T (p. 492)	8. F (p. 512)
4. F (pp. 495-96)	9. F (p. 516)
5. T (p. 507)	10. T (p. 526)

Key Concepts Matching Solutions

Exercise #1

1. D

Exercise #2

1. B, C, E, F
2. A, D, G

Exercise #3

1. B
2. E
3. C
4. A
5. D

Essay Solutions

1. The fundamental attribution error is the tendency to overattribute other people's behavior to personal causes, and the failure to recognize the importance of situational causes (p. 490). An example might be when you assume that your roommate's lateness in paying his or her share of the rent is due to his or her innate stinginess and irresponsibility, rather than to the fact that he or she had other more pressing financial concerns.

   The fundamental attribution error might occur as a result of the basic two-step process that perceivers follow when making an attribution. Gilbert argues, for example, that perceivers first identify the behavior and then make an immediate personal attribution, and then correct or adjust this personal attribution by taking situational causes into account. The first step is simple and automatic; the second requires attention, thought, and effort. Anything that prevents attention or impedes thought will prevent the second step from occurring, and perceivers will rely on the initial personal attribution (p. 491).

   The fundamental attribution error is not as fundamental as theorists originally assumed. Specifically, it appears to occur or be most pervasive in cultures that emphasize the person over the situation (i.e., that view individuals as autonomous and responsible for their own behaviors). Non-Western cultures that commonly take a more holistic, collective view that focuses on the relationship between individuals and their social roles are less prone to the fundamental attribution error (p. 491).

2. The primacy effect refers to the finding that people are influenced more by information that they receive early in an interaction than by information that appears later (p. 492). This effect occurs for two reasons. First, we become less attentive to later behavioral evidence once we have already formed an impression (perhaps out of fatigue or boredom); if we are alert and/or motivated, this bias is diminished. Second, once we form an impression, we interpret subsequent information in light of that initial impression (this is called the change-of-meaning hypothesis); so any new information merely bolsters the first impression, because it is interpreted in line with that impression (pp. 492-93).

3. Research on minority influence suggests that Nancy should state her case and stick to her position in a persistent, unwavering, and self-confident manner. This technique of minority influence may be effective in changing the opinions of the majority because it creates a conflict that prevents the smooth functioning of the group. This, in turn, may cause the majority to rethink its position and eventually be swayed by the minority's (by Nancy's) position (pp. 503-4).

4. Groupthink is a type of thinking in which group members share such a strong motivation to achieve consensus that they lose the ability to critically evaluate alternative points of view. Basically, they convince themselves that their policies are correct (p. 514).

Groupthink's defining symptoms are (1) an overestimation by the group of its own capacity (for example, members may harbor an illusion of invulnerability to error, fall prey to an illusion of unanimity, and hold an exaggerated belief that the group's views are moral, just, or right); (2) closed-mindedness (the group members rationalize their own actions and stereotype the targets of those actions); and (3) increased pressure toward uniformity and conformity (for example, members self-censor their thoughts and function as "mind guards" who protect the group from divergent or contradictory information) (p. 515).

There are a number of ways to prevent the occurrence of groupthink. First, Lena and the other partners could avoid isolation and increase the quality and quantity of information available to the group (perhaps by inviting experts who represent a wide divergence of views to participate in the group's deliberations). Second, to reduce conformity pressures, Lena (in her role as group leader) might encourage criticism from the other members and might refrain from voicing an opinion in the early stages of group discussion. Third, the group can establish a norm of critical review (perhaps someone could play "devil's advocate," and the group could hold later meetings once a tentative decision has been reached in order to air any remaining doubts or provide subsequent information that members have) (p. 515).

5. According to Latané and Darley's (1970) analysis of the decision-making process in emergency situations, Buddy must (1) notice the incident, (2) interpret the incident as an emergency, (3) take responsibility for helping the fallen rollerblader, (4) decide to intervene, and (5) act on his decision (p. 525). The presence of others can inhibit helping at each of these five stages. For example, if he sees the woman fall and also sees that others are not reacting, he may interpret the incident as a nonemergency (step 2). In addition, the presence of others may lead to diffusion of responsibility, which is the belief that others will intervene; assuming that others will help, he may not take responsibility (step 3) (pp. 525-26).

14 Social and Cultural Groups

Chapter Overview

This chapter expands upon the previous chapter by exploring the ways in which people are influenced by their own culture and the situations in which they find themselves. First, your author considers how the human population is distributed cross-culturally and examines how the implicit rules of conduct (called social norms) may differ across cultures. Then, the chapter discusses differences in the extent to which cultures value individualism or collectivism, and the origins of these orientations. The development and the personal (e.g., self-concept) and social consequences of these different cultural orientations also are addressed. Next, the chapter turns to the topic of multiculturalism, including immigration, the acculturation process, and how immigrants form and maintain an ethnic identity. Gender—the ways in which men and women are similar and different, the biological and social origins of gender differences, and common gender stereotypes—then is explored. This section ends with a consideration of the challenges that face women as they move into a workplace that traditionally has been populated by men. The next part of the chapter concerns prejudice. This concept is defined, and its cognitive basis (including how stereotypes are formed and the process of social categorization) and motivational foundation (including realistic-conflict theory and social-identity theory) are discussed. The chapter concludes with a consideration of modern racism in America, and with an exploration of the various methods that social psychologists have used to reduce racism.

Chapter Outline

C. Individualism and Collectivism: A Tale of Two Cultural Worldviews
    1. Conceptions of the self
    2. Developmental influences
    3. The social consequences

III. Multicultural Perspectives

    A. Ethnic Diversity: A Fact of Life

    B. Acculturation and Ethnic Identity

IV. Gender: The Great Divide?

    A. How Are Men and Women Different?

    B. Why Are Men and Women Different?
        1. Biological perspectives
        2. Environmental perspectives
            a. Gender roles
            b. Gender stereotypes
            c. Social roots of sex differences

    C. *Psychology and . . . Business* Women in the Workplace

    D. Putting Sex Differences in Perspective

V. Prejudice

    A. The Cognitive Roots
        1. How stereotypes are formed
        2. Is stereotyping inevitable?

    B. The Motivational Roots
        1. Realistic conflict theory
        2. Social identity theory

    C. Racism in America
        1. The problem
        2. The symptoms
        3. The treatment

    D. *Psychology and . . . Education* Using Schools to Combat Racism

VI. The Big Picture

Learning Objectives

By the time you have read and reviewed this chapter, you should be able to:

1. Consider the numerous ways in which all people are similar, and some of the ways in which each person is unique (pp. 534-35).

2. Discuss how the world's population is distributed geographically (p. 536), and the ways in which social norms differ across cultures (pp. 538-40).

3. Distinguish between individualism and collectivism (p. 541), and discuss three key factors (i.e., complexity, affluence, and heterogeneity) that influence the development of these cultural orientations (pp. 541-42).

4. Consider how the cultural orientations of individualism and collectivism can influence the ways in which people view themselves and others (pp. 542-44).

5. Discuss the culturally prescribed socialization practices that foster individualism or collectivism (pp. 544-45).

6. Consider the social consequences of having an individualist or collectivist orientation (p. 545).

7. Describe sources of ethnic diversity within a culture (e.g., immigration). Explain the process of acculturation (p. 548) and the development of an ethnic identity (p. 549). Define the concepts of acculturative stress (p. 549) and discrimination (p. 550).

8. Consider how men and women are different, biologically and psychologically (pp. 552-54).

9. Consider the biological basis of psychological differences between men and women (pp. 554-55).

10. Explore the social/environmental basis of the same gender differences (pp. 555-61). Distinguish between gender roles and gender schemas (p. 556).

11. Describe gender stereotypes and how they influence the ways in which boys and girls are perceived and socialized (p. 557). Consider whether there is a "kernel of truth" to gender stereotypes (p. 557). Use social-role theory to explain the persistence of gender stereotypes (pp. 557-58). Consider the social origins of sex differences (pp. 558-61). In what ways are men and women similar? (p. 561).

12. Discuss sex differences in the workplace and gender gaps in positions of leadership (p. 559). Explain the possible origins of the gender gap in leadership positions (pp. 559-60).

13. Define prejudice (p. 561) and consider the extent to which prejudice is a product of the beliefs we hold (stereotypes) and the way we think (social categorization, outgroup-homogeneity bias) (pp. 562-63).

14. Define the concept of stereotype and discuss how the formation of stereotypes involves two related processes (p. 562). Explain how the process of social categorization contributes to the outgroup-homogeneity bias (p. 562).

15. Discuss the consequences of using stereotypes (pp. 562-63). Consider whether stereotypes can be automatically activated (p. 563) and the factors the increase or decrease the likelihood that we will rely on stereotypes when evaluating others (p. 563).

16. Consider how prejudice and stereotypes are a function of the way we feel about a social group and our need to perceive that group in a particular manner (p. 564). Describe the two major motivational theories of prejudice (pp. 564-65).

17. Describe realistic conflict theory (p. 564).

18. Describe social identity theory and explain how this theory accounts for ingroup favoritism in the absence of realistic conflict (pp. 564-66).

19. Define racism (p. 566) and consider the methods psychologists use to detect racist beliefs (pp. 568-69).

20. Explain the contact hypothesis and the conditions that are necessary for contact to change racist beliefs (p. 570).

Key Terms

The following key terms and concepts are featured in this chapter and are important for you to know. Write out definitions of each term and check your answers with the definitions in the text on the pages listed.

Social norms (p. 538)	Social-role theory (pp. 557-58)
Individualism (p. 541)	Prejudice (p. 561)
Collectivism (p. 541)	Stereotype (p. 562)
Multicultural research (p. 547)	Social categorization (p. 562)
Acculturation (p. 548)	Outgroup-homogeneity bias (p. 562)
Ethnic identity (p. 549)	Realistic conflict theory (p. 564)
Acculturative stress (p. 549)	Ingroup favoritism (p. 565)
Discrimination (p. 550)	Social identity theory (p. 565)
Gender roles (p. 556)	Racism (p. 566)
Gender schemas (p. 556)	Contact hypothesis (p. 570)

Test Questions

Multiple-Choice Questions

Circle the correct choice for each question and compare your answers with those at the end of the Study Guide chapter.

1. Individualistic cultures value traits associated with _____.
    A. cooperation
    B. independence
    C. social harmony
    D. interdependence

2. A collectivist culture tends to value characteristics and behaviors associated with
_____.
   A. autonomy
   B. self-reliance
   C. cooperation
   D. independence

3. Individualism is to lone wolf as collectivism is to _____.
   A. all-star
   B. national hero
   C. lame duck
   D. team player

4. Some psychologists speculate that there are a number of key factors that influence a culture's orientation toward individualism or collectivism, including
   A. complexity.
   B. affluence.
   C. heterogeneity.
   D. All of the above

5. Societies that are _____ tend to have a collectivist orientation.
   A. homogeneous
   B. highly industrialized
   C. financially prosperous
   D. All of the above

6. Parent A is from a collectivist culture. Parent B is from an individualistic culture. When asked to describe the characteristics that she/he would like her/his child to develop, Parent A is likely to say _____; Parent B is likely to say _____.
   A. tolerance of others; family loyalty
   B. loyalty; cooperation
   C. strict obedience; independence
   D. independence; tolerance of others

7. Jane is from an individualistic culture; Bibiana is from a collectivist culture. When asked, Jane is likely to describe herself as _____ and Bibiana is likely to describe herself as _____.
   A. shy; intelligent
   B. friendly; a college student
   C. a college student; shy
   D. a woman; a banker

8. One day while shopping, you enter a bookstore. As you browse through the racks, you come across the pop psychology section. Assuming that you are in a collectivist culture, what title might you expect to see?
   A. "Uncovering Your Hidden Potential"
   B. "How to Get Along With Others"
   C. "How to Speak Your Mind"
   D. "Learning How to Stand Out From the Crowd"

9. People tend to demonstrate lower levels of _____ in collectivist cultures than in individualistic cultures.
   A. emotionality
   B. conformity
   C. productivity
   D. social loafing

10. Dr. Phinney is interested in issues of race and ethnicity. Her program of research, called _____, concerns the study of racial and ethnic groups within a particular culture.
    A. multicultural research
    B. intracultural research
    C. cross-cultural research
    D. pluralistic field research

11. Cathy recently moved to Spain. Although she was born in America and is of Western European ancestry, she has thrown herself completely into her new culture. She speaks Spanish, follows the local customs, and eats only traditional Spanish foods. Cathy is using the acculturation strategy of _____.
    A. separation
    B. assimilation
    C. integration
    D. marginalization

12. Chris also recently moved to Spain. Unlike Cathy, however, he continues to speak his native English tongue, chooses not to follow the local customs, and continues to eat "American" food. Chris is using the acculturation strategy of _____.
    A. separation
    B. assimilation
    C. integration
    D. marginalization

13. Ethnic identify formation typically begins in _____ with an acceptance of the dominant culture, and is followed by a later awakening of interest in one's own ethnic roots.
    A. infancy
    B. adolescence
    C. middle adulthood
    D. old age

14. Signs or symptoms of acculturative stress include
    A. anxiety.
    B. depression.
    C. guilt feelings.
    D. All of the above

15. Ruben recently moved to the United States from Mexico. Although he is doing well at his new job and planning on taking the citizenship exam, he frequently feels anxious and guilty about leaving his family behind in Mexico. Lately, he has been having difficulty falling asleep at night. Ruben may be experiencing _____.
    A. culture calamity
    B. multicultural malaise
    C. acculturative stress
    D. biculturation blues

16. Research on the members of other cultures who move to the United States suggests that those who _____ experience the least acculturative stress.
    A. identify with their own culture and reject American culture
    B. identify with American culture and reject their own culture
    C. identify with American culture and their own culture
    D. reject both American culture and their own culture and embrace a non-culture, solo status

17. Psychologists have found robust evidence for which of the following?
    A. Men and women are equally aggressive.
    B. Men are more likely than women to perceive eye contact as a sign of sexual interest.
    C. Women typically outperform men on tasks involving spatial reasoning.
    D. Men generally outperform women on tasks involving verbal fluency.

18. Men with low levels of testosterone often report _____.
    A. decreased sexual desire
    B. increased physiological arousal
    C. visual problems
    D. increased feelings of hostility

19. Children can learn about gender roles from _____.
    A. parents
    B. television
    C. teachers and other adults
    D. All of the above

20. The beliefs that men are "independent and adventurous" and that women are "nurturant and emotional" reflect
    A. gender stereotypes.
    B. gender sociotypes.
    C. social norms.
    D. sex schemas.

21. Research on the "kernel of truth" hypothesis suggests that
    A. existing gender stereotypes are highly accurate.
    B. the actual differences between men and women are much larger than is suggested by the stereotypes of those differences.
    C. stereotypes about gender differences may be stronger than the differences themselves.
    D. existing gender stereotypes are completely and totally inaccurate.

22. Social-role theory suggests that our beliefs about the differences between men and women
    A. are based on real differences between the sexes.
    B. are the result of the unequal social roles occupied by men and women.
    C. develop during early infancy.
    D. are the direct result of cultural brainwashing that occurs during adolescence.

23. Research suggests that _____ will be liked the *least* by his or her subordinates.
    A. Cindy, who has a directive, task-oriented leadership style and who works in an investment firm
    B. Howie, who has a directive, task-oriented leadership style and who works in an investment firm
    C. Julie, who has a nondirective, person-oriented leadership style and who works in a daycare center
    D. Jim, who has a directive, task-oriented leadership style and who works in a daycare center

24. Thomas learns that Sally Jones is the name of the new company president. His first response to this information is, "Oh great, a woman president. I just know I'm going to hate working for her—in fact, I don't like her already. Why can't the company hire a man?" Thomas's response reflects _____.
    A. schemas
    B. discrimination
    C. stereotypes
    D. prejudice

25. Carla learns about the new company president the same time that Thomas does. "Yes, but she'll probably be easy to work with—it'll be great to have that feminine touch around the office, don't you think? We could sure use someone who is warm and nurturant—that last one was so darn assertive and rude." Carla's response reflects _____.
   A. discrimination
   B. stereotypes
   C. prejudice
   D. attitudes

26. Lori is homosexual and she views her homosexual friends as distinct and unique individuals. However, she assumes that all heterosexuals are the same. Lori's thinking reflects the _____.
   A. ingroup heterogeneity bias
   B. outgroup-homogeneity bias
   C. ingroup-outgroup bias
   D. person positivity bias

27. We are most likely to rely on stereotypes when forming an impression of another person when we are _____.
   A. busy and distracted
   B. mentally tired
   C. in a hurry
   D. All of the above

28. The view that prejudice is the result of direct competition between groups over valued but limited resources is called _____.
   A. competition theory
   B. social deprivation theory
   C. realistic conflict theory
   D. social identity theory

29. Joseph is Jewish and he has a strong sense of ethnic and religious pride. He has just failed a very important exam. According to social identity theory, Joseph will experience _____ attraction to other Jewish people and _____ attraction to nonJewish people.
   A. increased; decreased
   B. decreased; increased
   C. no change in; increased
   D. increased; increased

30. In order for contact between members of different groups to reduce prejudice, the two groups must _____.
   A. be of equal status and share the same goal
   B. be divided into a "leaders" and a "workers" group
   C. have different goals
   D. not personally interact

True-False Questions

Indicate which of the following statements are true or false, and compare your answers with those at the end of the chapter.

T   F   1. There are tremendous variations in the social norms that characterize different cultures.

T   F   2. There appears to be a close link between cultural orientation and the self-concept.

T   F   3. We are socialized to be independent or interdependent almost immediately after birth.

T   F   4. Conformity rates are generally lower in collectivist cultures.

T   F   5. Discrimination is a sin of the past.

T   F   6. Men seem to view the world in "sexualized" terms.

T   F   7. Stereotypes about men and women are much the same across cultures.

T   F   8. Men and women are more alike than they are different.

T   F   9. Stereotypes can be activated without our awareness.

T   F   10. Research indicates that mere contact between members of a majority and minority group effectively can reduce prejudice.

Key Concepts Matching Exercises

Exercise #1: Social and Cultural Groups

Match the key terms on the left with the definitions on the right.

_____ 1. Social norms

_____ 2. Individualism

_____ 3. Collectivism

_____ 4. Multiculturalism

_____ 5. Acculturation

_____ 6. Ethnic identity

_____ 7. Discrimination

_____ 8. Gender roles

_____ 9. Prejudice

_____ 10. Stereotype

_____ 11. Outgroup-homogeneity bias

_____ 12. Realistic-conflict theory

_____ 13. Ingroup favoritism

_____ 14. Social-identity theory

A. "I refuse to rent rooms to unmarried couples."

B. "It makes me feel better to hate you and your kind."

C. "They're all the same, every last one of them."

D. The part of someone's identity that is defined by his or her ethnic heritage

E. The implicit "dos" and "don'ts" that govern behavior in a particular culture

F. "I don't like my new neighbor. He's one of them, and I don't like his kind."

G. "My work involves the study of various racial and ethnic groups in the United States."

H. The notion that prejudice stems from competition over limited resources

I. The tendency to discriminate in favor of "me and mine" over "them and theirs"

J. "Personal glory is more important than group allegiance."

K. Beliefs about the characteristics of the members of particular social groups

L. The process by which individuals are changed by their immersion in a new culture

M. The sex-typed behaviors that are promoted by social learning

N. "Group harmony is more important than individual goals."

Exercise #2: Acculturation

Berry and colleagues (1989) noted that there are four ways in which people can cope with being immersed in a new culture. Match the statements on the right with the appropriate coping strategy.

_____ 1. Assimilation

_____ 2. Integration

_____ 3. Separation

_____ 4. Marginalization

A. "I'll still honor our family traditions and celebrate cultural holidays, but I'll also enjoy the new customs and way of life."

B. "I have no desire to explore my so-called ethnic roots, and I also refuse to be a part of my new host culture."

C. "I refuse to even speak my native tongue; I no longer follow that way of life. I want to fit in with my new host culture."

D. "I would rather live with members of my own culture and continue to follow our ethnic traditions. I do not consider myself part of the larger culture."

Essay Questions

Write out answers to the following brief essay questions. Compare your responses with the sample answers at the end of the Study Guide chapter.

1. List and describe the three key factors that determine whether a culture is individualistic or collectivistic in orientation.

2. Discuss the possible biological and social basis for the gender difference in visual-spatial performance.

3. What is a stereotype? In what way is stereotyping an adaptive or useful process? In what way is it a maladaptive process?

4. Stereotypes can be automatically activated and can color our judgments of others. Does this mean that we are inevitably "trapped" into using stereotypes when we evaluate others? Why or why not? In other words, what conditions increase or decrease the likelihood of stereotyping?

5. What is the contact hypothesis? What four conditions must be met in order for contact to "work"? Select any social group on your campus whom you feel is the target of prejudice, and discuss (specifically!) how you would use contact to reduce prejudice against this group.

Multimedia Study Resources

Several activities and articles in Chapter 16 (Social Psychology: The Individual in Psychology) of The Psychology Place™ supplement the material covered in your textbook. In particular, an article presented in Research News examines the possibility that positive and negative stereotypes about particular social groups may affect actual performance in testing situations ("How Stereotypes Affect Test Performance"). "Investigating Social Judgments" is a Learning Activity that provides the opportunity to explore personal attitudes and biases that may influence impression formation. And finally, the Op Ed Forum contains a fascinating piece on the "darker side" of culture (e.g., requiring obedience to authority, promoting ethnocentrism), called "Are We Sugarcoating Culture? Thinking Critically About the Study of Diversity."

Multiple-Choice Solutions

1. B (p. 541)	11. B (p. 548)	21. C (p. 557)
2. C (p. 541)	12. A (p. 548)	22. B (pp. 557-58)
3. D (p. 541)	13. B (p. 549)	23. A (p. 559)
4. D (pp. 541-42)	14. D (p. 549)	24. D (p. 561)
5. A (p. 542)	15. C (p. 549)	25. B (p. 562)
6. C (p. 542)	16. C (pp. 549-550)	26. B (p. 562)
7. B (p. 543)	17. B (p. 553)	27. D (p. 563)
8. B (pp. 541-44)	18. A (p. 554)	28. C (p. 564)
9. D (p. 545)	19. D (p. 556)	29. A (pp. 565-66)
10. A (p. 547)	20. A (p. 557)	30. A (p. 570)

True-False Solutions

1. T (p. 538)	6. T (p. 553)
2. T (p. 542)	7. T (p. 557)
3. T (p. 544)	8. T (p. 561)
4. F (p. 545)	9. T (p. 563)
5. F (p. 550)	10. F (p. 570)

Key Concepts Matching Solutions

Exercise #1

1. E
2. J
3. N
4. G
5. L
6. D
7. A
8. M
9. F
10. K
11. C
12. H
13. I
14. B

Exercise #2

1. C
2. A
3. D
4. B

Essay Solutions

1. Triandis (1995) suggests that there are three key factors that determine whether a culture is relatively collectivistic or individualistic in orientation. The first is the complexity of a society. Highly complex, industrialized cultures contain more groups with which individual members can identity (family, hometown, church, school, occupation, political party, etc.). This results in less loyalty to any one group and a greater focus on personal rather than collective goals and concerns. The second factor is the affluence of the society. Individuals in wealthy cultures are more mobile and socially independent than individuals who reside in less affluent cultures; consequently, they are also more independent and less interdependent in orientation. The third factor is heterogeneity. Societies that are heterogeneous (contain many diverse members) tend to be more permissive of difference or dissent, which allows for greater individualism (pp. 541-42).

2. There is some (albeit not entirely convincing) evidence that sex differences in visual-spatial skills are related to hormonal processes. Specifically, some researchers argue that the greater prenatal exposure to testosterone experienced by male fetuses accounts for men's later advantage in spatial tasks (the prenatal testosterone washes over the fetal brain, slowing the development of the left hemisphere, which is associated with language skills, and enhancing the development of the right hemisphere, which is associated with spatial skills) (p. 555).

   There also is evidence that socialization practices and environmental forces may contribute the sex difference in spatial skills. For example, boys receive more encouragement in math than do girls, and parents set higher expectations for their male children on math problems and in math courses. In addition, boys tend to have greater experience than girls with visual-spatial tasks—they are permitted to stray farther from home than girls, and are more likely to use toys and play games that require spatial manipulation. This differential experience has a clear impact on ability—in one experiment, boys and girls who were trained with various toys (e.g., Tinkertoys, dominoes, blocks) scored higher on a spatial test than children who did not receive training (p. 558).

3. A stereotype is a belief that associates a whole group of people with certain traits (p. 562). The process of stereotyping—social categorization—is to some extent adaptive; specifically, stereotypes allow us to make judgments about someone quickly and easily without taking the time to gather individualized information. The problem, of course (and here's where stereotyping can get us into trouble), is that these quick and easy judgments may be grossly inaccurate (p. 562).

4. No, we are not inevitably trapped into using stereotypes when evaluating others. In fact, research suggests that we have some degree of control over whether we rely on social categories when we perceive and form evaluations of others. For example, we are most likely to form an impression based on stereotypes when we are busy or distracted, pressed for time, mentally tired, under the influence of alcohol, or in an extremely positive or negative mood state. This means, of course, that we are less likely to stereotype—and more likely to gather accurate, individuating information about others—when we are mentally alert and motivated to be accurate (p. 563).

5. The contact hypothesis states that, under certain conditions, direct cooperative contact between the members of two or more social groups can reduce prejudice and improve social relations (p. 570). For contact to "work," four conditions must be met: (1) the groups should be of equal status (no leaders and followers) in the contact situation; (2) there should be personal interactions between the group members; (3) the groups must share a common goal that requires cooperation (for example, learning a particular set of material,

with each member holding certain information and being responsible for sharing it with the other members); and (4) the contact should be supported, maintained, and encouraged by social norms (the teacher, for example, could expect and encourage participation in the activity) (p. 570).

The next part is up to you! Select any group on your campus whom you feel experiences prejudice (could be a racial group, could be "athletes" or "men" or "women" or "homosexuals" or "the students who live in such-and-such dorm"—you get the picture). Then, in as specific a manner as possible, indicate how you would set up a situation in the classroom or on campus that would meet each of the four contact conditions.

15 Personality

Chapter Overview

In contrast to the last two chapters, which focused upon situational and cultural influences, this chapter explores personality, defined as an individual's distinct and enduring pattern of thoughts, feelings, motives, and behaviors. Four major approaches to personality are considered. First, the chapter examines Freudian psychoanalysis, including work by Charcot and Breuer that shaped Freud's theory of personality; the division of personality into id, ego, and superego structural components; the psychosexual stages of development that each of us passes through as our personalities form and take shape; and the dynamics involved in the use of defense mechanisms to guard against anxiety. The ways in which subsequent generations of psychoanalytic theorists have altered classic Freudian theory are discussed, as are the major limitations and legacies of psychoanalysis. Second, the cognitive social-learning approach to personality is discussed, including how Watson and Skinner applied principles of learning to the study of personality; how observational or social learning (modeling), locus of control, and self-efficacy affect behavior; and the methods used by this approach to assess personality. Third, the basic principles of the humanistic approach to personality are considered, as well as the tenets of the theories of Rogers (e.g., self-actualization, the need for positive regard, unconditional positive regard, conditional positive regard) and Maslow (e.g., self-actualization, peak experiences). The limitations and influence of humanistic personality theory are discussed. The fourth approach that is considered in this chapter is the trait approach. Early work on the basic units of personality conducted by Allport and Cattell is discussed, and the five-factor model of personality is presented. Assessment devices, the biological basis of various traits, and the trait dimension of introversion and extraversion are considered, and the debate about the existence of traits is explored.

Chapter Outline

B. Freud's Theory of Personality
   1. The unconscious
   2. The structure of personality
   3. Psychosexual development
   4. The dynamics of personality

C. Freud's Legacy
   1. Neo-Freudian theorists
   2. Projective personality tests
   3. Current perspectives on psychoanalysis

III. The Cognitive Social-Learning Approach

   A. Principles of Learning and Behavior

   B. Social-Learning Theory
      1. Locus of control
      2. Self-efficacy

   C. Perspectives on Cognitive Social-Learning Theory

IV. The Humanistic Approach

   A. Carl Rogers
      1. Rogers' theory
      2. The self-concept

   B. Abraham Maslow
      1. Maslow's theory
      2. The state of self-actualization

   C. Perspectives on the Humanistic Approach

V. The Trait Approach

   A. The Building Blocks of Personality

   B. Construction of Multitrait Inventories

   C. Biological Roots of Personality

   D. Introversion and Extraversion

   E. Perspectives: Do Traits Exist?

   F. *Psychology and . . . Business* Use of Personality Tests in the Workplace

VI. The Big Picture

By the time you have read and reviewed this chapter, you should be able to:

1. Define the concept of personality and list and describe the four major approaches to personality (p. 579).

2. Describe how Freud's early work with the neurologist Jean Charcot and with the physician Josef Breuer contributed to his notion of psychoanalysis (p. 580).

3. Describe the phenomenon of transference (p. 580). Describe the techniques and phenomena of psychoanalysis (e.g., free association, resistance) (p. 580).

4. Explain Freud's division of the mind and consider what is contained in each portion of the human mind (p. 581). Distinguish between the life and death instincts (p. 581).

5. Outline the structure of personality and describe the three parts of personality (pp. 581-82).

6. Describe Freud's two conclusions about personality development (p. 582) and outline the five psychosexual stages of personality development (pp. 582-83). Consider the concept of fixation and the three personality types that reflect fixation (p. 583-84).

7. List and describe six common defense mechanisms (pp. 584-85).

8. Discuss how the theories of the neo-Freudians (Jung, Adler, Fromm, Horney) and ego psychologists (A. Freud, Hartmann, Erikson, White, etc.) were similar to and different from classic Freudian theory (p. 586).

9. Describe the purpose of projective tests (p. 587). Explain the procedures used in the Rorschach and Thematic Apperception Test (TAT) (pp. 587-88).

10. Consider three major criticisms of psychoanalysis (pp. 588-89). Explore the continuing contributions of Freudian theory (pp. 589-590).

11. Describe the cognitive social-learning approach to personality (p. 590). Explain Skinner's definition of personality (p. 592) and describe how modeling (social learning) and expectancies and values can shape personality (p. 592).

12. Discuss Mischel's "cognitive" social-learning theory (pp. 592-93). Outline the five "person variables" that determine how we interact with our environments (pp. 592-93).

13. Define locus of control (p. 593) and explain how these expectancies can influence behavior (p. 593). Consider whether having an internal locus of control is always adaptive (p. 594).

14. Define self-efficacy, consider sources of self-efficacy, and describe the consequences of self-efficacy (p. 595).

15. Explain the concept of reciprocal determinism (p. 595) and discuss the methods used by cognitive social-learning theorists to assess personality (p. 596).

16. List and describe the four basic principles of the humanistic theory of personality (p. 596).

17. Describe Rogers' theory of personality and explain the need for self-actualization and the need for positive regard (p. 597). Compare unconditional positive regard and conditional positive regard (p. 597).

18. Explain how the self-concept may affect our emotional state (p. 598).

19. Describe Maslow's theory of personality (p. 599). Consider the state of self-actualization (pp. 599-600) and how this is related to peak experiences (p. 600).

20. Consider the limitations and the legacies of the humanistic approach (p. 601).

21. Explore the basic assumption of the trait approach to personality (p. 602) and list and describe the "big five" factors of personality (p. 602).

22. Describe multitrait inventories of personality (p. 603). Consider the development of the MMPI (p. 604).

23. Discuss research findings on the biological basis of personality (p. 606).

24. Compare introversion and extraversion (p. 607). Consider the biological basis for these traits, and discuss the relation between these traits and other personality characteristics (pp. 607-9).

25. Consider Mischel's critique of the trait approach to personality (p. 610). Discuss Epstein's response (p. 610). Explore the interaction between our traits and the situations in which we find ourselves (pp. 610-11). Consider whether personality is stable over time (pp. 611-12).

26. Discuss the use of personality tests for employment purposes (p. 611).

Key Terms

The following key terms and concepts are featured in this chapter and are important for you to know. Write out definitions of each term and check your answers with the definitions in the text on the pages listed.

Personality (p. 579)
Psychoanalysis (p. 580)
Id (p. 581)
Pleasure principle (p. 581)
Superego (p. 581)
Ego (p. 582)
Reality principle (p. 582)
Psychosexual stages (p. 582)
Oedipus complex (p. 582)
Identification (pp. 582-83)
Fixation (p. 583)
Defense mechanisms (p. 584)
Repression (p. 584)
Denial (p. 584)
Projection (p. 585)
Reaction formation (p. 585)
Rationalization (p. 585)
Sublimation (p. 585)
Collective unconscious (p. 586)
Projective tests (p. 587)

Rorschach (p. 587)
Thematic Apperception Test (TAT) (p. 587)
Cognitive social-learning theory (p. 590)
Modeling (p. 592)
Locus of control (p. 593)
Self-efficacy (p. 595)
Reciprocal determinism (p. 595)
Humanistic theory (p. 596)
Unconditional positive regard (p. 597)
Conditional positive regard (p. 597)
Self-schemas (p. 598)
Self-discrepancy theory (p. 598)
Self-actualization (p. 599)
Peak experience (p. 600)
Traits (p. 602)
Five-factor model (p. 602)
Minnesota Multiphasic Personality Inventory (MMPI) (p. 603)
Extravert (p. 607)
Introvert (p. 607)

Multiple-Choice Questions

Circle the correct choice for each question and compare your answers with those at the end of the Study Guide chapter.

1. The concept of "personality" refers to an individual's distinct pattern of _____.
   A. thoughts and feelings
   B. motives and values
   C. behaviors
   D. All of the above

2. Dr. S. has been seeing a client for two years. During this time, her client has become quite attached to her, and in fact is growing increasingly affectionate in their sessions. Dr. S. suspects that she is not the real target of her client's affection, and that his behavior may demonstrate
   A. free association.
   B. transference.
   C. resistance.
   D. hysteria.

3. Against her wishes, Andrea's parents have signed her up for psychoanalysis. She dislikes her therapy and constantly makes up excuses not to attend the sessions. When she does attend, she frequently is distracted and prone to lose her train of thought. Andrea may be experiencing _____.
   A. transference   C. resistance
   B. free association   D. insight

4. Conscious is to "tip of the iceberg" as unconscious is to _____.
   A. ice cube   C. ocean
   B. icicle   D. blue whale

5. The life instincts include _____.
   A. the need for food
   B. the need for sex
   C. the need for air
   D. All of the above

6. Which of the following statements illustrates the role of the superego?
   A. "You really shouldn't do that. Nice people don't act that way."
   B. "I want it all, and I want it now!"
   C. "Can't we all just be reasonable? I'm sure we can work out a compromise."
   D. All of the above

7. Which of the following statements illustrates the role of the ego?
   A. "You really shouldn't do that. Nice people don't act that way."
   B. "I want it all, and I want it now!"
   C. "Can't we all just be reasonable? I'm sure we can work out a compromise."
   D. All of the above

8. Weaning is to oral stage as _____ is to anal stage.
   A. Oedipal complex
   B. toilet training
   C. sexual attraction
   D. envy

9. Brant is an overweight man who eats, drinks, and smokes too much. He chews on pencils and his fingernails, and spends hours talking on the phone with friends and family. He also tends to be demanding and dependent in his relations with others. Freud might argue that Brant has a(n) _____ personality.
   A. oral
   B. anal
   C. phallic
   D. expulsive

10. Gloria is described by others as "uptight" and "rigid." She gets extremely upset when she is faced with events that are beyond her control, and insists on following an organized protocol or plan for each day of the week. She is stubborn and controlling in her relations with others. Freud would probably describe Gloria as having a(n) _____ personality.
    A. oral
    B. anal-retentive
    C. anal-expulsive
    D. phallic

11. When Art was a small child, his parents adopted a little girl. Art promptly "forgot" that he was potty-trained and began urinating in the closet. As an adult, Art cannot remember that he did this, despite what his parents tell him. This is an example of _____.
    A. projection
    B. reaction formation
    C. rationalization
    D. repression

12. A person who channels his or her aggressive impulses into a medical career has experienced _____.
    A. projection
    B. reaction formation
    C. sublimation
    D. repression

13. "Well, I never really wanted that class, anyway. It's just as well that it was full. I heard the professor was unfair and the book was way too hard. I'll be better off with this other class." This is an example of
    A. rationalization.
    B. sublimation.
    C. reaction formation.
    D. projection.

14. According to Jung, the collective unconscious
    A. is inherited.
    B. consists of universal symbols and memories from the ancestral past.
    C. explains why common themes occur in cultural myths and legends around the world.
    D. All of the above

15. Jung and Adler criticized Freudian theory as relying too heavily upon _____.
    A. consciousness
    B. sexuality
    C. tension
    D. irrationality

16. Scott volunteered for a psychology study. Upon arrival at the lab, he is asked to complete a series of statements (for example, "When I think of my father, I . . ."). The psychologist then examines Scott's responses for a pattern. Scott has taken a(n) _____.
    A. personality test
    B. multiphasic inventory
    C. projective test
    D. rejective test

17. Both the Rorschach and the TAT have been criticized for _____.
    A. lacking reliability and validity
    B. lacking subjectivity
    C. being too objective
    D. All of the above

18. The "person variables" that are considered important by cognitive social-learning theorists include
    A. mental and physical competencies.
    B. expectancies.
    C. subjective values.
    D. All of the above

19. The person variable called _____ encompasses the ability to set goals, monitor and evaluate our progress, plan for the future, and delay our short-term needs for gratification.
    A. self-regulatory systems   C. competencies
    B. expectancies   D. subjective values

20. According to the social-learning approach to personality, behavior is influenced by _____.
    A. unconscious drives
    B. only actual reinforcements
    C. observation and imitation
    D. All of the above

21. Lucia believes that she is in charge of her own destiny. She takes difficult classes and accepts responsibility for her successes and failures. Rowena is just the opposite. She attributes her successes to luck and her failures to misfortune or her professor's whim. Lucia has an _____ locus of control; Rowena has an _____ locus of control.
    A. internal; internal   C. external; external
    B. internal; external   D. external; internal

22. According to Rogers' humanistic theory, all people are motivated by a need for
    A. self-actualization.
    B. positive regard.
    C. inner wisdom.
    D. A and B

23. Ross has recently decided to leave medical school and pursue a career as an artist. His parents, however, are deeply disappointed with his decision. Ross is experiencing _____ from his parents.
    A. positive regard
    B. unconditional positive regard
    C. conditional positive regard
    D. negative regard

24. Research suggests that when our self-concept does not match our self-guides, we will experience which of the following?
    A. lowered self-esteem
    B. negative emotions
    C. depression
    D. All of the above

25. Maslow believed that self-actualized people are
    A. spontaneous.
    B. independent.
    C. creative.
    D. All of the above

26. A peak experience is defined as a moment of _____.
    A. self-actualization
    B. positive regard
    C. unconditional love
    D. being in the zone

27. Which of the following factors are members of the "big five?"
    A. neuroticism, openness, and extraversion
    B. conscientiousness, anxiety, and psychoticism
    C. introversion, sensation seeking, and neuroticism
    D. emotionality, agreeableness, and shyness

28. Bev is good-natured, soft-hearted, courteous, and sympathetic. She probably would score high on the factor called _____.
    A. neuroticism
    B. extraversion
    C. agreeableness
    D. conscientiousness

29. Research suggests which of the following about introversion and extraversion?
    A. Introverts are less aroused by social stimulation than are extraverts.
    B. Extraverts are more sensation-seeking than introverts.
    C. Introversion has a biological basis, whereas extraversion does not.
    D. Extraverts are more easily aroused by caffeine and other "uppers" than are introverts.

30. Traits are expressed
    A. only in relevant situations.
    B. only in situations that do not constrain our behavior.
    C. Both of the above
    D. None of the above

True-False Questions

Indicate which of the following statements are true or false, and compare your answers with those at the end of the chapter.

T   F   1. Personality does not appear to be highly stable over time.

T   F   2. Freudian psychoanalysis and theory focuses on the events and traumas of early childhood.

T F 3. Neo-Freudian theorists disagreed with Freud over the primacy of sex as a driving force in personality development.

T F 4. The TAT and the Rorschach test have high validity and reliability.

T F 5. The cognitive social-learning approach views personality as the product of an interaction between person variables and environmental variables.

T F 6. Research suggests that it is always "better" to have an internal locus of control.

T F 7. The humanistic theory of personality emphasizes the past rather than the present, and biological determinism rather than choice and free will.

T F 8. Most adults will reach a state of self-actualization.

T F 9. Empirical evidence generally supports the five-factor model of personality.

T F 10. Research suggests that personality characteristics are to some extent biologically determined.

Key Concepts Matching Exercises

Exercise #1: Personality

Match the key terms on the left with the definitions on the right.

_____ 1. Personality

_____ 2. Psychoanalysis

_____ 3. Id

_____ 4. Pleasure principle

_____ 5. Superego

_____ 6. Ego

_____ 7. Reality principle

_____ 8. Defense mechanisms

_____ 9. Collective unconscious

_____10. Rorschach

_____11. TAT

_____12. Cognitive social-learning theory

_____13. Self-efficacy

_____14. Humanistic theory

A. Controlled by the unconscious, these are methods of reducing anxiety by distorting or denying reality

B. The personality approach that focuses on social learning, cognitive factors, and the person-situation interaction

C. A person's distinct and stable pattern of thoughts, feelings, motives, and behavior

D. Associated with Jung, this is a memory bank that contains images from our evolutionary past

E. A stable predisposition to behave in a particular way

F. "I'll love you as long as you continue to be the kind of person I want you to be."

G. "Me, me, me. I want instant gratification, and make it snappy!"

H. The ego's capacity to delay gratification

I. The inkblot test

J. The drive for immediate gratification of desires

K. The personality approach that focuses on the self, subjective experience, and self-actualization

L. "I think that I can do the task and achieve the goal."

M. The "dos" and "don'ts" of our personality

N. "Be all that you can be."

O. Ambiguous pictures onto which people project their personalities

P. The part of personality that mediates the conflict between the id and the superego

_____15. Unconditional positive regard   Q. The theory of personality that is associated with Freud

_____16. Conditional positive regard   R. "I'll love you no matter what."

_____17. Self-actualization

_____18. Trait

Exercise #2: Defense mechanisms

Match the statements on the right with the appropriate defense mechanism.

_____ 1. Repression

_____ 2. Denial

_____ 3. Projection

_____ 4. Reaction formation

_____ 5. Rationalization

_____ 6. Sublimation

A. "I really do love you, sis! I enjoy spending time at home helping you—I'm not at all resentful of the fact that I've had to quit my job to help care for you, honest!"

B. "My painting really lets me express my creative urges. I enjoy the way the colors seem to melt and flow onto the canvas."

C. "What do you mean? My son never told me that he was gay. You must be insane."

D. "I really don't care if my friend heard me talking about him. I mean, it's not like I said anything untrue, and besides, I've never really liked him that much anyway."

E. "I have very little memory of the time I fooled around with my best friend's partner in high school."

F. "I just know that my neighbor dislikes me. I've never done anything to her, but she always acts like she hates me."

Essay Questions

Write out answers to the following brief essay questions. Compare your responses with the sample answers at the end of the Study Guide chapter.

1. Describe one of the first three stages of personality development in Freud's theory. Be sure to discuss the ages, focus of energy, and the crisis of this stage, how resolution is achieved, and personality disorders associated with this stage. THEN give an example (and be specific) of a person you know who appears to have one of these disorders (do not use names if you use someone besides yourself!).

2. What are the three major criticisms of classic Freudian theory? Discuss some enduring legacies of Freudian theory as well.

3. Explain the concept of locus of control. What is the difference between an internal and an external locus of control? What are the consequences of having an internal as opposed to an external locus of control? Is an internal locus always adaptive?

4. Describe the two needs that all humans have, according to Rogers. What happens when these needs conflict with one another? Describe the consequences of experiencing conditional positive regard.

5. Discuss evidence that personality may be influenced by genetic and other biological factors.

Multimedia Study Resources

Several activities and articles in Chapter 15 (Personality) of The Psychology Place™ supplement the material covered in your textbook. In particular, the Learning Activity called "Investigating Dreams" allows you to review various dream theories and then to record and analyze your own dreams. In addition, the Op Ed Forum piece "The Social Usefulness of Self-Esteem: A Skeptical View" discusses whether high self-esteem truly is a criterion of good mental health. And finally, Ask Dr. Mike provides the answers to various questions, including "Can a Personality Test Ever Be Wrong?"

Test Solutions

Multiple-Choice Solutions

1. D (p. 579)	11. D (p. 584)	21. B (p. 593)
2. B (p. 580)	12. C (p. 585)	22. D (p. 597)
3. C (p. 580)	13. A (p. 585)	23. C (p. 597)
4. C (p. 581)	14. D (p. 586)	24. D (p. 598)
5. D (p. 581)	15. B (p. 586)	25. D (p. 599)
6. A (pp. 581-82)	16. C (p. 587)	26. A (p. 600)
7. C (p. 582)	17. A (p. 587)	27. A (p. 603)
8. B (p. 582)	18. D (pp. 592-93)	28. C (p. 603)
9. A (pp. 583-84)	19. A (p. 593)	29. B (p. 608)
10. B (p. 584)	20. C (p. 592)	30. C (p. 610)

True-False Solutions

1. F (p. 578)	6. F (p. 594)
2. T (p. 580)	7. F (p. 596)
3. T (p. 586)	8. F (p. 599)
4. F (p. 587)	9. T (pp. 602-3)
5. T (p. 590)	10. T (p. 606)

Key Concepts Matching Solutions

Exercise #1

1. C	10. I
2. Q	11. O
3. G	12. B
4. J	13. L
5. M	14. K
6. P	15. R
7. H	16. F
8. A	17. N
9. D	18. E

Exercise #2

1. E
2. C
3. F
4. A
5. D
6. B

Essay Solutions

1. You should describe one of the following (pp. 582-84):

   Oral stage: This occurs during the first year of life, and the mouth is the focus of energy or attention. The crisis is weaning, which is resolved when the baby is weaned successfully. If the child receives too much or too little oral stimulation, he or she is said to be fixated at the oral stage of development. Someone with an oral personality (fixated at this stage) might focus a lot of energy on oral activities (eating, smoking, drinking, biting nails or pens, chewing gum, talking) and also might seek symbolic forms of oral gratification by becoming passive, dependent, and demanding (like a nursing infant).

   Anal Stage: This stage occurs during the second and third years of life (so from one to two years), the anus is the focus of energy, and the child derives pleasure from the sensation of retaining or expelling feces. The major crisis is toilet training, which is resolved when the child becomes toilet trained. If toilet training does not go well, the adult leaves too much psychic energy behind at this stage and may develop an anal personality. Specifically, he or she can become anal expulsive (rebellious, messy, prone to temper tantrums and disorganization) or anal retentive (stubborn, stingy, rigid, neat, obstinate, controlling).

   Phallic Stage: This stage occurs between the ages of four and six, and the genitals become the focus of energy. The major crisis is the Oedipal complex, which refers to the tendency for the child to become attracted to and desirous of the opposite-sex parent, and jealous of and angry with the same-sex parent. For boys, this crisis is resolved via castration anxiety (the fear that his much more powerful dad will cut off the son's genitals) and the subsequent identification with dad and development of the superego (an internalization of parental standards). For girls, this crisis is resolved when the girl realizes that her dad has a penis (power) and she doesn't, blames her mother (since mom also doesn't have a penis, mom must be to blame), realizes the futility of this, and identifies with her mother (this process is much less clear for girls). The phallic personality who is fixated in this stage is narcissistic, self-centered, vain, and arrogant. He or she needs constant attention and reassurance of his or her attractiveness.

2. There are three major criticisms of psychoanalysis. First, it paints a highly pessimistic view of human nature (e.g., we are driven by uncontrollable instincts, our personalities are largely determined by the events of early childhood and thus not capable of much change later in life). Second, psychoanalysis does not meet acceptable standards of science (i.e., it is based largely on after-the-fact theorizing about the early childhoods of mentally disturbed clients). Third, carefully controlled research has largely failed to support most of the basic tenets of Freudian theory. For example, who has ever seen an id? Similarly, parents and children do come into conflict during childhood events, but is it really the result of penis envy or castration anxiety? (pp. 588-89).

   Many of Freud's contributions, however, still stand. For example, he was one of the first individuals to really demonstrate that mental disorders can have psychological as well as physical origins. He also drew attention to the profound influence that early childhood events can have on personality development. Theoretically, his notion of the mind as an iceberg (levels of consciousness) has continued to inform contemporary work on consciousness, and his work on defense mechanisms also has received support (pp. 589-590).

3. Locus of control refers to people's generalized expectancy for the control of reinforcement (in others words, our beliefs about who is in charge of what happens to us). People with an internal locus of control believe that they themselves are responsible for their outcomes;

those with an external locus believe that their outcomes are due to luck, fate, or powerful others (doctors, teachers, officials, parents, etc.) (p. 593).

Research does suggest that an internal orientation is associated with emotional well-being; control allows us to feel successful, happy, and action-oriented. However, an internal orientation may not always be adaptive. For example, when events are truly uncontrollable, people with an internal orientation have difficulty managing the situation (believing that they are in control, they are incapable of recognizing when they really are not in control, and this may cause them to continue with a maladaptive behavior pattern). Your text mentions that a victim of a crime (a random act that one cannot control) who has an internal orientation (and blames him- or herself) may experience greater distress than someone with an external control (who blames the situation). In addition, having an internal orientation may lead to problems if it causes one to develop an overcontrolling, I'm-always-in-charge kind of style (p. 594).

4. According to Rogers, we have two competing needs. The first is a natural need for self-actualization, which is the drive to become all that we are capable of becoming and to fulfill our potential. The second is a social drive, the need for positive regard (for approval, support, and love) from others. These needs may cause us to experience conflict; for example, if what we want to become or what we actually are is not what others wish us to become or to be (in other words, the positive regard of these others is conditional upon us behaving in a certain way), then we will experience tension and a feeling of discrepancy within the self (pp. 597-98).

5. Research on twins demonstrates that, for a wide range of traits, identical twins (who share 100% of their genetic material) are more similar than fraternal twins (who share less genetic material), and twins raised apart (who are subject to different environmental influences) are as similar as twins raised together (p. 606).

Research on the personality dimension of introversion-extraversion supports the notion that traits are to some extent biologically influenced. For example, there is growing evidence that introversion-extraversion differences are rooted in differential sensitivities of the central nervous system; introverts have a CNS that is more sensitive to stimulation (and, indeed, they salivate more than extraverts when exposed to sour tastes, are more easily aroused by stimulant substances, and are less easily relaxed by depressant substances) (pp. 607-8).

16 Psychological Disorders

Chapter Overview

This chapter explores the world of psychological disorders, beginning with a discussion of how "normal" and "abnormal" are defined and with an overview of the three major models of abnormality (i.e., medical, psychological, sociocultural). The chapter then considers how to diagnose mental disorders and the impact that diagnostic labels can have on the way that people are perceived and treated. The rest of the chapter is divided between different classes of psychological disorders. First, anxiety disorders (including generalized anxiety disorder, panic disorder, phobic disorder, and obsessive-compulsive disorder) are discussed, followed by somatoform disorders (i.e., hypochondriasis and conversion disorder) and dissociative disorders (amnesia and fugue states, dissociative identity disorder). Next, mood disorders—the prolonged emotional extremes that prevent normal function—are considered. Specifically, your author defines major depression and reviews the biological and psychological explanations for this mood disorder, and discusses its "vicious cycle" and association with suicide. A related mood disorder, bipolar disorder, also is presented. The symptoms, types, and theories of schizophrenia then are discussed, and the chapter ends with a consideration of two personality disorders (borderline, antisocial).

Chapter Outline

C. Diagnosis: A Necessary Step

D. *Psychology and . . . Education* Attention-Deficit Hyperactivity Disorder

III. Anxiety Disorders

    A. Generalized Anxiety Disorder

    B. Panic Disorder

    C. *Through the Global Window . . .* The Culture of Anxiety Disorders

    D. Phobic Disorder

    E. Obsessive-Compulsive Disorder

IV. Somatoform Disorders

    A. Hypochondriasis

    B. Conversion Disorder

V. Dissociative Disorders

    A. Amnesia and Fugue States

    B. Dissociative Identity Disorder

VI. Mood Disorders

    A. Major Depression

    B. Theories of Depression
       1. Biological factors
       2. Psychological factors

    C. The Vicious Cycle of Depression

    D. Suicide: The Ultimate "Solution"

    E. *How To . . .* Know—and What to Do—If a Friend Is Suicidal

    F. Bipolar Disorder

VII. Schizophrenic Disorders

    A. The Symptoms of Schizophrenia

    B. Types of Schizophrenia

    C. Theories of Schizophrenia
       1. Biological factors
       2. Psychological factors

VIII. Personality Disorders

    A. The Borderline Personality

    B. The Antisocial Personality

    C. *Psychology and . . . Law* The Insanity Defense

IX. The Big Picture

Learning Objectives

By the time you have read and reviewed this chapter, you should be able to:

1. Explain the criteria used by the American Psychiatric Association to determine whether a pattern of behavior can be considered a psychological disorder (p. 622).

2. List and define the three models of abnormality (i.e., medical, psychological, sociocultural) (pp. 622-24).

3. Explain the basic assumptions of the medical model of abnormality and examine criticisms of this approach (pp. 622-23).

4. Discuss the psychological model of abnormality and consider how psychoanalysis, cognitive social-learning theory, and humanistic psychology understand abnormal behavior (p. 623).

5. Explain the sociocultural perspective and discuss evidence of sociocultural influence on disorders (pp. 623-24).

6. Define the term diagnosis and discuss the DSM-IV (its uses, contents, and shortcomings) (pp. 624-26).

7. Define Attention-Deficit Hyperactivity Disorder and examine its causes (pp. 627).

8. Distinguish between generalized anxiety disorder, panic disorder, phobic disorder (simple and social), and obsessive-compulsive disorder (pp. 628-36). Consider the causes, symptoms, and treatment of each type of anxiety disorder.

9. Explain somatoform disorders (pp. 637-39). Distinguish between hypochondriasis (p. 637) and conversion disorder (p. 638) and examine the causes of each type of somatoform disorder.

10. Define dissociative disorders and explain how dissociation may be a "normal" part of daily life (p. 639). Distinguish between amnesia and fugue states (pp. 639-40). Explain the characteristics, possible causes, and diagnostic controversies surrounding dissociative identity disorder (pp. 640-42).

11. List the symptoms and examine the biological and psychological causes of major depression (pp. 643-46). Define learned helplessness and the depressive explanatory style (pp. 645-46). Explain the "vicious cycle" of depression and discuss the relation between depression and suicide (p. 647). Consider suicide risk factors and how to respond if you suspect someone you know is suicidal (pp. 648-49).

12. Define bipolar disorder and describe its symptoms. Discuss the genetic basis of this disorder (pp. 649-51).

13. List and describe the five major symptoms of schizophrenia (pp. 652-54). Distinguish between delusions and hallucinations (pp. 652-53). Discuss the five types of schizophrenia and explain the difference between positive and negative symptoms (p. 655). Discuss biological and psychological influences on schizophrenia, and explain the diathesis-stress model (pp. 656-57).

14. Explain the diagnostic criteria for personality disorders (p. 657). List the different types of personality disorders described in the DSM-IV (p. 658).

15. Consider the major features of borderline (p. 658) and antisocial (p. 659) personality disorder. Speculate about the causes of antisocial personality disorder (p. 659).

16. Discuss the concept of insanity (p. 660). Consider the consequences of pleading insanity in a court of law (p. 660). Define the three key elements of insanity, from a legal perspective (p. 660). Discuss the problems (e.g., faking) with the insanity defense (p. 661).

17. Discuss how comorbidity can make it difficult to diagnose a disorder (pp. 659-61).

Key Terms

The following key terms and concepts are featured in this chapter and are important for you to know. Write out definitions of each term and check your answers with the definitions in the text on the pages listed.

Psychological disorder (p. 622)
Medical model (p. 622)
Psychological model (p. 623)
Culture-bound syndrome (p. 624)
Diagnosis (p. 624)
DSM-IV (p. 624)
Generalized anxiety disorder (p. 629)
Panic disorder (p. 629)
Agoraphobia (p. 629)
Phobic disorder (p. 631)
Simple phobia (p. 631)
Social phobia (p. 632)
Obsessive-compulsive disorder (OCD) (p. 635)
Somatoform disorder (p. 637)
Hypochondriasis (p. 637)
Conversion disorder (p. 638)
Dissociative disorder (p. 639)

Amnesia (p. 639)
Fugue state (p. 640)
Dissociative identity disorder (DID) (p. 640)
Mood disorder (p. 643)
Depression (p. 643)
Learned helplessness (p. 645)
Depressive explanatory style (p. 645)
Bipolar disorder (p. 649)
Schizophrenic disorders (p. 652)
Delusions (p. 652)
Hallucinations (p. 652)
Diathesis-stress model (pp. 656-57)
Personality disorder (p. 657)
Borderline personality disorder (p. 658)
Antisocial personality disorder (pp. 658-59)
Comorbidity (p. 659)

Multiple-Choice Questions

Circle the correct choice for each question and compare your answers with those at the end of the Study Guide chapter.

1. Women are more likely than men to experience _____; men are more likely than women to experience _____.
   A. anxiety; depression
   B. antisocial personality disorder; substance abuse
   C. depression; substance abuse
   D. schizophrenia; anxiety

2. According to the APA, a pattern of behavior that _____ may be classified as a psychological disorder.
   A. results in an increased risk of death
   B. is not a "normal" response to specific life events
   C. is not a deliberate reaction to social conditions
   D. All of the above

3. A doctor who views anxiety as the result of a neurotransmitter imbalance and who treats this disorder with drugs is following the _____ model.
   A. medical   C. sociocultural
   B. psychological   D. demonology

4. A doctor who views anxiety as a learned response to situations is following the _____ model of abnormality.
   A. medical   C. sociocultural
   B. psychological   D. demonology

5. Which of the following provides evidence for the sociocultural model of abnormality?
   A. Anxiety is found in all cultures around the world.
   B. Emotional problems occur in teenagers from all racial, ethnic, and cultural groups.
   C. Anorexia is almost exclusively found in Western cultures.
   D. All of the above

6. A major criticism of early versions of the DSM was that they
   A. could only be used to make diagnoses of individuals from Western cultures.
   B. were based on anecdotal evidence.
   C. had low levels of reliability.
   D. could only be used to make diagnoses of male patients.

7. Your text describes a study conducted by Rosenhan (1973) in which he and his colleagues were admitted to mental hospitals after complaining of certain symptoms. What was the main point of this classic study?
   A. Once a diagnostic label is applied to someone ("schizophrenic"), all behavior comes to be seen in terms of that label.
   B. It is hard to tell the difference between "normal" and "abnormal" behavior.
   C. The DSM cannot be used reliably to diagnose schizophrenia.
   D. Most people in psychiatric hospitals are not mentally ill.

8. A child with Attention-Deficit Hyperactivity Disorder (ADHD) tends to be
    A. inattentive.
    B. impulsive.
    C. hyperactive.
    D. All of the above

9. Kess goes through each day feeling uneasy and tense. She is very sensitive to criticism and has difficulty making decisions, even about little things. She constantly worries about her job, her financial situation, and family matters. Her symptoms fit the diagnostic category of
    A. generalized anxiety disorder.
    B. major depression.
    C. phobic disorder.
    D. somatoform disorder.

10. Which item is out of place here?
    A. phobic disorder
    B. panic disorder
    C. seasonal affective disorder
    D. obsessive-compulsive disorder

11. One day during his lunch hour, Geraldo suddenly couldn't breathe. He felt his heart racing, he began to hyperventilate, and he became worried that he was dying. He wanted to get help from his coworkers, but he was worried about embarrassing himself in front of them. If these episodes continue, Geraldo might be diagnosed with _____.
    A. bipolar disorder
    B. panic disorder
    C. generalized anxiety disorder
    D. simple phobia

12. Patricia seldom leaves her home. She works out of a home office, has friends visit her at home, and has most things delivered to her. The idea of being in a movie theater, going to a public park, or eating in a restaurant scares her. Such symptoms are typical of
    A. obsessive-compulsive disorder.
    B. agoraphobia.
    C. fugue states.
    D. panic disorder.

13. All during the day, Don has repetitive thoughts about dirt and germs. To deal with these unpleasant images, he carefully washes and disinfects his hands precisely three times each hour. Don's thoughts reflect _____ and his washing behavior reflects _____.
    A. generalized anxiety; panic disorder
    B. an obsession; a compulsion
    C. a simple phobia; a social phobia
    D. a compulsion; an obsession

14. Chuck complains of numbness and tingling in his fingertips, nausea, chest pains, and indigestion. He is intensely aware of his own bodily sensations, often becoming extremely alarmed the moment that he sneezes or coughs. Certain that he suffers from extremely poor health, Chuck has seen over a dozen doctors in the past two years. Chuck may have
    A. hypochondriasis.
    B. a social phobia.
    C. paranoid schizophrenia.
    D. bipolar disorder.

15. Jana's son was recently attacked by a snake. Although she tried to hit the snake with her fist before it reached her child, Jana was unable to prevent it from biting him. Her son is fine, but Jana's hand has become paralyzed. However, examination and testing show no physical damage to her hand. Jana's paralysis may reflect
    A. psychosomatic disorder.
    B. hypochondriasis.
    C. insanity.
    D. conversion disorder.

16. While driving to work one day, Eli debates what color to paint his new house. When he arrives at his parking spot, he realizes that he doesn't remember any of the details of his drive in to work. Eli has experienced
    A. a manic episode.
    B. an obsessive thought.
    C. dissociation.
    D. a fugue state.

17. During a soccer game at the local park, Sheila is hit on the head by the ball. For a short time afterward, she cannot remember the name of the park and the name and mascot of her soccer team. However, she remembers who she is and where she lives. Later, her memory clears up. This condition is called
    A. a fugue state.
    B. organic amnesia.
    C. dissociative identity disorder.
    D. dissociative amnesia.

18. After several years of living and working in a small town in Michigan, Paul wakes up one morning insisting that his name is Brian and that he has to report to his job in Atlanta, Georgia. He does not recognize the furniture in his apartment or the clothing hanging in his closet. He is completely confused about his current life. He may have experienced
    A. a fugue state.
    B. dissociative identity disorder.
    C. borderline personality.
    D. amnesia.

19. Which statement best describes dissociative identity disorder?
    A. The individual loses contact with reality and becomes incapable of perceiving objective events.
    B. The person often moves to a new community and takes on a new identity for a period of time.
    C. The individual seems to have two or more distinct psychological selves or identities.
    D. The individual's personality "splits" into two halves, one that is emotional and one that is cognitive.

20. Many clinicians and researchers are skeptical about the recent increase in diagnoses of dissociative identity disorder (DID) because
    A. examples of people with this condition cannot be found earlier than 1970.
    B. some criminals have tried to escape punishment by pretending to have DID.
    C. people with DID are often hypochondriacs.
    D. this condition exists only in Western cultures.

21. Glynnis just doesn't enjoy doing much of anything lately. She blames herself for all her failures in life. She has lost interest in food and social activities, and most days she just stays in bed. If these symptoms last for more than two weeks, she may be diagnosed as having
    A. bipolar disorder.
    B. antisocial personality.
    C. major depression.
    D. agoraphobia.

22. If one identical twin is diagnosed with depression, the likelihood that the other twin also will develop this disorder is
    A. 10 percent.
    B. 50 percent.
    C. 75 percent.
    D. 100 percent.

23. The phrase "vicious cycle of depression" refers to the fact that depressed people
    A. dislike social support and refuse to interact with their friends and partners.
    B. have learned to become helpless in the face of adversity.
    C. are prone to become aggressive and vicious toward others.
    D. need social support but behave in ways that almost always result in social rejection.

24. Which one of the following statements about suicide is inaccurate?
    A. More men than women complete their attempted suicides.
    B. More women than men attempt suicide.
    C. Depression is not associated with suicide attempts.
    D. One of the best predictors of suicide is a sense of hopelessness.

25. Mardie hasn't slept in several days. She alternates between writing what she believes will be a grammy-winning album of folk songs and going on expensive shopping sprees. She speaks in a loud, frenzied voice and explodes in anger when her roommate tells her to "calm down." If this pattern is followed by a period of depression, a diagnosis of _____ may be made.
    A. bipolar disorder
    B. major depression
    C. dissociative identity disorder
    D. seasonal affective disorder

26. The "split" in schizophrenia involves a split
    A. between two or more inner selves.
    B. between the two hemispheres of the cerebral cortex.
    C. between one's masculine and feminine traits and characteristics.
    D. between the various brain functions.

27. Which of the following symptoms are found in people with a schizophrenic disorder?
    A. incoherent thinking and bizarre behavior
    B. delusions and hallucinations
    C. disturbed affect
    D. All of the above

28. While completing your internship at a state institution, you observe a young man complaining about how the other patients are spying on him and trying to poison him. He is highly suspicious of other people and he also believes that the government is monitoring his activities through the television set. These features are characteristic of _____ schizophrenia.
   A. catatonic
   B. paranoid
   C. disorganized
   D. undifferentiated

29. When a person's overall behavior patterns are inflexible and maladaptive and cause distress, the person may be diagnosed with
   A. schizophrenia.
   B. dissociative identity disorder.
   C. a personality disorder.
   D. fugues.

30. Michelle has difficulty maintaining friendships and romantic relationships. She is uncertain about her own identity and about her goals in life, experiences extreme mood fluctuations, and is prone to inappropriate outbursts of anger. When Michelle meets a potential new friend, partner, or colleague, she clings to that person so fiercely that he or she becomes alienated and leaves the relationship. Michelle may have
   A. borderline personality disorder.
   B. antisocial personality disorder.
   C. disorganized schizophrenia.
   D. mania.

True-False Questions

Indicate which of the following statements are true or false, and compare your answers with those at the end of the chapter.

T F 1. Men and women are equally likely to develop a psychological disorder over the course of their lifetimes.

T F 2. There is a clear and distinct division between "normal" and "abnormal" behavior.

T F 3. There are a number of psychological models of abnormality.

T F 4. Clinical judgments may be biased by expectations, stereotypes, and diagnostic labels.

T F 5. The physiological symptoms of anxiety vary across cultures.

T F 6. Research suggests that phobias can be learned through classical conditioning and observation.

T F 7. There is some evidence that hypochondriasis is associated with nervous system oversensitivity.

T F 8. Dissociative identity disorder is one of the most common psychological disorders.

T F 9. Depression appears to be linked to both biological and psychological factors.

T F 10. People diagnosed with one disorder often have symptoms of others as well.

Key Concepts Matching Exercises

Exercise #1: Diagnosis

Match the psychological disorders listed on the left with the definitions or examples listed on the right.

_____ 1. Generalized anxiety disorder

_____ 2. Panic disorder

_____ 3. Agoraphobia

_____ 4. Obsessive-compulsive disorder

_____ 5. Hypochondriasis

_____ 6. Conversion disorder

_____ 7. Amnesia

_____ 8. Fugue state

_____ 9. Dissociative identity disorder

_____ 10. Depression

_____ 11. Bipolar disorder

_____ 12. Seasonal affective disorder

_____ 13. Paranoid schizophrenia

_____ 14. Residual schizophrenia

_____ 15. Borderline personality

_____ 16. Antisocial personality

A. "I don't know who I am or what I want to be. I am moody, and I can't seem to maintain a relationship even though I desperately want one."

B. "Thank goodness summer is here. I always feel better in the summer. Winter just gets me down."

C. "How am I? Just terrible! I'm sure I'm coming down with something—I've had this tight feeling in my throat all day and my skin is tingly. I'm certain that I have that new virus that's been in the news lately."

D. "Oh my gosh, am I having a heart attack? I can't breathe, I can't think, my throat is closing up, I think I'm going to pass out!"

E. "Why are you calling me 'Betty'? My name is Veronica. Whose clothes are these? They aren't mine—and I don't live in California, I'm from Massachusetts."

F. "One day I'm on top of the world, and the next I'm plunged into the depths of despair."

G. "Ever since I saw that terrible car accident, I've been blind."

H. "Well, I had some schizophrenic symptoms a few years ago, but the drugs seem to be working. I haven't had any major symptoms since then."

I. "Did I turn off the oven last night? I'd better check." "Maybe the oven is still on. I'd better check one more time."

J. "Sonny isn't here right now. I'm here, and my name is Justin. When I leave, you can talk with Sonny again."

K. "Did I hit my head? I can't remember any of the details!"

L. "I am so worried about everything—my car, my life, my job, my relationships, my pets, my own health. Everything seems to be a source of constant anxiety."

M. "I don't care about you. You exist only to serve my needs. I feel no guilt or remorse whatsoever—people get what they deserve, and I deserve everything."

N. "I can't seem to get up enough energy to do anything. My whole life is one big failure. Just leave me alone."

O. "Are you following me? Stop talking about me behind my back! I know I'm being watched. I hear the voices, and I see the signs."

P. "Oh no, I could never go out in public. The mere thought of being surrounded by all those people makes me really uncomfortable. I'd much rather stay at home, where it's safe."

Essay Questions

Write out answers to the following brief essay questions. Compare your responses with the sample answers at the end of the Study Guide chapter.

1. When is a pattern of behavior considered to be a psychological disorder, according to the American Psychiatric Association? Is there always a clear distinction between "normal" and "abnormal" behavior? Explain, using a specific example, how the same behavior could be viewed as "normal" in one situation and "abnormal" in another.

2. What are the three major concerns that critics have voiced about psychiatric diagnosis in general and about using the DSM in particular?

3. In what way is anxiety a universal phenomenon? In what way is it culture-specific?

4. Explain the "vicious cycle" of depression.

5. Consider the biological basis of schizophrenia. What is the diathesis-stress model?

Multimedia Study Resources

Several activities and articles in Chapter 13 (Psychological Disorders) of The Psychology Place™ supplement the material covered in your textbook. In particular, an article in *Scientific American* magazine, "Manic-Depressive Illness and Creativity," explores whether an association exists between some forms of mental illness and creativity. In addition, one Learning Activity allows you to complete an on-line, self-report measure of depression, and then to compare your score with national averages ("Investigating Sex Differences in Depression"). A second Learning Activity provides you with the opportunity to diagnose a sample of patients based on their clinical symptoms and case histories ("Recognizing Mood Disorders").

Test Solutions

Multiple-Choice Solutions

1. C (p. 620)	11. B (p. 629)	21. C (p. 643)
2. D (p. 622)	12. B (p. 629)	22. B (p. 644)
3. A (pp. 622-23)	13. B (p. 635)	23. D (p. 646)
4. B (p. 623)	14. A (p. 637)	24. C (p. 647)
5. C (p. 623)	15. D (p. 638)	25. A (pp. 650-51)
6. C (p. 625)	16. C (p. 639)	26. D (p. 652)
7. A (p. 626)	17. B (p. 639)	27. D (pp. 652-53)
8. D (p. 627)	18. A (p. 640)	28. B (p. 655)
9. A (p. 629)	19. C (p. 640)	29. C (p. 657)
10. C (p. 629)	20. B (p. 642)	30. A (p. 658)

True-False Solutions

1. T (p. 620)
2. F (p. 622)
3. T (pp. 622-23)
4. T (p. 626)
5. F (p. 630)
6. T (p. 633)
7. T (pp. 637-38)
8. F (p. 640)
9. T (pp. 644-46)
10. T (p. 659)

Key Concepts Matching Solutions

Exercise #1

1. L
2. D
3. P
4. I
5. C
6. G
7. K
8. E
9. J
10. N
11. F
12. B
13. O
14. H
15. A
16. M

Essay Solutions

1. According to the American Psychiatric Association, a pattern of behavior can be considered a psychological disorder if it satisfies three conditions. First, the person must experience significant pain or distress, an inability to work or play, an increased risk of death, or a loss of freedom in important areas in life. Second, the source of the problem must reside within the person (as the result of biological factors, learned habits, or mental processes) and must not be a reaction to specific life events (like the loss of a loved one). Third, the behavior must not be a deliberate reaction to conditions like poverty, prejudice, government policy, or other conflicts with society (p. 622).

   There really is no clear dividing line between "normal" and "abnormal" behavior; that is, although it is possible to identify behavior that is clearly abnormal, these labels lie upon a continuum. Thus, it is difficult, for example, to determine how much anxiety is "normal" and how much is "abnormal" (p. 622).

   You should select an example of a behavior that can be viewed as normal in one situation and as a disorder in another. In thinking of relatively recent events in the media, one example might be cannibalistic behavior (eating human flesh). Jeffrey Dahmer's cannibalistic behavior, discussed in your textbook in the section on the insanity defense, was clearly abnormal—the source of the behavior resided within him, and it was not a reaction to a specific life event (like poverty, starvation, etc.). The cannibalistic behavior of the surviving members of a soccer team whose plane crashed in the Andes (featured in the movie "Alive") is unpleasant to think about, but is not due to a psychological disorder. The behavior in this case came about as a result of a specific life event (the plane crash), was a deliberate reaction to a social condition (starvation, potential death), and did not continue once that condition was removed (they were rescued).

2. The first major concern is that the diagnostic system, which is based on the DSM-IV, lacks reliability. Certainly research on the first editions of the DSM demonstrated that the instrument lacked high reliability; however, later editions appear to produce higher reliability. The second concern involves the issue of bias. Research provides strong evidence that clinical judgments and diagnoses are influenced by stereotypes, expectations, and all the other biases the affect human judgment and decision making (after all, clinicians are human, too, and subject to the same factors that affect the rest of us!). For example, some studies find that the same symptoms are labeled "antisocial personality" (which is more common among men than women) when the patient is male and "borderline personality" (which is more common among women than men) when the patient is female. The third concern is related to the second, and involves the notion that diagnostic labels can adversely affect the way that we perceive and treat those with a particular disorder; in other words, we might view the most innocuous behaviors as "evidence" that someone is depressed, for example, if we have already been told that the person is depressed (pp. 625-26).

3. Anxiety is a universal phenomenon in two ways. First, anxiety is experienced by all people, of all ages, around the world. Second, the physiological symptoms of anxiety (e.g., shortness of breath, racing heart, trembling) are the same across cultures (p. 630). However, anxiety is also a culture-specific phenomenon in terms of its cognitive component—as noted by your textbook author, the types of symptoms that cause people anxiety, the interpretations placed on those symptoms, and beliefs about the causes of anxiety are different in different cultures. For example, Koro (the anxiety-producing belief that one's sexual organs will disappear into the body and cause death) is specific to Asian cultures, susto (an intense fear reaction brought on by the belief that one has been cursed by voodoo or black magic) is found in Central and Latin American cultures, and so on (p. 630).

4. The "vicious cycle" of depression refers to the fact that many men and women with depression are in desperate need of social support and friendship, but they behave in ways that almost always prevent them from achieving these things. In other words, depression causes social rejection, which increases the depression, which in turn causes more social rejection, and so on. There is research that people who are depressed avoid eye contact, speak softly, are slow to respond to others, and are negative in their emotional expressions and demeanor. They also tend to withdraw socially (one of the major symptoms of depression). All of these factors prevent successful social contact. Others may interpret these behaviors as a sign of rudeness, detachment, and a desire to be left alone (when in fact the opposite is often the case). The result is that people may react to depressed others with mixed emotions—sadness, a desire to help, irritation, anger, etc. (p. 646).

5. Schizophrenia has a strong genetic basis (the more closely related you are to someone with schizophrenia, the higher the likelihood that you will develop schizophrenia yourself). In addition, there are clear biological factors involved in this disorder, most notably an excess of, or an oversensitivity to, the neurotransmitter dopamine and structural defects in the brain (p. 656). However, there is also evidence for the impact of environmental or psychological factors in the development of schizophrenia (just because one identical twin has schizophrenia does not necessarily mean the other twin will develop it). The diathesis-stress model states that schizophrenia is the result of both a genetic, biological, or acquired predisposition (diathesis) toward schizophrenia and an environmental stressor (stress) that causes that predisposition to actually develop (pp. 656-57).

17 Treatment

In the last chapter, you were introduced to a variety of psychological disorders—their symptoms, prevalence, and causes. In this chapter, you will explore the many therapeutic approaches that have been developed to treat these disorders. The majority of the chapter is devoted to psychotherapy, or those forms of treatment that utilize psychological techniques. Your author discusses the major techniques and assumptions of both orthodox (classic Freudian) and modified (brief) psychoanalytic therapies, considers the criticisms and legacies of these forms of psychotherapy, and reviews research on the phenomenon of repressed memory. Next, the chapter explores behavioral therapies, including classical-conditioning techniques (i.e., flooding, systematic desensitization, aversive conditioning) and operant-conditioning methods (i.e., reinforcement programs or token economies, punishment, biofeedback techniques, social-skills training). Cognitive therapies, which focus on altering maladaptive thought patterns, then are presented. Specifically, your author discusses Ellis's rational-emotive therapy and Beck's cognitive therapy, and then examines alternative cognitive therapies (e.g., stress-inoculation training). The last psychotherapeutic approach to be discussed is the humanistic perspective. The assumptions and techniques of person-centered therapy (associated with Rogers) and Gestalt therapy (associated with Perls) are presented. Then, the chapter explores a variety of group therapy approaches, including transactional analysis, sensitivity training, encounter groups, and self-help groups. Family therapy also is discussed. At this point, your author considers the effectiveness of psychotherapy in general, whether one type of therapy is better than another, and the essential ingredients of a successful therapy. This section ends with a discussion of current trends in psychotherapy; namely, eclecticism. The final part of the chapter focuses on medical interventions, including drug therapies, electroconvulsive therapy, and psychosurgery.

Chapter Outline

I. *What's Your Prediction? Consumer Reports* Asks, Does psychotherapy help?

II. Psychological Therapies

    A. Psychoanalytic Therapies
        1. Orthodox psychoanalysis
            a. Free association
            b. Resistance
            c. Transference
        2. Brief psychoanalytic therapies
        3. Controversies in psychoanalysis

    B. *Psychology and . . . Law* Putting Repressed Memories on Trial

    C. Behavioral Therapies
        1. Classical-conditioning techniques
            a. Flooding
            b. Systematic desensitization
            c. Aversive conditioning
        2. Operant-conditioning techniques
            a. Reward and punishment
            b. Biofeedback
            c. Social-skills training

    D. *How To . . .* Use Biofeedback to Treat Headaches

    E. Cognitive Therapies
        1. Rational-emotive behavior therapy
        2. Beck's cognitive therapy

    F. Humanistic Therapies
        1. Person-centered therapy
        2. Gestalt therapy

    G. Group-Therapy Approaches

III. Perspectives on Psychotherapy

    A. The Bottom Line: Does Psychotherapy Work?

    B. Are Some Therapies Better than Others?

    C. What Are the Active Ingredients?
        1. A supportive relationship
        2. A ray of hope
        3. An opportunity to open up

    D. The Eclectic Alternative

IV. Medical Interventions

    A. Drug Therapies
        1. Antianxiety drugs
        2. Antidepressants
        3. Mood stabilizers
        4. Antipsychotic drugs

    B. *How To . . .* Beat the Winter Blues

    C. Perspectives on Drug Therapies

    D. Electroconvulsive Therapy

    E. Psychosurgery

V. The Big Picture

Learning Objectives

By the time you have read and reviewed this chapter, you should be able to:

1. Define the term psychotherapy and list the various types of professionals who can conduct psychotherapy (p. 670).

2. Describe the goals of orthodox (classical Freudian) psychoanalysis (p. 671). List and describe the three types of behavior—free association, resistance, transference—that a traditional psychoanalyst interprets during therapy (pp. 671-73).

3. Compare orthodox and brief psychoanalytic therapies (pp. 671-74). Discuss the ways in which brief therapies are similar to and different from Freud's original approach (p. 674).

4. Consider the three main criticisms of psychoanalysis as a form of treatment (p. 674). Consider the impact that psychoanalysis has had on clinical theories, practice, and research (p. 674).

5. Describe the phenomenon of repressed memory and consider the controversy surrounding repressed memory syndrome. List the conclusions about the issue drawn by the APA taskforce (pp. 675-76).

6. Describe the basic assumptions of the behavioral therapies, and compare them with the assumptions of psychoanalysis (p. 676).

7. List and describe the three classical-conditioning therapies (pp. 677-81).

8. Describe the technique of flooding (p. 677).

9. Consider the three steps involved in systematic desensitization (i.e., relaxation training, anxiety hierarchy creation, gradual exposure) (pp. 677-79).

10. Explain the technique of aversive conditioning (pp. 680-81).

11. Describe operant-conditioning techniques, including the ways in which reinforcement (token economies), punishment, biofeedback, and social-skills training can be used to change abnormal behavior (pp. 681-82).

12. Consider how biofeedback may be used to treat migraine headaches (p. 683).

13. Discuss the basic tenet of cognitive therapies (pp. 682-83).

14. Describe rational-emotive behavior therapy (REBT) and compare this technique with Beck's cognitive therapy (pp. 684-85). Consider other forms of cognitive therapy (e.g., stress-inoculation training) (p. 685).

15. List and describe the four assumptions and goals of humanistic therapy (p. 686).

16. Describe the features of person-centered therapy, including empathy, unconditional positive regard, genuineness, and reflection (pp. 686-87).

17. Explain the features of Gestalt therapy and compare this approach with that of person-centered therapy (p. 687).

18. Discuss group therapies, including transactional analysis, sensitivity training, encounter groups, and self-help groups (pp. 689-90).

19. Consider the features of family therapies (p. 690).

20. Consider the question of whether psychotherapy "works" (pp. 690-92). Explain why researchers are cautious about using clients' self-reports as a measure of the effectiveness of psychotherapy (p. 691).

21. Discuss whether some therapies might be more effective than others (pp. 692-93).

22. Explain the three features common to all successful psychotherapies (pp. 693-94).

23. Describe the eclectic approach to psychotherapy (p. 695).

24. Consider the three types of medical interventions used to treat abnormal behavior (pp. 695-701).

25. Distinguish between the various types of drug therapies, including those used to treat anxiety, to treat depression, to stabilize mood, and to reduce the positive symptoms of schizophrenia (pp. 696-99).

26. Describe electroconvulsive therapy—its history, procedures, and uses (pp. 700-1).

27. Define psychosurgery and explain why this is a controversial form of medical intervention. Consider its uses (p. 701).

28. Consider the types of mental-health care providers available to consumers (p. 702).

Key Terms

The following key terms and concepts are featured in this chapter and are important for you to know. Write out definitions of each term and check your answers with the definitions in the text on the pages listed.

Psychotherapy (p. 670)
Free association (p. 671)
Resistance (p. 672)
Transference (p. 672)
Behavioral therapy (p. 677)
Flooding (p. 677)
Systematic desensitization (p. 677)
Aversion therapy (p. 680)
Token economy (p. 681)
Biofeedback (p. 682)
Social-skills training (p. 682)
Cognitive therapy (p. 682)
Rational-emotive behavior therapy (REBT) (p. 684)

Person-centered therapy (p. 687)
Gestalt therapy (p. 687)
Group therapy (p. 689)
Family therapies (p. 690)
Placebo effect (p. 694)
Psychopharmacology (p. 695)
Antianxiety drugs (p. 696)
Antidepressants (p. 697)
Lithium (p. 697)
Antipsychotic drugs (p. 697)
Seasonal affective disorder (SAD) (p. 698)
Electroconvulsive therapy (ECT) (p. 700)
Psychosurgery (p. 701)

Test Questions

Multiple-Choice Questions

Circle the correct choice for each question and compare your answers with those at the end of the Study Guide chapter.

1. The goal of psychoanalytic therapy is
   A. insight.
   B. catharsis.
   C. free association.
   D. A and B

2. In order to deal with his recurrent bouts of anxiety, Charley is seeing a psychoanalyst. During each session, Dr. Farias encourages Charley to lie back, relax, and say whatever comes to his mind. This part of psychoanalysis is called _____.
   A. resistance
   B. free association
   C. transference
   D. catharsis

3. After about six months of therapy, Charley finds himself becoming more and more angry with Dr. Durvasala. Dr. Durvasala believes that Charley is really angry with his father and that the feelings he has for his therapist reflect _____.
   A. resistanc
   B. insight
   C. transferencee
   D. catharsis

4. When Dr. Durvasala suggests that Charley may have some buried feelings of anger and hostility toward his father, Charley laughs and quickly changes the subject. This happens several times. Charley's behavior may reflect
   A. transference.
   B. resistance.
   C. insight.
   D. catharsis.

5. Compared to traditional Freudian techniques, modern psychoanalytic therapies
   A. are less time-consuming and intense.
   B. focus more heavily on current life problems.
   C. minimize the use of transference and resistance.
   D. All of the above

6. A task force assembled by the APA reviewed evidence on repressed memories of childhood abuse. What conclusions did they draw?
   A. Most people who were abused as children remember all or part of what happened.
   B. It is possible to recall old memories that have been forgotten over time.
   C. It is possible to construct false memories of events that did not occur.
   D. All of the above

7. Which of the following is out of place?
   A. flooding
   B. token economies
   C. systematic desensitization
   D. aversive conditioning

8. Sharon is extremely afraid of snakes. To eliminate her phobia, the therapist locks her in a room with a caged snake. Although she experiences an initial panic reaction, her fear subsides after 45 minutes. This procedure is repeated several times until the phobia is completely gone. The therapist has used the classical conditioning technique of _____.
   A. flooding
   B. systematic desensitization
   C. anxiety hierarchies
   D. relaxation training

9. Lee is also extremely afraid of snakes and has sought treatment for his phobia. During his therapy, he is trained in relaxation techniques, he and his therapist construct an anxiety hierarchy, and he is gradually exposed over several sessions to the items on the anxiety hierarchy. Lee has experienced _____.
   A. flooding
   B. aversion therapy
   C. systematic desensitization
   D. modeling

10. Classical conditioning techniques have been used successfully to treat which disorders?
    A. phobias
    B. obsessive-compulsive disorders
    C. eating disorders
    D. All of the above

11. Donna works with autistic children. When a child engages in "good" behavior (for example, picking up his or her toys), she gives the child a plastic chip that can be exchanged for tv privileges, candy, and other treats. Donna has established a _____.
    A. biofeedback system
    B. token economy
    C. social skills workshop
    D. conditioning system

12. Ryan was diagnosed with schizophrenia a few years ago. In order to help Ryan learn how to more effectively interact with people, his therapist demonstrates appropriate forms of eye contact, social distance, and conversational style. Ryan then imitates and rehearses the same behaviors while his therapist provides praise and constructive feedback. Ryan is receiving _____.
    A. social-skills training
    B. biofeedback
    C. interpersonal perception training
    D. systematic sensitization

13. Which one of the following statements about cognitive therapy is accurate?
    A. Cognitive therapy is long-term therapy.
    B. Cognitive therapy centers on unconscious conflicts rooted in early childhood.
    C. Cognitive therapy is designed to alter maladaptive thought processes and beliefs.
    D. Cognitive therapy focuses on concrete behaviors that can be changed via conditioning principles.

14. Jay is about to begin rational-emotive behavior therapy. Which of the following might he expect to experience during the course of his treatment?
    A. flooding   C. psychoeducation
    B. pain exercises   D. catharsis

15. Compared with Ellis's rational-emotive therapy, Beck's cognitive therapy is
    A. less successful.
    B. gentler and more collaborative.
    C. more behaviorally-oriented.
    D. less focused on changing cognitions.

16. Rogers redefined the role of the therapist as being that of a(n) _____.
    A. detective   C. teacher
    B. adviser   D. facilitator

17. Person-centered therapists must demonstrate which qualities for a successful therapeutic experience?
    A. unconditional positive regard
    B. genuineness
    C. empathy
    D. All of the above

18. The technique of _____ involves actively listening to a client's statements without interrupting or evaluating, paraphrasing those statements in response to the client, and seeking clarification when needed.
    A. reflection
    B. transference
    C. unconditional regard
    D. empathic interaction

19. Which of the following individuals would play the least directive role in the therapeutic process?
    A. Lisa, a Beckian cognitive therapist
    B. Louie, a rational-emotive therapist
    C. Lana, a person-centered therapist
    D. Luke, a psychoanalyst

20. Compared to Rogerian therapy, Gestalt therapy is
    A. more confrontational.
    B. less directive.
    C. more focused on early childhood experience.
    D. All of the above

21. Psychoanalysis is to _____ as humanistic therapy is to sensitivity-training.
    A. orthodox therapy
    B. transactional analysis
    C. encounter group
    D. self-help group

22. Family therapies view the family as
    A. a "salad" composed of individual, separate ingredients.
    B. a "universe" composed of distinct planets.
    C. a "system" composed of interdependent parts.
    D. a "battleground" composed of warring factions.

23. Research suggests that people will experience improvements in what order during the course of therapy?
    A. feeling "better;" more effective functioning at work, home, and in relationships; relief from specific symptoms
    B. more effective functioning at work, home, and in relationships; feeling "better;" relief from specific symptoms
    C. relief from specific symptoms; feeling "better;" more effective functioning at work, home, and in relationships
    D. feeling "better;" relief from specific symptoms; more effective functioning at work, home and in relationships

24. Cognitive therapies appear to be most effective for treating
    A. phobic disorders.
    B. depression.
    C. low self-esteem.
    D. obsessive-compulsive disorder.

25. Behavioral therapies are most effective at treating
    A. mood disorders.
    B. anxiety disorders.
    C. low self-esteem.
    D. repressed hostility.

26. Which term is out of place?
    A. drug therapy   C. REBT
    B. ECT   D. psychosurgery

27. Panic attack is to benzodiazepines as bipolar disorder is to _____.
  A. lithium
  B. barbiturates
  C. prozac
  D. thorazine

28. Parker is taking chlorpromazine for schizophrenia. What might he expect to experience?
  A. reduced negative symptoms
  B. increased negative symptoms
  C. reduced muscle control
  D. increased positive symptoms

29. Considerations in using drug therapy include
  A. side effects.
  B. physical dependence.
  C. psychological dependence.
  D. All of the above

30. Electroconvulsive therapy (ECT) is likely to result in which of the following?
  A. a temporary state of confusion
  B. death
  C. severe brain damage
  D. significant alterations in personality

True-False Questions

Indicate which of the following statements are true or false, and compare your answers with those at the end of the chapter.

T   F   1. Survey reports indicate that most people are dissatisfied with the outcomes of their therapy.

T   F   2. Modern psychoanalysis has eliminated the classic Freudian focus on unconscious processes and past experiences.

T   F   3. Psychoanalysis is on the increase in the United States.

T   F   4. It is possible to create a memory for an event that did not take place.

T   F   5. Systematic desensitization is a highly effective form of treatment for anxiety disorders.

T   F   6. Biofeedback allows people to control parts of the autonomic nervous system.

T   F   7. Cognitive therapy is the most frequently taught orientation in American clinical psychology graduate programs.

T   F   8. Research suggests that no single therapeutic approach is consistently superior to another.

T   F   9. Most psychotherapists identify themselves with a single orientation (e.g., cognitive, behavioral, Freudian).

T   F   10. The number of people who seek professional help for psychological problems has increased in recent years.

Key Concepts Matching Exercises

Exercise #1: Psychotherapy

Match the disorders or phenomena listed on the right with the most effective treatment. Each treatment may be used for more than one disorder.

_____ 1. Psychoanalysis   A. Obsessive-compulsive disorder

_____ 2. Behavioral therapies   B. Repressed conflicts

_____ 3. Cognitive therapies   C. Low self-esteem

_____ 4. Humanistic therapies   D. Depression

                                     E. Unconscious anxiety

                                     F. Phobias

Exercise #2: Drug Therapies

Match the drug therapy listed on the left with the symptoms it relieves, disorders it treats, and effects it produces.

_____ 1. Benzodiazepines   A. Mood stabilizer

_____ 2. Prozac   B. Tranquilizing agent

_____ 3. Lithium   C. Used to treat schizophrenia

_____ 4. Thorazine   D. Reduces manic symptoms

                                     E. Produces mood elevation

                                     F. Used to treat bipolar disorder

                                     G. Reduces hallucinations and delusions

                                     H. Used to treat generalized anxiety disorder

                                     I. May relieve depression

Essay Questions

Write out answers to the following brief essay questions. Compare your responses with the sample answers at the end of the Study Guide chapter.

1. Discuss how modern psychoanalysis differs from traditional Freudian psychoanalysis. In what ways does modern psychoanalysis resemble traditional psychoanalysis?

2. Toby is terribly afraid of spiders. In fact, his fear is so excessive that he decided to take a leave of absence from his job at the local zoo when he learned that a new exhibit on spiders would soon open. Desperately seeking a cure for his phobia, he turns to you for help. Explain how you would use systematic desensitization to treat Toby.

3. What is a token economy? Is it ever appropriate to use punishment as a form of therapy?

4. What four features characterize the humanistic approach to therapy? How is person-centered therapy different from Gestalt therapy?

5. Consider the positive and negative aspects of drug therapies.

Multimedia Study Resources

Several activities and articles in Chapter 14 (Therapy) of The Psychology Place™ supplement the material covered in your textbook. In particular, three articles presented in Research News explore topics related to the treatment of psychological disorders. "Beyond Shyness: Diagnosing and Treating Social Phobia", discusses the concept of social phobia and examines possible ways of treating this disorder. "Childhood and Adolescent Depression: To Medicate or Not?" considers the controversial topic of drug treatments for depression in children and young adults. And finally, "Feeling Low this Winter? A 'Sunny Disposition' May Help", presents ways to treat seasonal affective disorder (SAD).

Test Solutions

Multiple-Choice Solutions

1. D (p. 671)	11. B (p. 681)	21. B (p. 689)
2. B (p. 671)	12. A (p. 682)	22. C (p. 690)
3. C (p. 672)	13. C (p. 682)	23. D (p. 692)
4. B (p. 672)	14. C (p. 684)	24. B (p. 693)
5. D (p. 674)	15. B (p. 685)	25. B (p. 693)
6. D (p. 676)	16. D (pp. 686-87)	26. C (p. 695)
7. B (pp. 677-681)	17. D (p. 687)	27. A (pp. 696-97)
8. A (p. 677)	18. A (p. 687)	28. C (p. 699)
9. C (p. 677)	19. C (p. 687)	29. D (p. 699)
10. D (p. 679)	20. A (p. 687)	30. A (p. 700)

True-False Solutions

1. F (p. 667)	6. T (p. 682)
2. F (p. 674)	7. T (p. 685)
3. F (p. 674)	8. T (pp. 692-93)
4. T (p. 676)	9. F (p. 695)
5. T (p. 677)	10. T (p. 702)

Key Concepts Matching Solutions

Exercise #1

1. B, E
2. A, F
3. D
4. C

Exercise #2

1. B, H
2. E, I
3. A, D, F
4. C, G

Essay Solutions

1. Modern psychoanalysis tends to be briefer (and therefore less expensive), less intense, and more flexible than classic techniques. For example, to accelerate the process, many analysts sit face-to-face with their clients and take a more active, engaging conversational role rather than relying on long-term free association. However, many aspects of Freud's original approach remain, including the emphasis on the importance of past experiences and unconscious processes, and the use of resistance and transference (p. 671).

2. Systematic desensitization is designed to condition people to respond to a feared stimulus, like a spider, with calmness rather than with anxiety. There are three basic procedures in systematic desensitization. The first step involves relaxation training. You will teach Toby how to relax the muscle groups throughout his body in response to a cue from you. Next, you will help Toby to create an anxiety hierarchy; this is defined as a graduated sequence of fear-provoking situations that are rated on a 100-point scale from mild ("you see a photograph of a spider's web") to terrifying ("a large, hairy spider is crawling on your arm"). Finally, you will talk Toby into a state of relaxation and then guide him through a gradual series of exposures to these fear-provoking situations. As soon as he is able to remain relaxed while visualizing a particular situation, you will move him onto the next one. This routine will last for several sessions (probably). For long-term success, you will also want to use *in vivo* exposure, which involves having Toby actually confront the feared situations in real life (pp. 677-79).

3. A token economy is a large-scale reinforcement program in which individuals earn "tokens" for engaging in desired behaviors. For example, a developmentally disabled individual might receive a token every time he or she remembers to put away his or her clothing before bedtime, an anorexic client might receive a token for every ounce of weight he or she gains, and a hospitalized child might receive a token for participating in physical therapy sessions. These tokens then can be exchanged for various resources (e.g., candy, movie passes, play time) (p. 681).

   Yes, punishment is sometimes necessary to eliminate dangerous or self-destructive behavior (p. 681). For example, a squirt of water from a spray bottle may be used to stop autistic children from injuring themselves by banging their heads against the wall.

4. The humanistic approach has four main features: (1) Trust is placed on the client's "growth" instincts; (2) the focus is upon feelings and not cognitions or behavior; (3) the orientation is toward the here-and-now rather than toward the past; and (4) the client is believed to be responsible for his or her own change (p. 686).

   Person-centered therapy tends to be a "nicer" experience than Gestalt therapy. By this, I mean that the therapist's whole focus is upon creating a warm and caring relationship with the client that fosters self-exploration and discovery. To do this, the therapist offers unconditional positive regard, exhibits empathy, is genuine (honest and sincere), and uses nondirective reflection. Gestalt therapists also are interested in self-discovery, but they are more directive, less reflective, and brutally honest (the client is on the "hot seat") (p. 687).

5. Drug therapies definitely have positive effects. They have been used successfully to treat a variety of disorders, ranging from depression to bipolar disorder to some of the symptoms of schizophrenia. However, some drugs produce negative physical side effects (and even fatal illnesses) and some produce physical and psychological dependence (p. 699). More worrisome is the fact that drugs do not deal with underlying problems—if someone's depression, for example, is due to an unresolved childhood conflict, then the depression is likely to return as soon as the client stops taking the drug. A more effective therapeutic strategy might be to use drugs in conjunction with psychotherapy—for example, antidepressants might increase an extremely depressed or suicidal person's level of functioning to the point where he or she is able to benefit from cognitive and behavioral therapies.

18 Health and Well-Being

Chapter Overview

The final chapter in your text considers issues that relate to health and well-being. First, the chapter considers the mind's influence over the body, including the placebo effect and other ways in which we are able to influence our physical state through positive expectations. Next, the text discusses the importance of self-esteem (e.g., its relation to physical and mental health), and examines how self-awareness and self-discrepancies can influence our self-esteem. The ways in which self-esteem and psychological well-being are affected by the beliefs, positive illusions, and biases that we hold about ourselves and our relations to others also are examined. Then, the chapter considers the causes of stress, including catastrophes, major life events, and microstressors. The short-term and long-term (e.g., general adaptation syndrome, coronary heart disease, immune system malfunction) physiological consequences of stress are examined, as are the various ways that people cope with stress. The chapter ends with a discussion of personality factors (hardiness) and social factors (social support) that appear to act as buffers against stress.

Chapter Outline

I. *What's Your Prediction?* Does Stress Lower Resistance?

II. Mind Over Matter

    A. *Debunking the Myth* . . . That Placebo Effects are "All in the Mind"

III. The Self and Well-Being

    A. The Need for Self-Esteem

    B. The Self-Awareness "Trap"
        1. Is self-consciousness an adaptive trait?

C. Positive Illusions
    1. Are positive illusions adaptive?

IV. Stress and Health

  A. The Sources of Stress
    1. Catastrophes
    2. Major life events
    3. Microstressors

  B. The Physiological Effects of Stress
    1. Coronary heart disease

  C. The Immune System
    1. What stress does to the immune system
    2. The link between stress and illness

V. Coping with Stress

  A. Coping Strategies
    1. Thought suppression
    2. Relaxation
    3. Aerobic exercise

  B. The "Self-healing Personality"
    1. Hardiness
    2. Optimism and hope

  C. Social Support

VI. The Big Picture

Learning Objectives

By the time you have read and reviewed this chapter, you should be able to:

1. Discuss the placebo effect and explain how positive expectations may reduce anxiety and trigger physiological responses (pp. 711-13).

2. Define self-esteem (p. 713). Consider the consequences of high and low self-esteem (p. 713).

3. Explain the relation between self-esteem and self-discrepancy (p. 714).

4. Discuss the self-awareness "trap" and consider how self-awareness may produce lowered self-esteem. Describe the situations that increase self-awareness. Consider two ways to reduce the discomfort produced by self-awareness (pp. 714-15).

5. Describe the positive illusions that characterize how we think of ourselves (e.g., unrealistic optimism, exaggerated control over life events) (pp. 715-16).

6. Consider whether positive illusions are adaptive (pp. 716-17).

7. Explain the main sources of stress, including catastrophes, major life events, and microstressors (pp. 718-21).

8. Describe the short-term and long-term effects of stress and define general adaptation syndrome (pp. 721-22).

9. Examine the relation between stress and coronary heart disease (p. 723). Distinguish between a Type A and a Type B personality, and consider the relation between Type A behavior and coronary heart disease (pp. 723-24).

10. Describe methods of assessing immune system function (p. 726), and describe how stress affects the immune system (pp. 726-27). Examine the relation between stress and physical illness (pp. 727-28).

11. Explain the difference between problem-focused and emotion-focused coping (pp. 728-29). Describe thought suppression and self-distraction as coping strategies (pp. 729-30).

12. Discuss ways to manage the physical symptoms of stress, including relaxation (pp. 730-31) and aerobic exercise (p. 731).

13. Consider the "self-healing personality" (pp. 731-34). Define the concept of hardiness and explain how this personality style may help us manage stress (p. 732). Consider optimism and its relation to coping with stress (pp. 732-34).

14. Explain the relation between social support and psychological and physical health (pp. 735-36). Discuss why social support has beneficial consequences (pp. 735-36).

Key Terms

The following key terms and concepts are featured in this chapter and are important for you to know. Write out definitions of each term and check your answers with the definitions in the text on the pages listed.

Psychoneuroimmunology (PNI) (p. 710)
Self-esteem (p. 713)
Self-awareness theory (p. 714)
Health psychology (p. 717)
Stress (p. 718)
Posttraumatic stress disorder (PTSD) (p. 719)
General adaptation syndrome (pp. 721-22)

Type A personality (p. 723)
Type B personality (p. 723)
Immune system (p. 724)
Lymphocytes (p. 724)
Hardiness (p. 732)
Social support (p. 735)

Multiple-Choice Questions

Circle the correct choice for each question and compare your answers with those at the end of the Study Guide chapter.

1. Psychoneuroimmunology is a new field that focuses on _____.
   A. the relation between personality factors and mental health
   B. the development of antipsychotic drug therapies
   C. the relation between the immune system and psychotic personality tendencies
   D. the association between physical and mental health

2. A placebo is able to improve someone's condition by
   A. altering the physical structure of the brain.
   B. increasing the rate of neurotransmitter activity.
   C. providing the suggestion that he or she will improve.
   D. decreasing physiological arousal.

3. Placebos have been used successfully to treat
   A. allergies.
   B. headaches.
   C. chronic pain.
   D. All of the above

4. Positive expectations about a particular treatment may trigger the release of _____.
   A. anxiety   C. dopamine
   B. endorphins   D. glucose

5. Shaquawn has high self-esteem. It is likely that she is also
   A. happy.
   B. productive.
   C. successful.
   D. All of the above

6. Kenneth has low self-esteem. It is likely that he is also
   A. anxious.
   B. depressed.
   C. prone to illness.
   D. All of the above

7. People with high self-esteem tend to have _____ self-discrepancy than people with low self-esteem, and they tend to focus _____ on their self-discrepancies than people with low self-esteem.
   A. more; less   C. less; less
   B. less; more   D. more; more

8. According to self-discrepancy theory, which situations can cause us to become self-aware?
   A. an audience
   B. a video camera
   C. a mirror
   D. All of the above

9. When people are self-focused, they are _____ likely to behave in accord with their values and _____ likely to behave in line with socially accepted ideals.
   A. more; more
   B. more; less
   C. less; less
   D. less; more

10. People who are chronically self-aware may
    A. develop extremely high self-esteem.
    B. experience temporary illness.
    C. become insane.
    D. overuse alcohol.

11. Research reveals that the majority of people tend to
    A. rate negative traits as more self-descriptive than positive traits.
    B. rate themselves more highly on positive traits than they rate others.
    C. underestimate their contribution to team efforts.
    D. exaggerate their lack of control over life events.

12. Which of the following statements reflects "unrealistic optimism"?
    A. "I'm going to escape from this unpleasant state of self-awareness by drinking myself into oblivion."
    B. "I'm much more intelligent, compassionate, and generous than he is."
    C. "I have a brighter future than the rest of you."
    D. "I contribute much more to the team than you all do."

13. People often exhibit unrealistic optimism with respect to which of the following events?
    A. Jobs and career success
    B. Marriage and interpersonal success
    C. Physical and mental health
    D. All of the above

14. Which of the following "illusions" may be associated with mental health and better psychological functioning?
    A. Holding unrealistically positive evaluations of the self
    B. Being unrealistically optimistic
    C. Having an exaggerated sense of control over the events in one's life
    D. All of the above

15. Which of the following statements is supported by social psychological research on mental health?
    A. People who are depressed tend to exaggerate their faults and shortcomings.
    B. People who are mentally healthy tend to have accurate and clear perceptions of themselves.
    C. People with low self-esteem are more likely to exaggerate their sense of control over events that are not easily controlled.
    D. People who are mentally healthy tend to have inaccurate, overly positive views of themselves.

16. Positive illusions may _____ our self-esteem and at the same time may _____ affect our relationships with others.
    A. increase; negatively
    B. decrease; positively
    C. increase; positively
    D. decrease; negatively

17. An unpleasant state of arousal that we experience in response to threatening events is defined as _____.
    A. anxiety
    B. stress
    C. reactance
    D. coping

18. Three months after Warren and Deb moved to California they lost their house in a major earthquake. Now, Warren is having problems sleeping at night and Deb frequently finds herself thinking about the original moments of the earthquake. What are Warren and Deb experiencing?
    A. posttraumatic stress disorder
    B. personal stressors
    C. psychosomatic disorder
    D. catastrophic flashbacks

19. Stressors may include
    A. catastrophes.
    B. major life events.
    C. microstressors.
    D. All of the above

20. To assess a person's risk for developing coronary heart disease, you might ask him or her which of the following questions?
    A. "Do you smoke?"
    B. "Do you have high blood pressure and/or high cholesterol?"
    C. "Are you often under stress?"
    D. All of the above

21. Nan works hard at all that she does. She is impatient and competitive with her coworkers and friends, and often feels frustrated and hostile when she is unable to meet her goals. Nan's actions reflect _____.
    A. hardiness
    B. Type A behavior
    C. Type B behavior
    D. defense mechanisms

22. When Jim sees the work schedule for December, he realizes that he will be unable to go home and see his family during the holidays. "Oh well," he says, "There's a silver lining in every cloud. This will give me more time to work on the house." Jim is using _____ to deal with his stressful situation.
    A. defense mechanisms
    B. social support
    C. problem-focused coping
    D. emotion-focused coping

23. Julie also sees that she is scheduled to work over the holidays. However, she seeks out the boss and asks that her schedule be changed to accommodate her travel plans. Julie is using _____ to deal with her stressful situation.
    A. defense mechanisms
    B. social support
    C. problem-focused coping
    D. emotion-focused coping

24. What would you recommend to someone who wants to become less stressed?
    A. "Relax."
    B. "Go for a run."
    C. "Look on the bright side of things."
    D. All of the above

25. Hardy people have which characteristics?
    A. commitment; challenge; control
    B. control; self-efficacy; self-actualization
    C. self-esteem; Type B personality; no self-discrepancy
    D. All of the above

26. _____ is a personality characteristic associated with a lower rate of stress-related illness.
    A. Hardiness
    B. Type B behavior pattern
    C. Pessimism
    D. Defensiveness

27. Francisco did not get the lead in the school play, even though he practiced his lines every day for a month before auditions. "Oh well," he says, "The director must have thought that the other guy would be better for this particular part. I'll get the next one." Francisco is a(n)
    A. pessimist.
    B. optimist.
    C. Type A personality.
    D. Type B personality.

28. Optimists tend to attribute their successes to _____ factors and their failures to _____.
    A. external; internal
    B. temporary; stable
    C. internal; external
    D. specific; global

29. Carmen also did not get the lead in the school play, and he practiced even harder than did Francisco. His friends tell him that he did not succeed because the director was new and didn't know what he was doing. Carmen listens to his friends and now feels better about himself. His friends provided _____.
    A. social support
    B. optimistic support
    C. emotion-focused coping
    D. hardiness

30. Which of the following individuals can provide social support?
    A. a dog
    B. a friend
    C. a family member
    D. All of the above

True-False Questions

Indicate which of the following statements are true or false, and compare your answers with those at the end of the chapter.

T   F   1. Once we are infected, stress appears to lower our resistance to illness.

T   F   2. Positive expectations can influence the mind (e.g., self-esteem) but not the body.

T   F   3. The placebo effect is not a purely mental phenomenon.

T   F   4. Self-esteem is related to physical and mental health.

T   F   5. Some situations can cause us to become self-aware.

T   F   6. Self-awareness is often an unpleasant state.

T   F   7. Most mentally healthy people hold realistic views about themselves and their relation to others.

T   F   8. The impact of a stressful life event depends in part on how we interpret it.

T   F   9. Small daily hassles may contribute more to stress and illness than major life events.

T   F   10. Any supportive relationship—with a friend, family member, or pet—may contribute to our mental and physical health.

Key Concepts Matching Exercises

Exercise #1: Health and Well-being

Match the phenomena listed on the left with the examples listed on the right.

_____ 1. Self-esteem

_____ 2. Self-awareness

_____ 3. Self-deception

_____ 4. Pessimism

_____ 5. Optimism

_____ 6. Posttraumatic stress disorder

_____ 7. General adaptation syndrome

_____ 8. Type A personality

_____ 9. Type B personality

_____ 10. Hardiness

A. "Why are people so slow? I can't wait any longer. I have things to do, places to go, people to see. Let's move it, folks!"

B. "I try to look at the bright side of life. When things go well, I know that it's because I made them happen. When things don't go so well, it's probably just a fluke that won't happen again."

C. "At first, I was really energized—my body and mind were so aroused and alert. But after a few weeks, I just got really worn out. Now, I can't seem to shake this cold I've picked up."

D. "I refuse to think about my past mistakes. I am completely in control of my life, and I can tell that good things are more likely to happen to me than to anyone else."

E. "Oh, I don't mind waiting. It'll give me a chance to relax and think. After all, we all need to stop and smell the flowers once in a while."

F. "You know, I really feel good about myself. I'm happy, productive, and successful."

G. "Face it, the glass is always half empty. I didn't get the raise because I'm just doomed to failure. They probably only hired me in the first place because they were desperate; it certainly wasn't because of my qualifications."

H. "If I had to describe myself, I'd say that I'm open to new experiences, that I embrace change, that I have a sense of purpose in my life, and that I am in control of my future outcomes."

I. "Ever since the flood, I've been unable to sleep, I feel anxious all the time, and I keep having these horrible flashbacks."

J. "I feel so self-conscious! Do you always have to bring that darn camera along?"

Essay Questions

Write out answers to the following brief essay questions. Compare your responses with the sample answers at the end of the Study Guide chapter.

1. How might a discrepancy between a person's actual self and his or her personal standards produce both positive and negative consequences?

2. While standing in line at the movie theater, you hear the following statement: "The single most important hallmark of mental health is holding a clear and accurate view of oneself." What would you say to the person who made this statement?

3. Diana just moved to a new town and started an extremely challenging job. On the first day of her new job, what immediate reactions might she experience? What long-term reactions might she experience? Discuss the circumstances under which her reactions may be beneficial or harmful (include Selye's general adaptation syndrome in your discussion).

4. Explain the difference between problem-focused coping and emotion-focused coping.

5. Charles is experiencing a great deal of stress in his daily life. He knows you are taking a psychology course and asks for your advice on ways that he might more effectively reduce or manage his level of stress. What will you tell him?

Multimedia Study Resources

Several activities and articles in Chapter 15 (Health Psychology) of The Psychology Place™ supplement the material covered in your textbook. In particular, two articles presented in Research News explore topics related to health. "Classes, Computers, Exams . . . and Beer: College Drinking" discusses the phenomenon of binge drinking among college students. "Procrastination May Be Dangerous to Your Health and Performance" considers whether procrastination is really an effective way of dealing with stress (it isn't). In addition, Ask Dr. Mike provides answers to a number of health-related questions, including whether repeated exposure to stress can result in autoimmune diseases.

Test Solutions

Multiple-Choice Solutions

1. D (p. 710)	11. B (p. 715)	21. B (p. 723)
2. C (p. 712)	12. C (p. 715)	22. D (p. 729)
3. D (p. 712)	13. D (pp. 715-16)	23. C (pp. 728-29)
4. B (p. 712)	14. D (p. 716)	24. D (pp. 730-32)
5. D (p. 713)	15. D (p. 716)	25. A (p. 732)
6. D (p. 713)	16. A (p. 717)	26. A (p. 732)
7. C (p. 714)	17. B (p. 718)	27. B (p. 732)
8. D (p. 714)	18. A (p. 719)	28. C (p. 732)
9. A (p. 714)	19. D (p. 718)	29. A (p. 735)
10. D (p. 715)	20. D (pp. 722-23)	30. D (pp. 735-36)

True-False Solutions

1. T (p. 709-10)	6. T (p. 714)
2. F (p. 712)	7. F (p. 716)
3. T (p. 712)	8. T (p. 720)
4. T (p. 713)	9. T (p. 720)
5. T (p. 714)	10. T (pp. 735-36)

Key Concepts Matching Solutions

Exercise #1

1. F
2. J
3. D
4. G
5. B
6. I
7. C
8. A
9. E
10. H

Essay Solutions

1. A discrepancy between people's self-concept and the standards that they strive to attain can have both negative and positive consequences. Sometimes, people who experience a discrepancy feel unhappy and experience lowered self-esteem (p. 714). Some individuals may attempt to withdraw from this unpleasant state of self-awareness by using drugs or alcohol (p. 715). However, these self-discrepancies may also spark people to behave in constructive ways that reduce the discrepancy (p. 714).

2. You would probably cite the research findings of social psychologists Shelley Taylor and Jonathan Brown (1988), who argue that mental health may be associated with holding certain positive illusions about oneself. For example, people who are depressed or low in self-esteem seem to view themselves clearly and accurately, and are less apt to exaggerate their sense of control over events that are not easily controlled. In fact, better psychological functioning and mental health seem to be associated with several basic illusions, including holding unrealistically positive views of the self, having an exaggerated sense of control over the occurrences in one's life, and being unrealistically optimistic. People who hold these illusions tend to be happy, content, productive, creative, and able to care about others. Thus, although it may be maladaptive to ignore or twist reality too much, some biased self-perceptions appear to be beneficial. It's also important to keep in mind, however, that there may be a downside to these positive illusions — for example, people with an inflated self-image may be more sensitive to criticism, and they appear to be viewed by others as somewhat inconsiderate, hostile, and condescending. In sum, positive illusions can be personally adaptive but interpersonally destructive (pp. 716-17).

3. According to Selye, Diana will first experience an "alarm" reaction to any stressor. This reaction includes a rise in heart rate, blood pressure, and breathing rate, and the secretion of certain adrenal gland hormones. In the short term, these physiological reactions may be beneficial or adaptive. For example, Diana may experience a burst of energy that helps her to cope with her job's challenges. If the stress continues over time, however, she may experience deterioration of body tissues due to the ongoing secretion of stress-related hormones (this occurs during the "resistance" stage, when the body remains aroused and alert). Over time, Diana may become more susceptible to disease and illness, either because her antistress resources are limited or because the overuse of these resources has caused other systems in her body to break down (this is referred to as the "exhaustion" phase, according to Selye's model). In general, then, reactions to long-term, sustained stress are harmful (p. 722).

4. Problem-focused coping is designed to reduce stress by overcoming the source of the problem. For example, if you were having difficulty with a class, you might seek out a school counselor, your academic adviser, your course professor, and people you knew had successfully passed that particular class. In other words, you go to the root of the problem itself. Emotion-focused coping does not focus on the source of the problem, but rather on the emotional aftermath of the problem. For example, if your class was causing you to feel anxious and depressed, you might decide to simply tough it out and make the best of the situation, hoping that you would feel better at the end of the term. Problem-focused coping is more likely to occur when we feel that we can actually control the situation; emotion-focused coping is more likely in situations that we feel cannot be controlled (pp. 728-29).

5. Charles has several options available to him. As noted in the answer to the previous question, he can employ problem-focused coping and reduce his stress level by removing the source of stress, and he can also employ emotion-focused coping strategies (including thought suppression and focused self-distraction) to manage his emotional response to a stressor (pp. 728-29). He also can manage the physical symptoms of stress by taking a class in relaxation training and by engaging in systematic aerobic exercise (pp. 730-31). Charles might also use or learn to use an "optimistic" explanatory style—for example, he could learn to blame failures on external, temporary, and specific factors, and to credit successes to internal, permanent, and global factors (p. 732). Finally, he could seek out social support and ask for assistance from caring others (pp. 735-36).